GW00711496

Matrix 2006

The Schools'
Cricket Almanac 2006

The Schools' Cricket Almanac 2006

Edited by
Grenville Simons and Andrew Fraser

Foreword by
Christopher Martin-Jenkins

Wisteria Books

Birtsmorton

First published in 2006

by
Wisteria Books
Wisteria Cottage
Birt Street
Birtsmorton
Malvern
Worcs. WR13 6AW
www.wisteriabooks.co.uk

British Library Cataloguing in Publication Data

ISBN 0 9527760 3 0

Design and Typesetting by George Simons

Set in Times and Din-Medium

Printed by Aldine Print Ltd., Malvern

Bound by JWB Finishers Ltd., Wolverhampton

CONTENTS

continued

(In all team lists * denotes colours)

Articles

Illustrations

FOREWORD

by Christopher Martin-Jenkins

Early last October I was passing a large playing field at Hunstanton in Norfolk, an area better known for golf, birds and beaches than for cricket. There, however, was a group of youngsters of about 12 playing cricket, the batsman fully padded up, complete with helmet and what looked like a new bat. It is a fair bet that a year previously these boys would have been playing football.

This heartening scrap of evidence of a cricketing renaissance amongst the young was only one of many. The best thing about England's overdue success in the series against Australia that had finished, amidst much national excitement, a month before, was indeed the stimulus it gave to youthful enthusiasm for cricket. It is no good telling grown children that they should have a go at the best of all games: they have to want to try it for themselves. Once bitten by cricket, in my experience, you are hooked for life.

That is probably truer now than it was when, in my own youth, England's regaining of the Ashes in 1953 made the game front page news in the same way, because most organised games for the young at cricket clubs these days give more opportunities to players of all ability to have a go at batting and bowling. On the other hand, as everyone who follows the game knows, the chances to play the game at state schools are far fewer than they were 50 years ago.

Great efforts are being made to arrest that decline, so the first appearance of this Almanac, giving the sort of prominence to the cricket season in schools that was once the provenance of Wisden, is happily timed. Independent schools occupy the most space because that is where the game is strongest, but the hope and expectation of the enterprising editors of this deserving new publication is that in future years there will be more solid evidence of organised cricket returning to all secondary schools.

It is an exciting thought that there will probably be a future Test player or two in the pages of this inaugural volume.

EDITORIAL

In life, taking part is what really matters. Schools encourage and instil this philosophy in children from a very young age. This publication – the first of its kind – records the achievements of well over one thousand teenagers who have 'taken part' during the memorable summer of 2005, a summer when fond memories of performances and events on the school cricket field were entwined and enriched with 'Ashes' fever.

Publishing *The Schools' Cricket Almanac* was a logical step forward after the launch of *The Preparatory Schools' Cricket Almanac* in 2005. It is the editors' wish that both books should reflect a celebration of the game, and not produce a league table of the most successful schools.

It is our hope that *The Schools' Cricket Almanac* will help to promote interest in the game and stimulate involvement in all senior school cricket. The details of any senior school 1st XI (U18) are welcome. We want to encourage players to improve their skills and enjoy the benefits of team spirit and, at the same time, engender within all pupils an appreciation of the game's traditions, etiquette, history, art and literature. We hope that this Almanac will inspire youngsters to share our passion for the game and see what is on offer.

It would not have been possible to produce the Almanac without the help and support of many people. We are indebted to the dedicated staff who organise and coach cricket at all the schools included for completing and returning forms, and for the enthusiastic response to our various communications. How encouraging it is to read so many optimistic school reports from heads of cricket, and with many schools reporting a young team with several players returning for the summer of 2006, prospects are promising for the forthcoming season.

With this in mind, in order to ensure the growth and success of the Almanac, the editors would like to take this opportunity to urge those schools who have not submitted their results this year to do so in the future!

Accuracy in this publication was one of the highest priorities. All reasonable care has been taken regarding the use of photographs and we thank parents who have kindly given permission for images to be reproduced.

We welcome suggestions and criticisms about the Almanac and would gratefully receive any historical or contemporary articles and photographs concerning senior school cricket.

Our sincere thanks go to Christopher Martin-Jenkins for writing the foreword and for his interest and support. We wish to acknowledge, with gratitude, the following for their valuable contributions: David Birks, Ian Botham OBE, George Chesterton, Clare Connor OBE, Dr David English MBE, Nick Gandon, Phil Harding, Andrew Radd, Jack Russell MBE and Glenys Williams.

Our thanks also go to Kathy Botham, Andy Murtagh, Jim Ruston and Tom Southall for providing information and assistance in a variety of ways; particular thanks go to Barnaby Simons who has worked with unending enthusiasm, offering constructive suggestions and giving the editors his wholehearted support.

Grenville Simons and Andrew Fraser
January 2006

The Editors SCA
Wisteria Cottage, Birt Street, Birtsmorton, Nr Malvern, Worcs WR13 6AW
Tel/Fax 01684 833578 Email sca@wisteriabooks.co.uk
www.wisteriabooks.co.uk

ALDENHAM SCHOOL

Elstree, Hertfordshire WD6 3AJ

Tel: 01923 858122 Fax: 01923 854410
Email: aps@aldenham.com

Master i/c Cricket: A.P. Stephenson Coach: D.W. Goodchild

2005 SEASON

Played: 18 Won: 10 Lost: 6 Drawn: 2

Captain: M. Karani Vice-captain: A. Sharma

Team selected from: M. Karani*, A. Sharma*, B. Frais, B. Ireson*,
C. Woolley*, R. Stone, A. Vijh, J. Thakrar*, S. Thakrar, D. Fraser,
P. Gregory*, M. Wallace, T. Pettet, D. Ben-Ari, J. Harris*, I. Fraser.

SUMMARY

This was a very exciting summer with the school playing some positive cricket. A mixture of formats were played, including a mini Twenty20 tournament. Five games were decided in the final over and the season ended with a memorable festival, hosted over three sun-drenched days.

Runs and wickets were shared around, with six players scoring a fifty at some point. Andre Sharma was the player of the season for his all-round contribution, and the captain, Manish Karani, recorded the highest score. Five of the side played representative cricket for either Middlesex or Hertfordshire and with many of them returning next year, prospects for the future are good.

AVERAGES

BATSMAN	INNINGS	NOT OUT	RUNS	H. SCORE	AVERAGE
A. Vijh	12	4	276	70	34.5
M. Karani	13	3	333	81	33.3
A. Sharma	16	5	356	62	32.4
P. Gregory	9	2	182	66	26.0
C. Woolley	14	1	239	54	18.4
R. Stone	13	2	193	55	17.5

BOWLER	OVERS	MAIDENS	RUNS	WICKETS	AVERAGE
A. Sharma	97	5	391	29	13.5
P. Gregory	48	3	189	13	14.5
J. Thakrar	89	13	312	18	17.3
M. Karani	106	15	382	21	18.2
S. Thakrar	53	3	201	11	18.3
A. Vijh	69	3	243	10	24.3

AMPLEFORTH COLLEGE

York YO62 4ER

Tel: 01439 766729 Fax: 01439 766854
Email: gdt@ampleforth.org.uk

Master i/c Cricket and Coach: G.D. Thurman

2005 SEASON

Played: 14   Won: 4   Lost: 1   Drawn: 9

Captain: A. Kisielewski   Vice-captain: A. Faulkner

Team selected from: A. Kisielewski*, A. Faulkner*, T. Bromet*,
C. O'Kelly*, L. Codrington, M. Forsythe, D. Tulloch*, B. Thurman,
I. Wright, S. Biker, F. Woodhead.

SUMMARY

The XI was captained by Alex Kisielewski who led from the front with the bat. His aggressive style gave confidence to the rest of the side. Charlie O'Kelly batted supremely and was rarely equalled by any bowler. He formed a powerful opening partnership with Tom Bromet. They scored 1,181 runs between them, which underpinned the side's batting success.

Alex Faulkner led the attack and his fine figures do not show how well he bowled. He could easily have doubled his wickets tally.

The team started their season slowly, not quite able to complete victories and drawing many games. They learnt from all their slips and mistakes and soon became an imposing side. Their fielding backed up the bowling with Thurman, Kisielewski and Bromet claiming crucial run outs.

As a side, the boys played exciting cricket, giving enjoyment to themselves and to those who were lucky enough to work with them or watch their matches.

AVERAGES

BATSMAN	INNINGS	NOT OUT	RUNS	H. SCORE	AVERAGE
C. O'Kelly	14	4	635	105*	63.5
T. Bromet	13	0	546	102	42.0
A. Kisielewski	14	2	447	72	37.3
D. Tulloch	9	3	170	55	28.3
M. Forsythe	9	3	142	24*	23.7
L. Codrington	14	4	122	43	12.2

BOWLER	OVERS	MAIDENS	RUNS	WICKETS	AVERAGE
F. Woodhead	69.2	12	310	17	18.2
A. Faulkner	180.1	39	549	28	19.6
S. Biker	74.2	15	262	11	23.8
D. Tulloch	103	8	433	18	24.1
C. O'Kelly	44	5	247	10	24.7
A. Kisielewski	85.1	9	353	6	58.8

WICKET-KEEPER	PLAYED	CAUGHT	STUMPED
M. Forsythe	14	-	-

NOTABLE BATTING PERFORMANCES

PLAYER	OPPOSITION	SCORE
C. O'Kelly	OACC	100*
T. Bromet	OACC	102
T. Bromet	OACC	83
A. Kisielewski	Bradford GS	72
C. O'Kelly	King's Parramatta (Australia)	105*
T. Bromet	Taunton	74

NOTABLE BOWLING PERFORMANCES

PLAYER	OPPOSITION	FIGURES
A. Faulkner	MCC	4-22
A. Faulkner	Sedbergh	4-54
F. Woodhead	OACC	5-21
A. Faulkner	Bradford GS	5-47
F. Woodhead	King's Parramatta (Australia)	4-24
C. O'Kelly	Durham	5-39

ARDINGLY COLLEGE

College Road, Ardingly, West Sussex RH17 6SQ

Tel: 01444 893000 Fax: 01444 893001
Email: head@ardingly.com

Master i/c Cricket: R.A. King   Coach: C. Waller

2005 SEASON

Played: 20   Won: 12   Lost: 6   Drawn: 2

Captain: G. Martin   Vice-captain: B. Brown

Team selected from: G. Martin, B. Brown, E. Long, M. McGahan,
S. Lambert, L. Wisdom, T. Edwards, J. Knight, S. Runham, J. Bennett,
S. Wates, C. Towner, J. Howie, B. Coombs.
Scorer: Mrs D. Brown

SUMMARY

We had an extremely successful two week tour to Cape Town in March
and April, combining seven days of cricket with sight-seeing trips. The
team recorded two wins, two losses and two draws, with captain
George Martin and vice-captain Ben Brown both scoring over 250
runs.

The domestic season saw victories over Hurstpierpoint College,
Lancing College, Seaford College and the Old Ardinians. Ed Long
scored a century against Hurstpierpoint in sixty-nine balls, Joe Bennett
took 6-9 against Seaford and Sam Wates took a hat trick against the
OAs.

We lost to Brighton College by 1 run, to Worth by 2 runs and to
Eastbourne by a count-back of wickets after a tie in the Sussex
Schools' Twenty20 Cup. Our other defeat was to Butterflies by 4
wickets.

There were three wins in a week against the MCC (George Martin
75 and Lawrence Wisdom 6-37), the XL Club and St. Bede's (James
Howie 5-16). Finally, the team swept to a convincing win against
Ardingly College Common Room.

Ben Brown (our 16-year-old wicket-keeper/batsman) has made
several appearances for the full Sussex 2nd XI, the Sussex Academy
and the South of England, making great strides towards a career as a
professional cricketer.

AVERAGES

BATSMAN	INNINGS	NOT OUT	RUNS	H. SCORE	AVERAGE
B. Brown	19	1	820	99*	45.6
G. Martin	20	1	772	75	40.6
E. Long	19	2	614	102	36.1
S. Lambert	15	2	191	36*	14.7

BOWLER	OVERS	MAIDENS	RUNS	WICKETS	AVERAGE
G. Martin	108	10	409	25	16.4
M. McGahan	107	18	391	23	17.0
J. Bennett	66	5	292	16	18.3
L. Wisdom	115	7	459	22	20.9

WICKET-KEEPER	PLAYED	CAUGHT	STUMPED
B. Brown	19	8	14

NOTABLE BATTING PERFORMANCES

PLAYER	OPPOSITION	SCORE
E. Long	Hurstpierpoint College	102
B. Brown	Hurstpierpoint College	99*
G. Martin	MCC	75
S. Runham	Ardingly Common Room	94

NOTABLE BOWLING PERFORMANCES

PLAYER	OPPOSITION	FIGURES
J. Bennett	Seaford College	6-9
L. Wisdom	MCC	6-37
J. Howie	St. Bede's	5-16

ARNOLD SCHOOL

Lytham Road, Blackpool FY4 1JG

Tel: 01253 346391 Fax: 01253 336251
Email: mevans@arnoldschool.com

Master i/c Cricket: Mr Evans   Coach: Mr McKeown

2005 SEASON

Played: 18 Won: 7   Lost: 7   Drawn: 4

Captain: M. Cowburn   Vice-captain: P. Moss

Team selected from: M. Cowburn*, M. Blackburn, P. Moss*,
J. Cain, J. Heald, P. Storey*, M. Wells, R. Simpson*,
J. Thornton*, N. Vann.

SUMMARY

After a tough six match pre-season tour to Trinidad and Tobago, Arnold 1st XI enjoyed one of their most successful domestic seasons for many years, losing just one match against Woodhouse Grove.

Captain Matthew Cowburn led by example with both bat and ball, taking 27 wickets and scoring 365 runs. James Cain had another good season opening the innings. He has now scored over 1,100 runs in the last three years for the school.

Our leading wicket-taker, Mark Blackburn, enjoyed his best school season taking 40 wickets, of which 19 were gathered in Trinidad and Tobago. Phil Moss was the other success with the ball, taking 30 wickets.

Notable victories were against Stockport GS, Kirkham GS, Cheadle Hulme, Bury GS, Tobago Schools, Bangor GS and Hutton GS.

AVERAGES

BATSMAN	INNINGS	NOT OUT	RUNS	H. SCORE	AVERAGE
J. Cain	19	3	419	77*	26.2
M. Cowburn	16	2	365	81	26.1
J. Heald	13	3	258	75	25.8
M. Blackburn	17	1	306	60	19.1

BOWLER	OVERS	MAIDENS	RUNS	WICKETS	AVERAGE
M. Blackburn	110	21	439	40	11.0
P. Moss	115	20	446	30	14.9
M. Cowburn	127	19	498	27	18.4

WICKET-KEEPER	PLAYED	CAUGHT	STUMPED
J. Thornton	9	6	3

NOTABLE BATTING PERFORMANCES

PLAYER	OPPOSITION	SCORE
J. Heald	QEGS Wakefield	75
M. Cowburn	Bury GS	81
J. Cain	Bangor GS	77*

NOTABLE BOWLING PERFORMANCES

PLAYER	OPPOSITION	FIGURES
M. Blackburn	Trinidad	6-25
M. Cowburn	Cheadle Hulme	5-12
P. Moss	Stockport GS	6-22

BANCROFT'S SCHOOL

Woodford Green, Essex IG8 0RF

Tel: 020 8505 4821 Fax: 020 8559 0032
Email: office@bancrofts.essex.sch.uk

Master i/c Cricket and Coach: J.K. Lever

2005 SEASON

Played: 18 Won: 12 Lost: 3 Drawn: 3

Captain: J. Lever Vice-captain: F. Khan

Team selected from: J. Lever*, R. Thompson*, J. Patel,
S. Ganandran, F. Khan*, A. Jeyadevan, D. Samuel, J. Lewis,
T. Kopelman, A. O'Leary, M. Henry*, T. Saull*.

SUMMARY

Following a reasonably successful winter tour to Namibia and South
Africa (P9 W5 L4), this young Bancroft's side enjoyed an excellent
season.

In both batting and bowling the depth of talent was self-evident.
Sixteen-year-old opening batsman Robin Thompson top scored with
626 runs, including one century and four fifties. His solid batting
provided the foundation for many wins.

Four all-rounders dominated the middle-order. Captain James Lever
amassed 340 runs and was the team's strike bowler, taking 29 wickets,
bowling left-arm as his father did. Jatan Patel was a strong striker of
the ball (339 runs) and picked up 13 wickets with his useful off-breaks.
16-year-olds Faiz Khan (469 runs and 22 wickets) and Jack Lewis (191
runs and 17 wickets) completed the quartet. They also recorded a
school record partnership of 210 for the sixth wicket versus Enfield
GS, coming together with the score on 33-5.

Special mention must be made of the outstanding contribution made
by wicket-keeper Matthew Henry - he kept wicket excellently and his
24 victims were crucial to the team's success.

Most of the XI will be back next season and will be reinforced by
some tremendous young talent coming through the school. 2006 should
prove exciting.

AVERAGES

BATSMAN	INNINGS	NOT OUT	RUNS	H. SCORE	AVERAGE
R. Thompson	16	4	626	117	52.2
A. Jeyadevan	7	2	185	48	37.0
J. Patel	12	2	339	73	33.9
F. Khan	17	3	469	117*	33.5
J. Lever	16	4	340	70*	28.3
J. Lewis	11	4	191	87*	27.3

BOWLER	OVERS	MAIDENS	RUNS	WICKETS	AVERAGE
J. Lever	123.3	14	438	29	15.1
J. Patel	60	3	259	13	21.0
F. Khan	107	15	461	22	21.4
J. Lewis	87	8	363	17	21.3
D. Samuel	51.4	2	286	13	22.0
T. Kopelman	102	14	416	18	23.1

WICKET-KEEPER	PLAYED	CAUGHT	STUMPED
M. Henry	17	16	8

NOTABLE BATTING PERFORMANCES

PLAYER	OPPOSITION	SCORE
R. Thompson	St. Dunstan's	117
F. Khan	Enfield GS	117*
J. Lewis	Enfield GS	87*

NOTABLE BOWLING PERFORMANCES

PLAYER	OPPOSITION	FIGURES
T. Kopelman	Ilford CHS	4-14
D. Samuel	Colfe's	4-6
J. Lever	Eltham College	4-18
J. Lever	Aylesbury GS	4-11
J. Lever	Old Bancroftians	4-16

BANGOR GRAMMAR SCHOOL

College Avenue, Bangor, County Down BT20 5HJ

Tel: 028 9147 3734 Fax: 028 9127 3245
Email: info@bgs.bangor.ni.sch.uk

Master i/c Cricket: D.J. Napier   Coach: C.C.J. Harte

2005 SEASON

Played: 20   Won: 10   Lost: 5   Drawn: 4   Tied: 1

Captain: T. Speers   Vice-captain: A. Titmus

Team selected from: R. Adair*, M. Allen, J. Cherry, M. Dhanjal,
R. Garrett*, R. Law*, P. McCalister*, A. Nixon*,
M. Nixon*, J. Parker*, T. Speers*, N. Spiers*,
A. Titmus*, T. Watson.

SUMMARY

The 1st XI enjoyed a fairly productive season. They were a team very short on batting experience, but with a mature seam attack. The fourth form Nixon twins led the way, playing well beyond their years and, like Jonathan Parker towards the end of the season, often performing best when their side was in trouble.

Ross Garrett's medium-pace bowled us back into games which could have run away, while Tom Speers and Andrew Titmus kept the earlier batsmen on their toes.

Of the defeats, it was only those against Royal Belfast Academical Institution and Arnold School, in the final tour match, which were poor performances. On the credit side, wins at Wesley College and St. Columba's, both in Dublin, got the campaign off to a great start.

A six run victory in the Plate Final at Foyle College in Derry and a second successive win at King's Macclesfield were late June delights!

AVERAGES

BATSMAN	INNINGS	NOT OUT	RUNS	H. SCORE	AVERAGE
A. Nixon	19	4	423	62*	28.2
M. Nixon	16	2	301	61*	21.5
N. Spiers	14	3	152	24	13.8
J. Parker	17	1	197	42*	12.3
R. Adair	20	1	221	30	11.6
R. Law	18	4	154	19*	11.0

BOWLER	OVERS	MAIDENS	RUNS	WICKETS	AVERAGE
R. Garrett	130.5	16	447	35	12.8
T. Speers	142.1	24	423	32	13.2
A. Titmus	150	27	386	24	16.1
A. Nixon	83.1	6	235	13	18.1

WICKET-KEEPER	PLAYED	CAUGHT	STUMPED
M. Nixon	12	8	2
N. Spiers	8	4	1

NOTABLE BATTING PERFORMANCES

PLAYER	OPPOSITION	SCORE
A. Nixon	Methodist College Belfast	62*
M. Nixon	Methodist College Belfast	61*

NOTABLE BOWLING PERFORMANCES

PLAYER	OPPOSITION	FIGURES
R. Adair	Wallace HS 2nd XI	6-6
A. Titmus	Banbridge Academy	5-5
T. Speers	Wesley College Dublin	5-15
R. Garrett	Sullivan US Holywood	5-27

BEDFORD MODERN SCHOOL

Manton Lane, Bedford MK41 7NT

Tel: 01234 332500 Fax: 01234 332550
Email: reception@bedford.co.uk

Master i/c Cricket: N. Chinneck
Coaches: R. Bailey and P. Woodroffe

2005 SEASON

Played: 16   Won: 6   Lost: 5   Drawn: 5

Captain: T. Gill   Vice-captain: J. Kerr

Team selected from: T. Gill, R. Godfrey, J. Kerr, C. Comer, C. Downes,
J. Lord, L. Presswell, L. Kendall, R. Chandarana, S. Kanugo,
P. Katechia, G. Hill, J. Cakebread, P. Datta.
Scorer: C. Webb

AVERAGES

BATSMAN	INNINGS	NOT OUT	RUNS	H. SCORE	AVERAGE
G. Hill	6	1	211	67	42.2
P. Datta	2	1	34	22	34.0
T. Gill	15	4	310	60*	28.2
J. Kerr	13	2	307	79	27.9
P. Katechia	6	4	47	30*	23.5
C. Downes	15	4	245	41	22.3

BOWLER	OVERS	MAIDENS	RUNS	WICKETS	AVERAGE
J. Lord	147.4	25	485	33	14.7
C. Downes	5	0	19	1	19.0
P. Katechia	83.1	12	313	13	24.1
L. Kendall	108	22	385	13	29.6
R. Chandarana	73.2	11	300	8	37.5
S. Kanugo	57.2	3	273	7	39.0

MY SCHOOL MEMORIES

by Ian Botham OBE

One of England's greatest all-rounders, Ian Botham played in 102 Test matches scoring 5200 runs, taking 383 wickets and 120 catches. He is President of Leukaemia Research, the charity for which he has raised millions of pounds.

I am delighted to have been asked to contribute to the very first edition of *The Schools' Cricket Almanac*.

During my own school years, I was very lucky to have attended schools where cricket was included in the curriculum, and to have teachers who were willing to give freely of their time and energy to coach and accompany us around the county to play matches against other schools. This was at a time – the sixties and early seventies – when many state school pupils were having to look further afield than their schools for adequate coaching and match practice.

My own teachers at both junior and senior school, Mr Hibbert and Mr Burgh respectively, were a major influence in my early sporting life. Many days I was able to stay at school until 6 or 7pm practising.

During the summer holidays, when there were no school matches, I would turn up at the Westland Cricket Club in Yeovil and stand at the gate waiting for the teams to turn up, offering my services to any team short of players, no matter what age or status. I would play anywhere just to get a game.

There were many special moments and I remember them all. Most of all, however, I remember the opportunities I was given and that I had the foresight and the will to grasp those opportunities eagerly.

BEDFORD SCHOOL

De Parys Avenue, Bedford MK40 2TU

Tel: 01234 362200 Fax: 01234 362283
Email: jfarrell@bedfordschool.org.uk

Master i/c Cricket: Jeremy Farrell   Coach: Derek Randall

2005 SEASON

Played: 18   Won: 5   Lost: 5   Drawn: 8

Captain: O. Yew   Vice-captain: R. Patel

Team selected from: A. Wakely*, A. Bird*, A. Burrows*, J. Murphy,
H. Fell*, E. Waite*, T. Elliot*, R. Patel*, J. Richardson*, C. Wren*,
O. Yew*, T. Warfield, K. Patel, M. Parmar.
Scorer: Tom Day

SUMMARY

Whilst there was a predominance of draws for the 1st XI, much good
cricket was played on a circuit with many talented sides. There were
excellent wins against the MCC and a strong Old Boys team.

A young batting line-up performed very well, whilst Oliver Yew
captained the side for a second season.

Did you know? **. . .** The highest England Test total is 903-7
declared scored against Australia at The Oval in 1938. The
lowest England total in Tests was 45 made at Sydney in
1886/7. In 1993/4 England narrowly avoided breaking this
record when they were dismissed for 46 by the West Indies at
Port-of-Spain.

AVERAGES

BATSMAN	INNINGS	NOT OUT	RUNS	H. SCORE	AVERAGE
A. Bird	19	4	830	110*	55.3
A. Wakely	16	1	786	144	52.4
J. Murphy	15	3	285	58*	23.8
A. Burrows	16	3	303	71*	23.3
H. Fell	12	0	184	34	15.3

BOWLER	OVERS	MAIDENS	RUNS	WICKETS	AVERAGE
R. Patel	129.2	21	511	24	21.3
T. Elliot	96.1	9	345	15	23.0
A. Wakely	51.1	4	256	11	23.3
E. Waite	119.3	13	468	16	29.2
O. Yew	175.1	19	791	23	34.4
C. Wren	177.2	20	747	19	39.3

WICKET-KEEPER	PLAYED	CAUGHT	STUMPED
J. Richardson	16	15	5
T. Warfield	2	4	0

NOTABLE BATTING PERFORMANCES

PLAYER	OPPOSITION	SCORE
A. Wakely	Old Boys	144
A. Bird	Tonbridge	110*
A. Bird	Old Boys	103*
A. Bird	Dulwich College	101

NOTABLE BOWLING PERFORMANCES

PLAYER	OPPOSITION	FIGURES
K. Patel	Caulfield GS (Australia)	5-36
R. Patel	MCC	4-30
E. Waite	Stowe	4-38
R. Patel	Harrow	4-39

BIRKENHEAD SCHOOL

58 Beresford Road, Oxton, Wirral CH43 2JD

Tel: 0151 652 4014 Fax: 0151 653 7412
Email: enquiries@birkenheadschool.co.uk

Master i/c Cricket: P. Lindberg Coach: B. Donelan

2005 SEASON

Played: 15 Won: 9 Lost: 5 Drawn: 1

Captain: A. Tyler Vice-captain: D. Hurst

Team selected from: A. Tyler*, D. Hurst*, O. Jones*, E. Rendle*,
G. Goodwin*, C. Mathieson, D. Sandhu, A. Greenfield, A. Lee,
G. Baxter, C. Diable, T. Hickley, A. Syed, H. Masters,
J. Masters, A. Clarke.

SUMMARY

A young side performed very encouragingly, with David Hurst (only Year 10) the outstanding player. He scored over 700 runs, including two big hundreds. His 176* versus Cheadle was a school record score. Consistent support was provided by captain Alex Tyler and big-hitting left-hander Ed Rendle.

The bowling was less impressive, but Grant Goodwin was aggressive and quick, while David Hurst was our stock bowler with his accurate off and leg-spinners. The fielding was massively improved from last season, very few catches were dropped and some outstanding ones were taken.

The highlight of the season was the thrilling victory over King's Macclesfield, where an imperious 97* from Ed Rendle led the team to victory after we had slumped to 36-4, chasing 227.

In the last game, against Abingdon, we scored 257-7, while our hosts could only limp to 54 all out (from 28-9).

We had a comprehensive win over local rivals Merchant Taylors' Crosby. Our opponents were bowled out for 135, which we surpassed for the loss of only 2 wickets.

Low points were in the match versus Sedburgh and the MCC, as understrength batting line-ups (due to exam commitments) meant we could only manage 73 and 105 all out respectively. Both games resulted in heavy defeats.

AVERAGES

BATSMAN	INNINGS	NOT OUT	RUNS	H. SCORE	AVERAGE
D. Hurst	13	2	705	176*	64.1
T. Hickley	6	2	174	63	43.5
E. Rendle	13	4	380	96*	42.2
A. Tyler	11	3	305	61*	38.1
O. Jones	11	0	276	74	25.1
A. Greenfield	9	3	148	47	24.7

BOWLER	OVERS	MAIDENS	RUNS	WICKETS	AVERAGE
A. Clarke	34	10	119	9	13.2
D. Hurst	114	23	265	16	16.6
G. Goodwin	107.1	19	345	18	19.2
J. Masters	61	5	283	12	23.6
E. Rendle	67.3	5	314	12	26.2
A. Syed	61	15	187	7	26.7

WICKET-KEEPER	PLAYED	CAUGHT	STUMPED
A. Greenfield	13	6	3

NOTABLE BATTING PERFORMANCES

PLAYER	OPPOSITION	SCORE
D. Hurst	William Hulme's GS	139
D. Hurst	Cheadle Hulme	176*
E. Rendle	King's Macclesfield	96*
D. Hurst	University College	86*
D. Hurst	Abingdon	73
O. Jones	William Hulme's GS	74
D. Hurst	Bury GS	68

NOTABLE BOWLING PERFORMANCES

PLAYER	OPPOSITION	FIGURES
D. Hurst	Abingdon	5.1-2-7-5
G. Goodwin	Abingdon	6-4-3-3
J. Masters	Cheadle Hulme	7-1-23-4

THE BISHOP'S STORTFORD HIGH SCHOOL

London Road, Bishop's Stortford, Hertfordshire CM23 3LU

Tel: 01279 868686 Fax: 01279 868687
Email: ian.athill@tbshs.herts.sch.uk

Master i/c Cricket: I. Athill Coach: M. Dale

2005 SEASON

Played: 12 Won: 4 Lost: 7 Drawn: 1

Captain: L. Padgett Vice-captain: S. Ali

Team selected from: L. Padgett*, S. McConnell, A. Lewin*, N. Bishop, H. Bass, S. Ali, E. Sellears, O. Williams, C. Armstrong, A. Bishop, D. Rose, R. Horne, H. Barrett, L. Heskett, A. Osbourne, P. Clarke, J. Agnew, T. Ryder.

SUMMARY

We have endured a frustrating season where winning games seemed to be a small step too far early on. A very good performance against a competitive Felsted side did not seem to raise the confidence that it might have done, and games seemed to simply slip away at crucial moments.

The future looks bright with some strong young players coming through. Simon McConnell was the pick of them, averaging over 40 for the 1st XI.

Though 2005 has proved a little disappointing, a major cricket tour and specialist coaching beckons for next year and there is certainly a great deal more to come.

AVERAGES

BATSMAN	INNINGS	NOT OUT	RUNS	H. SCORE	AVERAGE
S. McConnell	7	1	248	66	41.3
S. Ali	11	3	319	63	39.9
L. Padgett	7	0	202	50	28.9
H. Bass	10	2	215	59	26.9

BOWLER	OVERS	MAIDENS	RUNS	WICKETS	AVERAGE
N. Bishop	54.3	6	83	14	5.9
O. Williams	50	9	145	14	10.4
D. Rose	28.2	2	104	8	13.0
C. Armstrong	32	6	138	8	17.2
E. Sellears	49	6	232	11	21.1
R. Horne	65.2	12	209	9	23.2

NOTABLE BATTING PERFORMANCES

PLAYER	OPPOSITION	SCORE
S. McConnell	Glen HS (Australia)	66
S. Ali	Knox GS (South Africa)	63
S. Ali	Felsted	43
L. Padgett	Haberdashers' Aske's	50

NOTABLE BOWLING PERFORMANCES

PLAYER	OPPOSITION	FIGURES
N. Bishop	Enfield GS	10.3-31-5
N. Bishop	Haberdashers' Aske's	8-45-4
E. Sellears	MCC	6-18-3
D. Rose	Forest	6.3-16-3

BLOXHAM SCHOOL

Banbury, Oxon OX15 4PE

Tel: 01295 720222 Fax: 01295 721714
Email: registrar@bloxhamschool.com

Master i/c Cricket: N. Furley   Coach: R. Kaufman

2005 SEASON

Played: 15   Won: 3   Lost: 6   Drawn: 6

Captain: H. Ahmed   Vice-captain: N. Mawby

Team selected from: H. Ahmed*, N. Mawby, T. Loxton*, D. Smith,
C. Hudson-Evans, C. Harper, M. Boscott, L. Andre, E. Byass,
A. Boyle, T. Gurmani, S. Cox, N. Putt.

SUMMARY

The most encouraging feature of the 2005 season was the steady and significant progress the boys made during the term. Five of the six defeats were suffered before half-term, whilst all three wins were enjoyed in the second half. The batting especially showed better technique and application so that challenging totals were set. Bowling sides out remained a problem, but with the attempt to widen the variety of the bowling attack, results did improve.

Tim Loxton was the backbone of the batting, consistently making scores in the forties, but puzzlingly never going on to make more. Other batsmen sometimes scored more runs, but none as reliably.

Similarly in the bowling, Dan Smith shouldered the majority of the burden without getting his just rewards. In fact Loxton bowled more wicket-taking balls and achieved better figures. Again the other bowlers had their moments, but no-one bowled so consistently. Ned Mawby, in his third year in the side, helped to raise the fielding standard to a high level, making four stumpings in ten matches.

With several promising young players coming through and Loxton and Smith remaining, we are optimistic about next year.

AVERAGES

BATSMAN	INNINGS	NOT OUT	RUNS	H. SCORE	AVERAGE
T. Loxton	13	1	337	49*	28.1
T. Gurmani	9	4	134	38	26.8
A. Boyle	13	4	166	44*	18.4
D. Smith	13	0	220	59*	16.9
M. Boscott	9	0	143	65	15.9
N. Mawby	10	0	115	40	11.5

BOWLER	OVERS	MAIDENS	RUNS	WICKETS	AVERAGE
C. Harper	20	1	73	5	14.6
L. Andre	20	0	101	6	16.8
T. Loxton	84.3	4	364	19	19.2
H. Ahmed	42.5	4	201	9	22.3
A. Boyle	52.4	5	218	9	24.2
D. Smith	109	20	392	14	28.0

WICKET-KEEPER	PLAYED	CAUGHT	STUMPED
N. Mawby	10	3	4

NOTABLE BATTING PERFORMANCES

PLAYER	OPPOSITION	SCORE
M. Boscott	Wellingborough	65
D. Smith	MCC	59*

NOTABLE BOWLING PERFORMANCES

PLAYER	OPPOSITION	FIGURES
T. Loxton	Ellesmere College	5-23
D. Smith	King Edward's Stratford	5-16
C. Harper	Shiplake College	4-24

BOLTON SCHOOL

Chorley New Road, Bolton BL1 4PA

Tel: 01204 840201 Fax: 01204 849477
Email: hm@boys.bolton.sch.uk

Master i/c Cricket: A.C.R. Compton   Coach: P. Fernside

2005 SEASON

Played: 11   Won: 4   Lost: 4   Drawn: 3

Captain: T. Liversedge   Vice-captain: P. Rainford

Team selected from: T. Liversedge*, M. Fray*, T. Mallinson*,
J. Reynard, P. Rainford*, P. Busby, L. Casey, B. Reynard, N. Eastham,
S. Jiva, A. Lockett*, J. Ariyaratnam, J. Edmundson, H. Hibbert,
R. Mellalieu, M. Entwistle, J. Cross, S. Burns, J. Greville.

SUMMARY

Following an extremely successful tour of Grenada in July 2004, the 2005 season began with great promise. We had assembled a squad with a mixture of experience and talent throughout the winter, which we hoped a season-opener away to Giggleswick would confirm. Bolton restricted Giggleswick to 167 and the team's chase got off to a commanding start. Despite a mini collapse, the middle-order batsmen guided Bolton home with overs to spare.

Unfortunately, the next two fixtures were blighted by bad weather, but normal service was quickly resumed with a home fixture against Stockport GS. In a rather one-sided match, a first innings total of 150 by Stockport proved not to be a enough against a Bolton side in good form with the bat.

We went into our next game against Bury GS with confidence high. The result emphasised this, with a comfortable victory by 5 wickets. Having been brought down to earth in previous matches versus Manchester GS, this year's fixture with them was eagerly anticipated. We were confident of chasing the 176 runs which Manchester set us. However, despite valiant attempts, we fell an agonising 17 runs short of the final total.

A well-earned draw against Sedbergh was followed by the annual week of cricket at Bolton School. A pleasing win over the XL Club and a hard-fought draw against MCC rounded off a busy week.

Glenwood School from Durban were our final opponents. An impressive all-round game, especially in the field, restricted Bolton to 163 off 40 overs. Controlled batting by Glenwood resulted in an easy win for the tourists by 8 wickets.

AVERAGES

BATSMAN	INNINGS	NOT OUT	RUNS	H. SCORE	AVERAGE
N. Eastham	4	3	51	40*	51.0
M. Fray	8	3	242	55*	48.4
T. Mallinson	8	1	204	58	29.1
J. Reynard	8	1	165	49	23.6
P. Rainford	8	2	122	49*	20.3
T. Liversedge	5	2	57	22	19.0

BOWLER	OVERS	MAIDENS	RUNS	WICKETS	AVERAGE
S. Jiva	40	5	178	10	17.8
N. Eastham	28	4	89	4	22.2
T. Liversedge	59	16	201	8	25.1
M. Fray	86	16	304	12	25.3
L. Casey	40.2	5	174	5	34.8
P. Busby	37	5	149	3	49.7

WICKET-KEEPER	PLAYED	CAUGHT	STUMPED
A. Lockett	9	4	2
T. Mallinson	2	1	0

NOTABLE BATTING PERFORMANCES

PLAYER	OPPOSITION	SCORE
T. Mallinson	Giggleswick	51
J. Reynard	Giggleswick	49
T. Mallinson	Stockport GS	58
M. Fray	Manchester GS	52*
M. Fray	XL Club	52
M. Fray	Glenwood (South Africa)	55*
P. Rainford	Glenwood (South Africa)	49*

NOTABLE BOWLING PERFORMANCES

PLAYER	OPPOSITION	FIGURES
M. Fray	Stockport GS	10-2-39-4
T. Liversedge	Bury GS	6-4-9-3
S. Jiva	Bury GS	6-2-28-5

BRADFORD GRAMMAR SCHOOL

Keighley Road, Bradford BD9 4JP

Tel: 01274 542492 Fax: 01274 548129
Email: ags@bradfordgrammar.co.uk

Master i/c Cricket: A.G. Smith

2005 SEASON

Played: 17   Won: 6   Lost: 7   Drawn: 4

Captain: J. Robinson   Vice-captain: J. Dangerfield

Team selected from: J. Robinson*, J. Dangerfield*, J. Shaw*,
A. Sutcliffe*, O. Collinge*, S. Stockill*, S. Lawrence*, J. Hill,
T. Slater, A. Mahmood, J. Lee, S. Shah, I. Mahomed, T. Watson.
Scorer: J. Cooke

SUMMARY

This was a season of consolidation with a young and inexperienced team. More composure could have seen us win three of the games we lost, while the defeat at RGS Lancaster only came with a dismissal on the last ball of the game. Throughout the season, the side lacked a dominant batsman capable of ensuring we made competitive totals.

The older batsmen, James Shaw and captain Jonathan Robinson, contributed well, but the positives came from the development of some of the younger players. U14 batsman Tom Slater, in particular, had a very promising first season with two half-centuries, while James Hill showed increasing confidence as an opener. Tom Watson produced some excellent performances at the end of the season after promotion from the 2nd XI, and Sam Lawrence made real progress with both bat and ball.

The bowling was dominated by the opening attack of Oliver Collinge and Adam Sutcliffe, who both had impressive seasons. They were well supported by off-spinner Josh Dangerfield, who ended up as the leading wicket-taker and produced the bowling highlight with a hat trick against RGS Lancaster.

The season ended with a successful tour of Denmark, where the team played their best cricket. We recorded three notable victories, including a seven wicket win against the Denmark U19 side. Twelve of the tour squad will be available next year, when the real benefits of this season should be seen.

AVERAGES

BATSMAN	INNINGS	NOT OUT	RUNS	H. SCORE	AVERAGE
T. Watson	3	1	125	73*	62.5
J. Shaw	16	1	397	82	26.5
T. Slater	14	3	253	56	23.0
J. Robinson	12	0	264	68	22.0
S. Lawrence	16	1	303	52	20.2
J. Dangerfield	12	2	150	30*	15.0

BOWLER	OVERS	MAIDENS	RUNS	WICKETS	AVERAGE
O. Collinge	160.5	33	526	25	21.0
J. Robinson	48	11	182	8	22.7
A. Sutcliffe	144.2	25	500	21	23.8
J. Dangerfield	138	9	672	28	24.0
A. Mahmood	58	7	210	8	26.2
S. Lawrence	103.3	16	404	13	31.1

WICKET-KEEPER	PLAYED	CAUGHT	STUMPED
S. Stockill	17	14	2

NOTABLE BATTING PERFORMANCES

PLAYER	OPPOSITION	SCORE
J. Shaw	Glostrup CC (Denmark)	82
T. Watson	Denmark U19	73*
J. Hill	Ampleforth College	71
J. Robinson	MCC	68
T. Slater	St. Peter's York	56
T. Slater	Bury GS	55*
J. Shaw	Bury GS	54*

NOTABLE BOWLING PERFORMANCES

PLAYER	OPPOSITION	FIGURES
J. Dangerfield	Silcoates	5-47
J. Dangerfield	RGS Lancaster	5-94
J. Dangerfield	Woodhouse Grove	4-19
A. Sutcliffe	Svanholm CC (Denmark)	4-19
S. Lawrence	Denmark U19	4-28

BRENTWOOD SCHOOL

Ingrave Road, Brentwood CM15 8AS

Tel: 01277 243204 Fax: 01277 243325
Email: brhardie@brentwood.essex.sch.uk

Master i/c Cricket: B.R. Hardie

2005 SEASON

Played: 13   Won: 5   Lost: 6   Drawn: 2

Captain: C. Prowting   Vice-captain: K. Sohal

Team selected from: K. Sohal*, N. Wickramasinge, R. Bull,
C. Prowting*, A. West, R. Bray, B. Washington, W. Stock,
J. Chavhan, D. Gulrajani, M. Geggus, T. Barbone, J. Turnbull,
C. Boon, R. Rajani, N. Childs.
Scorer: G. Belchamber

SUMMARY

The season was disappointing for the inconsistency of performances and availability of senior players. In thirteen matches we were able to select our strongest XI only once, and in fact did not field the same line-up on any two occasions. This meant we lacked consistency, strength and depth.

We relied heavily on Karn Sohal and Christopher Prowting for stability in our batting. The four main bowlers, seamers Will Stock and Michael Geggus, and spinners Tim Barbone and Dayan Gulrajani, were left to do most of the hard work with the ball.

The best batting and bowling figures were achieved in the same game. Richard Bray, our U15 captain, hit a positive 113*, and Michael Geggus ran through the Colfe's batting with 5 wickets. The best performance, however, was reserved for our captain, whose well-compiled and paced hundred gave us victory over a strong MCC side. This was closely followed by some tight leg-spin and four quick wickets to give us an unlikely win over Bishop's Stortford HS.

With such a young team this year, we look forward to more consistency next season.

AVERAGES

BATSMAN	INNINGS	NOT OUT	RUNS	H. SCORE	AVERAGE
K. Sohal	11	2	412	98	45.8
C. Prowting	10	2	344	102*	43.0
R. Bray	5	1	168	113*	42.0
D. Gulrajani	10	4	206	42	34.3
N. Childs	8	0	158	39	19.8
W. Stock	10	2	156	38	19.5

BOWLER	OVERS	MAIDENS	RUNS	WICKETS	AVERAGE
M. Geggus	84	7	337	15	22.5
T. Barbone	128	34	426	15	28.4
D. Gulrajani	94	12	510	17	30.0
W. Stock	123	23	391	13	30.1

WICKET-KEEPER	PLAYED	CAUGHT	STUMPED
C. Prowting	10	-	-

NOTABLE BATTING PERFORMANCES

PLAYER	OPPOSITION	SCORE
R. Bray	Colfe's	113*
C. Prowting	MCC	102*
K. Sohal	The Perse	98

NOTABLE BOWLING PERFORMANCES

PLAYER	OPPOSITION	FIGURES
M. Geggus	Colfe's	5-43
T. Barbone	Framlingham College	4-34
D. Gulrajani	Bishop's Stortford HS	4-36

BRIGHTON COLLEGE

Eastern Road, Brighton BN2 0AL

Tel: 01273 704200 Fax: 01273 704204
Email: jspencer@brightoncollege.net

Master i/c Cricket: Michael Edmunds   Coach: John Spencer

2005 SEASON

Played: 21   Won: 12   Lost: 6   Drawn: 2   Tied: 1

Captain: R. Young   Vice-captain: M. Thornely

Team selected from: R. Young, M. Thornely, A. Sumner, C. Saville,
K. Stevenson, M. Garth, M. Hume, J. Austin, C. Foreman, N. Seager,
T. Hayward, A. Thornely, O. Gatting, Miss H. Colvin, Miss S. Taylor.

SUMMARY

Following our tour to Sri Lanka in December 2004, the 1st XI enjoyed reasonable success in 2005. We have a young squad, with nine of the listed players available for two more seasons. With most of our matches played as limited overs, it is all or nothing with nowhere to hide!

Our best days coincided with the rich form of Michael Thornely and, before exams, Richard Young. Thornely became the sixth Brighton College cricketer to score 1000 runs in a season. His six centuries equalled the Brighton record set by C.R. Maxwell in 1931. Richard Young and Matt Hume broke the record for an opening partnership, adding 271 versus Epsom. In scoring 367-2 against Ipswich in our 50 over festival, the College created a new record for the school in the UK.

Brighton won the inaugural Sussex Schools' Twenty20 Competition, complete with coloured clothing, however there was no pop music to accompany dismissals and sixes! Our best performances were against Tonbridge and Eton, whom we beat in exciting contests. Our defeats to English schools were by Whitgift, Harrow and Wellington.

Against Wellington we selected two girls, 15-year-old Holly Colvin and 16-year-old Sarah Taylor, both likely to be regulars next term. With Clare Connor in 1993 we were the first school to play a girl regularly in a public school 1st XI.

Matt Hume, Charlie Foreman and Ollie Gatting also played important knocks, while Adam Sumner was the most penetrating bowler and Andrew Thornely the most economical.

AVERAGES

BATSMAN	INNINGS	NOT OUT	RUNS	H. SCORE	AVERAGE
M. Thornely	21	6	1360	182*	90.7
R. Young	18	1	791	125	46.5
M. Hume	12	1	331	136	30.1
C. Foreman	15	4	317	57	28.8
O. Gatting	16	1	414	94	27.6
J. Austin	16	3	212	49	16.3

BOWLER	OVERS	MAIDENS	RUNS	WICKETS	AVERAGE
A. Sumner	115.1	7	463	30	15.4
J. Austin	77.2	6	322	17	18.9
A. Thornely	164	20	519	21	24.7
M. Thornely	115.5	7	598	22	27.2
C. Saville	97	12	432	15	28.8
M. Garth	83	5	429	14	30.6

NOTABLE BATTING PERFORMANCES

PLAYER	OPPOSITION	SCORE
M. Thornely	Ipswich	182*
M. Thornely	MCC	177
M. Thornely	Dulwich College	127*
M. Thornely	Eastbourne College	115*
M. Thornely	Lancing College	109*
R. Young	Epsom College	125
M. Hume	Epsom College	136

NOTABLE BOWLING PERFORMANCES

PLAYER	OPPOSITION	FIGURES
A. Sumner	St. Bede's	4-11
M. Garth	Eastbourne College	4-33
A. Sumner	Eton College	3-26
A. Sumner	Ipswich	4-30

In August 2005, Brighton's Holly Colvin became England's youngest Test player. On day one of the first Ashes Test match, she took three wickets with her left-arm spin. At one stage, she was on a hat trick.

BRISTOL GRAMMAR SCHOOL

University Road, Bristol BS8 1SR

Tel: 0117 973 6006 Fax: 0117 946 7485
Email: kblackbu@bgs.bristol.sch.uk

Master i/c Cricket: Kevin Blackburn   Coach: Roy Jones

2005 SEASON

Played: 15   Won: 5   Lost: 4   Drawn: 6

Captain: T. Parnell   Vice-captain: C. Gwyther

Team selected from: T. Parnell, J. Neale, T. O'Gallagher, C. Gwyther, S. Leonard, R. Murley, N. Luker, B. Trembath, J. Taylor, F. Currell, W. Tavaré, W. Fishley.

SUMMARY

Well led by T. Parnell, who once again scored over 300 runs, we had a good season with a young team enjoying five wins in school matches.

Star of the season was F. Currell, who scored a superb 129 against Wellington School and took 17 wickets with his leg-spin. Another highlight was the second wicket partnership of 231 by T. Parnell and C. Gwyther against Prior Park.

Did you know? . . . The highest individual score for England in Tests remains the 364 scored by Len Hutton against Australia at The Oval in 1938. The record partnership for England was made at Birmingham in 1957 against the West Indies where Colin Cowdrey and Peter May put on 411 for the fourth wicket.

AVERAGES

BATSMAN	INNINGS	NOT OUT	RUNS	H. SCORE	AVERAGE
T. Parnell	10	1	309	104	34.3
F. Currell	11	2	295	129	32.8
S. Leonard	7	1	192	76	32.0
T. O'Gallagher	4	1	86	38	28.7
C. Gwyther	10	0	244	128	24.4
W. Tavaré	8	1	170	89	24.3

BOWLER	OVERS	MAIDENS	RUNS	WICKETS	AVERAGE
F. Currell	53	8	196	17	11.5
J. Taylor	36	4	156	11	14.2
W. Tavaré	36	0	150	10	15.0
C. Gwyther	70	12	235	13	18.1
W. Fishley	76	14	224	12	18.7
J. Neale	80	12	314	12	26.2

WICKET-KEEPER	PLAYED	CAUGHT	STUMPED
R. Murley	10	9	3

NOTABLE BATTING PERFORMANCES

PLAYER	OPPOSITION	SCORE
F. Currell	Wellington School	129
C. Gwyther	Prior Park	128
T. Parnell	Prior Park	104
W. Tavaré	XL Club	89
T. Parnell	Kingswood	87*
S. Leonard	King Edward's Bath	76
T. Parnell	MCC	51

NOTABLE BOWLING PERFORMANCES

PLAYER	OPPOSITION	FIGURES
F. Currell	Prior Park	6-1-27-4
C. Gwyther	QEH Bristol	4-0-18-3
F. Currell	Wellington School	4-1-19-3
W. Tavaré	Clifton College	5-0-22-3
C. Gwyther	XL Club	15-1-45-3

BROMSGROVE SCHOOL

Worcester Road, Bromsgrove, Worcs B61 7DU

Tel: 01527 579679 Fax: 01527 576177
Email: pgreetham@bromsgrove-school.co.uk

Master i/c Cricket and Coach: Paul Greetham

2005 SEASON

Played: 17   Won: 12   Lost: 4   Drawn: 1

Captain: M. Mullan   Vice-captain: B. Dudley

Team selected from: M. Mullan*, B. Dudley*, J. Jones*, J. Chandler*,
N. Dallow*, D. Mumford*, B. Bales*, L. Mullan, J. Attwood,
J. Millington, R. Cleary, B. Rands, L. Radford.

SUMMARY

The 1st XI exceeded all expectations in 2005, posting one of the most impressive playing records in recent times. The core of the squad were upper sixth formers, meaning that in 2006 we will revert to a younger and potentially very promising XI. All of the twelve wins we achieved were team efforts. No one person stood out, with quality running through the side.

Following a disappointing warm-up game against Princethorpe College and a defeat to a strong MCC side, the highlight of the first half of the season was the 27 run victory over RGS Worcester. It was tight bowling and good fielding which swung the game in Bromsgrove's favour. Then followed more wins against Dean Close, where James Chandler saved the day with a half-century after Bromsgrove were 0-3, and, perhaps most impressively, against a rather strong Loughborough GS team (Liam Mullan 6-16).

The 1st XI enjoyed taking part in the second year of the Independent Schools' Twenty20 Competition. All of our group matches took place on one Sunday in May at Cheltenham College. Unfortunately, not much respect was shown to any bowler all day - many of our bowlers pleaded that their figures should not be included in the season averages!

After half-term, we beat Trent College, Old Swinford Hospital and the XL Club, but we were then defeated by the touring Wesley College Melbourne.

Matthew Mullan won the school batting trophy for the third successive year. He has scored over 2000 runs during his time in the 1st XI. Equally impressive is Jonny Jones's 100 wickets over his five years in the team.

AVERAGES

BATSMAN	INNINGS	NOT OUT	RUNS	H. SCORE	AVERAGE
M. Mullan	17	4	528	132*	40.6
B. Dudley	15	1	411	73	29.4
J. Chandler	16	3	279	77*	21.5
D. Mumford	13	7	123	29*	20.5
R. Cleary	13	0	236	53	18.2
B. Bales	14	1	216	50	16.6

BOWLER	OVERS	MAIDENS	RUNS	WICKETS	AVERAGE
L. Mullan	56.2	10	211	16	13.2
J. Jones	149.4	34	406	29	14.0
L. Radford	106	18	317	19	16.7
D. Mumford	99.2	11	347	18	19.3
B. Bales	95	12	310	16	19.4
N. Dallow	94.4	10	374	19	19.7

WICKET-KEEPER	PLAYED	CAUGHT	STUMPED
B. Dudley	15	6	11

NOTABLE BATTING PERFORMANCES

PLAYER	OPPOSITION	SCORE
M. Mullan	Geelong College (Australia)	132*
J. Chandler	Cheltenham College	77*
B. Dudley	Old Swinford Hospital	73
B. Dudley	Geelong College (Australia)	72
M. Mullan	XL Club	69
M. Mullan	Stowe	65*
B. Dudley	Worcestershire U17	57

NOTABLE BOWLING PERFORMANCES

PLAYER	OPPOSITION	FIGURES
L. Mullan	Loughborough GS	6-16
J. Jones	Geelong College (Australia)	4-21
J. Jones	Warwick	4-24
J. Jones	XL Club	4-28
N. Dallow	Trent College	4-32
L. Radford	Wycliffe College	3-3

BRYANSTON SCHOOL

Blandford Forum, Dorset DT11 OPX

Tel: 01258 452411 Fax: 01258 484657
Email: tjh@bryanston.co.uk

Master i/c Cricket: T.J. Hill   Coach: P.J. Norton

2005 SEASON

Played: 11   Won: 6   Lost: 3   Drawn: 2

Captain: C. Cosgrove   Vice-captain: J. Gibbs

Team selected from: C. Cosgrove*, J. Gibbs*, W. Dobbs*, S. Street*,
I. Pearce, J. Pearce, H. Pyrgos, R. Alexander, J. Barnes, T. Turney,
J. Irwin-Brown, O. Williams, J. Marshall*, J. Forster, G. Ledger,
F. Strange, C. Lorkin, D. Pearce, N. Marshall, R. Turner, M. Woods,
C. Rawlings, O. Bowring.
Scorer: Dr M. Kearney

SUMMARY

Before half-term, five 1st XI matches were not played because of rain. Then, with public examinations and recurring injuries, the side was seldom the same. Indeed twenty-one boys played, including two U14s. One was Dean Pearce, who joined his older brothers John and Iain in the defeat of Aldenham.

Jamie Gibbs, an excellent vice-captain, topped batting and wicket-taking aggregates. His captain, Christopher Cosgrove, handled the side shrewdly and took 11 wickets with his off-spin. Apart from these two, nine other players took wickets!

The U15 starlet, Sebastian Street, continued to be unplayable and received his colours. Unfortunately, a serious back injury in the week leading up to the Bunbury Festival prevented him from representing the West. He had been outstanding in the Easter Tour of the West Indies by the West Region.

The side was often impressive, but Exeter brought us down with a bump, only for the boys to rise to the occasion and beat Victoria College Jersey in a two day game the following weekend.

AVERAGES

BATSMAN	INNINGS	NOT OUT	RUNS	H. SCORE	AVERAGE
O. Williams	3	2	74	57*	74.0
J. Barnes	4	2	77	37	38.5
J. Pearce	5	4	30	26	30.0
J. Gibbs	10	1	247	54	27.4
I. Pearce	10	1	189	48	21.0
O. Bowring	4	1	63	47	21.0

BOWLER	OVERS	MAIDENS	RUNS	WICKETS	AVERAGE
M. Woods	15	4	46	6	7.7
S. Street	50.3	21	104	13	8.0
J. Gibbs	72.5	18	176	22	8.0
R. Alexander	31	6	106	7	15.1
J. Pearce	60.1	8	211	12	17.6
W. Dobbs	56	14	221	11	20.1

WICKET-KEEPER	PLAYED	CAUGHT	STUMPED
I. Pearce	4	6	0
O. Bowring	7	0	0

NOTABLE BATTING PERFORMANCES

PLAYER	OPPOSITION	SCORE
J. Gibbs	Monkton Combe	54
H. Pyrgos	King Edward VI Southampton	78
O. Williams	Victoria College Jersey	57*

NOTABLE BOWLING PERFORMANCES

PLAYER	OPPOSITION	FIGURES
S. Street	Monkton Combe	6.3-2-12-4
J. Gibbs	King's Bruton	10-3-25-5
J. Gibbs	King Edward VI Southampton	5.4-1-13-5
S. Street	Victoria College Jersey	5-2-8-3

CATERHAM SCHOOL

Harestone Valley Road, Caterham, Surrey CR3 6YA

Tel: 01883 343028 Fax: 01883 344248
Email: sandy.ross@caterhamschool.co.uk

Master i/c Cricket: Sandy Ross   Coach: Craig Carolan

2005 SEASON

Played: 17   Won: 5   Lost: 6   Drawn: 3   Abandoned: 3

Captain: M. Joiner   Vice-captain: H. Jones

Team selected from: M. Joiner*, H. Gooden*, A. Patel*, S. Long*,
H. Jones, M. Valia, S. Purnell, L. Barnard, N. Patel, C. Waud,
M. Waud, S. Chaudhry, J. Leck, T. Lewis, D. Shearman, A. Long,
L. McAuliffe, R. Willson.

SUMMARY

The 1st XI had a highly enjoyable season, with six very close last over finishes. The team was ably led by Michael Joiner, who was the leading run-scorer. He hit a magnificent 106* against Alleyn's in the first match played in a wet April.

Lorne Barnard, Sam Long, Arjun Patel and Nirau Patel all had good days with the bat, but it was the outstanding bowling which caught the eye. Harry Gooden, Madhav Valia, Henry Jones and leg-spinner Arjun Patel made up a very talented attack, well supported by Shabaz Chaudhry. Arjun Patel claimed several 4 or 5 wicket hauls, Harry Gooden had three 4 wicket returns, while Madhav Valia bagged 6 wickets on one occasion and 4 wickets twice.

Four of the eighteen who played in 2005 will not be back in 2006. Following a short April tour to Malta, it should be another exciting summer which, if matched by the energy and enthusiasm shown in 2005, will be great fun to look forward to.

AVERAGES

BATSMAN	INNINGS	NOT OUT	RUNS	H. SCORE	AVERAGE
M. Joiner	13	2	484	106*	44.0
L. Barnard	14	1	343	69*	26.4
S. Long	11	0	224	40	20.4
A. Patel	11	1	155	94	15.5
N. Patel	12	1	164	48	14.9
M. Valia	11	3	118	29	14.8

BOWLER	OVERS	MAIDENS	RUNS	WICKETS	AVERAGE
H. Gooden	98.2	10	321	25	12.8
A. Patel	121	20	375	26	14.4
M. Valia	123	17	410	28	14.6
H. Jones	107.1	11	461	15	30.7

WICKET-KEEPER	PLAYED	CAUGHT	STUMPED
S. Long	14	6	1
M. Waud	3	2	0

NOTABLE BATTING PERFORMANCES

PLAYER	OPPOSITION	SCORE
M. Joiner	Alleyn's	106*
M. Joiner	Seaford College	84*
M. Joiner	MCC	72
M. Joiner	City of London Freemen's	71
A. Patel	Lancing College	94
L. Barnard	King's Rochester	69*
L. Barnard	John Fisher	52

NOTABLE BOWLING PERFORMANCES

PLAYER	OPPOSITION	FIGURES
A. Patel	Seaford College	8-3-8-5
A. Patel	MCC	20-7-45-5
M. Valia	King's Rochester	12-6-10-6

CHARTERHOUSE

Godalming, Surrey GU7 2DX

Tel: 01483 291671 Fax: 01483 291594
Email: admissions@charterhouse.org.uk

Master i/c Cricket: P.J. Deakin   Coach: R.V. Lewis

2005 SEASON

Played: 17 Won: 5   Lost: 7   Drawn: 5

Captain: T. Lumsden Vice-captain: H. Schofield

Team selected from: T. Lumsden*, H. Schofield*, R. Aldridge*,
R. Greensmith*, P. Summers*, M. Carr-Jones*, B. Ryder-Smith*,
A. Proctor*, C. Clinton*, S. Cussins*, G. Adolphus*, S. Fawcett,
D. Bowman, B. Hitchcock, W. Bowlby, E. Walford, T. Davey, H. Don.
Scorer: T. Bryers

SUMMARY

Although the final record of results may not reflect a good season, the team played well and saved some of their best performances for the Cowdrey Cup. We enjoyed wins over Tonbridge and Wellington and came within a whisker of winning the competition for the first time, after narrowly losing to Harrow by one wicket and Eton by eight runs.

The XI has a very strong fixture list and with some extra luck and a more clinical edge, we could have reversed the season's records with eight or nine wins. Other victories included Westminster, Charterhouse Friars and Whitgift.

The batting featured two centuries. Vice-captain and Surrey U17 wicket-keeper/batsman Harry Schofield batted excellently (101*) in the thrilling and victorious run-chase over Wellington, when 39 runs were scored in the last three overs. U16 batsman Sam Cussins hit 100 versus Eton. Fellow fifth former, Charlie Clinton, topped the batting aggregate with 497 runs for the season.

Although Peter Summers was leading wicket-taker for the season, with 26 wickets, he often conceded too many runs. With the exception of left-arm seamer and captain Lumsden, the attack lacked the penetration needed to bowl out strong school XIs. Ben Ryder-Smith developed into a useful opening bowler and Matt Carr-Jones produced the best spell with 6-11 against Westminster. The team often relied on the off-spin pairing of Rob Aldridge and U15 Surrey representative George Adolphus. They regularly bowled well in tandem and with their respective flighted and flatter off-spin they complemented each other to restrict the opposition.

AVERAGES

BATSMAN	INNINGS	NOT OUT	RUNS	H. SCORE	AVERAGE
C. Clinton	14	0	497	81	35.5
S. Cussins	16	2	334	100	23.9
H. Schofield	16	1	356	101*	23.7
M. Carr-Jones	15	4	248	51	22.5
T. Lumsden	15	1	295	84*	21.1
R. Greensmith	17	2	306	53	20.4

BOWLER	OVERS	MAIDENS	RUNS	WICKETS	AVERAGE
P. Summers	116.2	13	509	26	19.6
R. Aldridge	127	32	420	17	24.7
T. Lumsden	148.4	25	563	22	25.6
G. Adolphus	129	19	460	17	27.1
B. Ryder-Smith	111.1	14	420	14	30.0
M. Carr-Jones	86	8	411	13	31.6

WICKET-KEEPER	PLAYED	CAUGHT	STUMPED
H. Schofield	17	11	4
H. Don	1	2	1

NOTABLE BATTING PERFORMANCES

PLAYER	OPPOSITION	SCORE
S. Cussins	Eton College	100
H. Schofield	Wellington College	101*
T. Lumsden	Charterhouse Friars	84*
C. Clinton	MCC	81

NOTABLE BOWLING PERFORMANCES

PLAYER	OPPOSITION	FIGURES
P. Summers	Leinster U19	7-0-32-5
M. Carr-Jones	Westminster	6-1-11-6
G. Adolphus	Dulwich College	17-1-55-4
R. Aldridge	Charterhouse Friars	10-6-8-3

CHATHAM GRAMMAR SCHOOL FOR BOYS

Holcombe, Maidstone Road, Chatham, Kent ME4 6JB

Tel: 01634 830083 Fax: 01634 826320
Email: info@cgsb.co.uk

Master i/c Cricket and Coach: G. Benwell

2005 SEASON

Played: 6   Lost: 5   Drawn: 1

Captain: T. Bhopara

Team selected from: T. Bhopara, L. Short, A. Jackson, B. Arnold, O. Barnard, C. David, D. Andrews, M. Porter, B. Ford, L. Lockhart, M. Loveridge, D. Curtis, S. Rodwell.

NOTABLE BATTING PERFORMANCES

PLAYER	OPPOSITION	SCORE
M. Porter	Borden GS	71

***Did you know?* . . .** Graham Gooch holds the record for the most runs in Tests for England. He amassed 8,900 runs with a highest score of 333 in the first innings against India at Lord's in 1990. In the second innings he made 123. This remains the only instance of a triple century and a century by the same player in a game of first-class cricket. Fifteen years earlier he had started his Test career with a pair against Australia at Edgbaston.

Normandie à la Carte

Educating Children with a Real Taste of France

Carefully tailored Language and Activity programmes

- Ideal for all types of Schools and Groups
- Courses that motivate and stimulate
- Exclusive use of accommodation

Choose an activity in French from:

Mountain biking - Kayaking - Climbing
High Ropes Course - Sailing - Orienteering

Meet French people:

In the market - At a Goat's Cheese Farm
Walking across the Bay of Mont St. Michel
On the Landing Beaches - Baking croissants
At a Cider Farm

For more information please contact Andrew Caverhill
Email: Acaverhill@aol.com   Tel: 07971 816 931

6 Route des Esnaudières, 50870 Subligny, Normandie, France
Normandie à la Carte is a trading name of European Study Visits Limited.
Reg. in UK No. 3387925

CHEADLE HULME SCHOOL

Claremont Road, Cheadle Hulme, Cheshire SK8 6EF

Tel: 0161 488 3330 Fax: 0161 488 3344
Email: winterj@chschool.co.uk

Master i/c Cricket: J.C. Winter

2005 SEASON

Played: 10   Won: 3   Lost: 5   Drawn: 2

Captain: A. Fleming

Team selected from: M. Bennett*, A. Fleming*, W. Dougal,
W. Ashraf, E. Davidson, K. Koch, S. Wood, J. McClements,
J. Burke, M. Parr, A. Lingard, J. Williams, B. Malloy,
G. Watmore, A. Mohammed.

Scorer: Mrs N. Bennett

SUMMARY

A young 1st XI, superbly led by Alex Fleming, achieved three notable victories against Stockport GS, St. Bede's and Bury GS. The nucleus of the team will be available for the next three years.

15-year-old Mark Bennett scored his maiden century at home against Rydal Penrhos, and carried his bat (61*) for 43 overs against KEQMS Lytham.

The opening bowlers, Kai Koch and Josh Burke, also 15-year-olds, proved a formidable partnership and should be a genuine threat next season. Retiring captain Alex Fleming scored his maiden fifty in the total of 281-4 against Rydal Penrhos.

Mark Bennett represented Cheshire at U15 and U16 level. The future appears very bright for a committed and talented squad - we look forward to 2006!

AVERAGES

BATSMAN	INNINGS	NOT OUT	RUNS	H. SCORE	AVERAGE
M. Bennett	9	1	280	112	35.0
M. Parr	4	0	89	46	22.3
J. Burke	4	2	43	24	21.5
A. Fleming	8	2	106	54	17.7

BOWLER	OVERS	MAIDENS	RUNS	WICKETS	AVERAGE
A. Lingard	8	0	53	4	13.2
J. Burke	40	2	136	9	15.1
K. Koch	45.1	7	179	7	25.6
W. Ashraf	30.3	6	95	3	31.7
M. Bennett	41	4	200	6	33.3

WICKET-KEEPER	PLAYED	CAUGHT	STUMPED
A. Fleming	10	3	3

NOTABLE BATTING PERFORMANCES

PLAYER	OPPOSITION	SCORE
M. Bennett	KEQMS Lytham	61*
M. Bennett	Rydal Penrhos	112
A. Fleming	Rydal Penrhos	54

Did you know? . . . Walter Hammond holds the record for the most Test centuries for England. He reached the notable milestone on no less than twenty-two occasions.

Top Left: Ben Brown (Ardingly College) 820 runs and 22 dismissals
Top Right: Mark Blackburn (Arnold) 40 wickets at 11.0
Bottom Left: Andy Bird (Bedford) 830 runs at 55.3
Bottom Right: Michael Thornely (Brighton College) 1360 runs at 90.7, including six centuries

Top Left: Seren Waters (Cranleigh) 525 runs at 65.6
Top Right: Dhyan Ranatunga (Dulwich College) 482 runs and 34 dismissals
Bottom Left: Robert Newton (Framlingham College) 947 runs at 94.7, including five centuries
Bottom Right: Felix Flower (Gresham's) 943 runs at 67.4, including four centuries

CHELTENHAM COLLEGE

Bath Road, Cheltenham GL53 7LD

Tel: 01242 513540 Fax: 01242 265630
Email: registrar@cheltcoll.gloucs.sch.uk

Master i/c Cricket: M.W. Stovold   Coach: M.P. Briers

2005 SEASON

Played: 23   Won: 9   Lost: 10   Drawn: 4

Captain: S. Mason   Vice-captain: A. Sherwood

Team selected from: S. Mason*, A. Sherwood*, B. Cowap*,
J. Mills, K. Stovold, G. Hughes*, C. Hall, W. Johnston, S. Kemp,
W. Davies*, R. Islam*.
Scorer: Mrs G. Howell

SUMMARY

A mixed season of results, featuring various types of cricket which ranged from traditional timed, 40 and 50 overs through to the instant Twenty20. The season was drier than recent years and more fixtures were completed.

The XI was well led by Sam Mason. The cricket was positive but not always consistent, and at times the various departments did not complement each other. When runs flowed, the bowlers struggled and vice versa. As a result, there were excellent victories and disappointing defeats.

The side reached the final of the Chesterton Cup. A Twenty20 day with Bromsgrove, Stowe and Wycliffe proved enjoyable and exciting in coloured clothing. The annual festival with Sherborne, Marlborough and Haileybury continues, despite the difficulties of raising full strength teams, due to fluctuating term dates.

The senior boys will be missed, but hopefully they will continue to play at suitable levels. The younger players are maturing and given time and exposure, they will maintain the strength in the future.

Sadly, limited-overs has become a major feature in school fixtures, but the ability to bowl sides out or chase down a score within timed conditions should not be forgotten, or the game will lose a unique art and the skill of captaincy.

AVERAGES

BATSMAN	INNINGS	NOT OUT	RUNS	H. SCORE	AVERAGE
G. Hughes	17	3	506	106	36.1
A. Sherwood	21	3	608	82*	33.8
J. Mills	21	3	605	103*	33.6
K. Stovold	21	3	473	113	26.3
B. Cowap	21	0	524	73	25.0
S. Mason	20	1	382	52	20.1

BOWLER	OVERS	MAIDENS	RUNS	WICKETS	AVERAGE
W. Johnston	125.2	26	429	29	14.8
W. Davies	161.2	23	590	31	19.0
S. Kemp	68	13	286	14	20.4
C. Hall	148.5	18	596	26	22.9
S. Mason	125.4	15	506	16	31.6
R. Islam	86.1	9	396	10	39.6

WICKET-KEEPER	PLAYED	CAUGHT	STUMPED
G. Hughes	21	22	4

NOTABLE BATTING PERFORMANCES

PLAYER	OPPOSITION	SCORE
K. Stovold	Dean Close	113
J. Mills	Sherborne	103*
G. Hughes	Haileybury	106

NOTABLE BOWLING PERFORMANCES

PLAYER	OPPOSITION	FIGURES
W. Johnston	Dean Close	9-15
W. Davies	Old Cheltonians	5-60
R. Islam	Wycliffe College	5-4

CONNOR ON CRICKET

In August 2005, the England Women's cricket team regained the Ashes.
Their captain, Clare Connor, reflects on her life in the game.

It gives me great pleasure to contribute to the inaugural edition of *The Schools' Cricket Almanac*. My love of the game, whilst engendered by my father, really exploded when I started life at Brighton College Prep School as a ten-year-old, where I was given the opportunity to play alongside the boys - something that was pretty much unheard of in the mid-eighties. I captained the U10s to an unbeaten season in my first year so it all got off to a flying start!

As each new season approached, my friends and the staff at school all wondered whether I would continue to play alongside the boys or join the girls on the rounders pitch or on the tennis court. And each season saw my love of the game intensify and my ambition grow. My school cricket career blossomed under the guidance and commitment of John Spencer, former Sussex fast bowler. He would spend hours with me in the nets, sometimes until dark, and he always said that if I was good enough then I would earn a place in the Brighton College 1st XI. This became my goal, and I achieved it in the summer of 1993. I had two fantastic years in the 1st XI, with an amazing tour to Zimbabwe, and I attribute so much of my international success to that time in my development.

It wasn't until I was in my mid-teens that I turned my attentions to the opportunities within the world of women's cricket. Very quickly, after junior girls' county trials with Sussex, I was selected for the senior county side and also for Young England. By 1994, at the age of 18, I was fully involved with the full England set-up and in November 1995 during my first term at Manchester University, I went on my first major tour: eight weeks to India! It was tough balancing Uni commitments and getting a 2:1 in my English degree with a rapidly progressing international career and all the time, travel and training that that entails. But I loved every moment and would not change a thing.

I am now teaching English back at Brighton College. I had four years here from 1999-2003 and then took a two year sabbatical during which time I was, essentially, a full-time cricketer and presenter with Channel 4's *The Cricket Show*. That sabbatical gave me the chance to commit myself wholly to World Cup preparations and obviously our Ashes campaign. It is a wonderful feeling to know that the time away from teaching has been justified by the success we have enjoyed as a team. The media work was also fun and exciting but I am back now where my heart is.

The success enjoyed by the England Women's Cricket Team over the last two years reached unparalleled heights with the obvious highlight being the regaining of the Ashes in August 2005. That moment, that winning run, that utterly united team huddle on the players' balcony at Worcester will be forever etched in my memory as the realisation that we were having a taste of being at the top. Where do we go from here? Well, the only way to say you are the best team in the world is not by simply by winning the next World Cup but by winning series upon series upon series during the coming summers and winter tours. We have enjoyed consecutive series wins over South Africa (home and away) and New Zealand, and now we hold the Ashes. We are well on our way.

Clare Connor holding the Ashes Trophy

CHIGWELL SCHOOL

Chigwell, Essex IG7 6QF

Tel: 020 8501 5700 Fax: 020 8500 6232
Email: hm@chigwell-school.org

Master i/c Cricket: D.N. Morrison   Coach: F. Griffith

2005 SEASON

Played: 16   Won: 8   Lost: 5   Drawn: 3

Captain: S. Martin   Vice-captain: W. Higgins

Team selected from: N. Amin, R. Bhome, W. Taylor, S. Higgins,
S. Martin, T. Kerr, D. Majeed, P. Sekhon, T. Galvin, L. Waller,
H. Virdee, S. Ahmed.

Scorers: T. Abraham and Claudia Koch

SUMMARY

After a promising six match tour to Barbados during the 2004
summer holidays, the 1st XI squad lost eight players from a highly
successful team who played together for three seasons. The new 1st
XI captain, Sean Martin, had to lead a young and inexperienced
squad. In the event, both he and the team played remarkably well in
an interesting and varied season.

The 1st XI played many different formats, including one day and
afternoon timed, declaration matches, straight limited-overs cricket
and split limited-overs cricket, as we tried to encourage versatility
and adaptability in developing our young players. By the end of the
season, the 1st XI had also enjoyed the experience of playing four
international matches against opposition from Northern Ireland,
South Africa, Australia and Barbados, as well as our traditional
independent school fixtures, the MCC and the Hackney College
Cricket Academy (an inner city initiative we partner). This provided
our players with a breadth of experience and a real learning curve,
which benefited them greatly.

The team possessed six excellent players, four of them genuine
all-rounders, in captain Sean Martin (25 wickets and 269 runs), Nik
Amin (16 wickets and 231 runs), Rohan Bhome (30 wickets and 343

runs) and Dean Majeed (21 wickets and 276 runs). The batting was aided and abetted by wicket-keeper William Taylor (410 runs including a rapid 110 versus The Perse) and vice-captain William Higgins (318 runs) who took countless slip catches and is undoubtedly the best schoolboy slip-fielder I have ever seen in my thirty years as master i/c cricket.

Parvan Sekhon's conversion to open at the end of the season provided additional support, while Luke Waller's seam bowling (10 wickets) was a useful back up.

The most exciting victory was against the MCC, with captain Sean Martin scoring the winning run on the penultimate ball to win by two wickets. This was followed by the two wicket win over Bancroft's, as Dean Majeed's 64* carried the 1st XI home.

The best all-round team performances were the 113 run victory over Brentwood and the 115 run win over St Philip's Parish Barbados. Despite the margin of victory, both were strong teams who met our 1st XI at their best.

AVERAGES

BATSMAN	INNINGS	NOT OUT	RUNS	H. SCORE	AVERAGE
D. Majeed	11	3	276	64*	34.5
W. Taylor	15	0	410	110	27.3
S. Martin	14	4	269	42	26.9
R. Bhome	16	1	343	60	22.9
W. Higgins	14	0	318	81	22.7
N. Amin	15	1	231	47	16.5

BOWLER	OVERS	MAIDENS	RUNS	WICKETS	AVERAGE
S. Martin	98.3	21	292	25	11.7
L. Waller	34.4	3	130	10	13.0
D. Majeed	103	29	321	21	15.3
R. Bhome	157	27	465	30	15.5
N. Amin	106.5	34	261	16	16.3

Above: Brothers Edward (28 wickets) and
Robert Clements (726 runs and 32 wickets)
(Haberdashers' Aske's)

Top Right: Nick Jones (KEQMS Lytham) 492 runs and 42 wickets
Bottom Left: William Bruce (King's Canterbury) 702 runs and 33 wickets
Bottom Right: Harry Sperling (King's Ely) 812 runs at 81.2

The best value cricket tours

Please call our specialist playing tours department for a quote when planning your next tour.

Some popular destinations include…

COUNTRY	PRICES FROM	NIGHTS
EUROPE		
Holland	£174	3
South of France	£320	4
Malta	£450	7
Majorca	£390	4
THE CARIBBEAN		
Barbados	£950	7/10/14
Grenada	£850	7/14
St Lucia	£850	7/10/14
St Kitts	£850	7/14
NEW DESTINATION		
St Vincent [combined with another island for 7 days for a 14 day tour]	£950	7
Trinidad & Tobago	£1275	14
WORLDWIDE		
Australia	£1450	14
British Columbia	£1100	10
Dubai	£759	7
Goa	£1100	14
New Zealand	£1450	14
South Africa	£995	10
Sri Lanka	£1050	12
India (Golden Triangle)	£1300	14

Your next step call us on **01684 293175**
or visit www.**gulliversports**.co.uk

Fiddington Manor Tewkesbury Glos GL20 7BJ
email gullivers@gulliversports.co.uk   Fax 01684 297926
ABTA V8321   ATOL 3720   IATA 91201670

GULLIVERS
sports Travel

CHISLEHURST & SIDCUP GRAMMAR SCHOOL

Hurst Road, Sidcup, Kent DA15 9AG

Tel: 020 8302 6511 Fax: 020 8309 6596
Email: chislehurst-sidcup-gmr.bexley@lgfl.net

Master i/c Cricket: R.A. Wallbridge

2005 SEASON

Played: 21   Won: 5   Lost: 13   Drawn: 2   Tied: 1

Captain: J. West   Vice-captain: J. Bond

Team selected from: B. Carey*, T. Clarke, D. Meeking, M. Fergerson,
J. Ahmed*, S. Ahmed, B. Mills, J. West, J. Bond, J. Matkins, J. Dawes,
J. Dawkins, O. Brend, M. Moshiri, S. Brady, N. Abbott, M. Whinney,
R. Morgan, N. Kraus, M. Stokes, J. Doyle, A. Hilliker,
R. McDonald, H. Ryan-Smith.

SUMMARY

The pre-season tour to St. Kitts and Nevis allowed our young and inexperienced squad to gain a lot of knowledge in a very short time. It took them a few games to adjust to the conditions, the intensity of the cricket and the strict umpiring. However, two wins out of seven was a good return considering the circumstances. The highlight of our first victory was Junaid Ahmed's century. The people were very welcoming, helpful and generous. Off the field of play, the boys enjoyed the beaches, diving, sailing, island tours and the food.

So, with great optimism we returned home to take up the challenge of the Kent U19 League. I was hopeful that this would be our breakthrough season. In previous years we were always beaten by teams returning from Caribbean tours; I was optimistic that it would be our time to return the favour. So there we were, kitted out in our tour garb, ready to sweep the board. Unfortunately, in my meticulous planning I had failed to take into consideration one thing - reverse culture shock! This phenomenon lasted for all our league games; the break for the exams was welcomed.

The second half of the season proved to be a much more positive experience. A victory over our local rivals, Dartford GS, breathed new confidence into the team. This was followed by an enthralling tie on a sticky wicket against Judd, with opening bowler Blaine Carey taking 4-13. Blaine also hit a memorable quickfire 60 during Cricket Week against the MCC.

Captain Jonathan West did an admirable job in his first season in charge. It is hoped that the experience he gained will stand him, and the team, in good stead for next season.

AVERAGES

BATSMAN	INNINGS	NOT OUT	RUNS	H. SCORE	AVERAGE
J. Ahmed	13	2	507	110*	46.1
S. Ahmed	16	1	272	102*	18.1
J. Dawes	13	4	162	55	18.0
J. West	20	1	339	77	17.8
N. Abbott	13	2	144	42	13.1
T. Clarke	17	5	147	54*	12.3

BOWLER	OVERS	MAIDENS	RUNS	WICKETS	AVERAGE
M. Moshiri	13	0	97	8	12.1
J. Bond	52	8	187	15	12.5
J. Doyle	19.4	2	73	5	14.6
B. Carey	114.3	21	433	21	20.6
J. West	102	16	434	20	21.7
T. Clarke	17	0	126	5	25.2

WICKET-KEEPER	PLAYED	CAUGHT	STUMPED
M. Whinney	18	12	3
J. Matkins	3	2	1

NOTABLE BATTING PERFORMANCES

PLAYER	OPPOSITION	SCORE
J. Ahmed	Staff	110*
J. Ahmed	St. Kitts U15	105*
S. Ahmed	XL Club	102*
J. West	Sevenoaks Wednesday	77
B. Carey	MCC	60

NOTABLE BOWLING PERFORMANCES

PLAYER	OPPOSITION	FIGURES
J. Bond	MCC	5-60
B. Carey	Judd	4-13
B. Mills	Staff	4-25
J. Dawes	Sandy Point HS (St. Kitts)	4-35
M. Moshiri	Nevis	4-21

CHRIST COLLEGE BRECON

Brecon, Powys, LD3 8AE

Tel: 01874 615440 Fax: 01874 615475
Email: enquiries@christcollegebrecon.com

Master i/c Cricket: C.J. Webber   Coach: N.C. Blackburn

2005 SEASON

Played: 12 Won: 3   Lost: 8   Drawn: 1

Captain: A. Wells   Vice-captain: E. Rees

Team selected from: A. Wells, E. Rees, G. Webber, A. Teale, B. Painter,
H. Rich, N. Vaughan, A. James, S. Frazer, J. Faull, D. Layton, B. Jones,
J. Wells, K. Marmion.
Scorer: W. Anthony

SUMMARY

The season ended rather disappointingly considering the potential
we had. The absence of upper sixth players with examination
commitments took its toll. On the bright side, a number of younger
players were given the opportunity during exam period. Greg Webber
played throughout the season, showing potential with both bat and ball,
and is only in the fourth year. Alex James, John Faull, Kieran Marmion
and Michael Painter all acquitted themselves competently. This augurs
well for the future.

The story of the season was that we could not get going when we
had the opportunity - whether fielding or batting first. Despite some
very promising stands, silly mistakes and dropped catches cost the
team dearly.

Aled Wells led by example and showed great enthusiasm behind the
stumps. Generally the team spirit was excellent and there were some
very good performances, the best probably against Monmouth. At the
time of playing Monmouth, no one had managed to bowl them out. We
were the first to do so, reducing our opponents to 108-6. Sadly, we let
them get away, allowing them to score over 200 in their 50 overs.

The message for the future is to be less generous and to really grasp
opportunities when they arise. Do not let good work to go to waste!

AVERAGES

BATSMAN	INNINGS	NOT OUT	RUNS	H. SCORE	AVERAGE
H. Rich	10	0	294	57	29.4
G. Webber	10	1	209	97*	23.2
A. Teale	11	0	241	60	21.9
K. Marmion	3	0	53	40	17.7
B. Painter	11	1	154	40	15.4
E. Rees	12	1	168	40	15.3

BOWLER	OVERS	MAIDENS	RUNS	WICKETS	AVERAGE
G. Webber	43	4	182	11	16.5
H. Rich	59	6	270	16	16.9
A. Teale	89	12	342	14	24.4
B. Painter	103	13	418	14	29.9
A. James	37	2	201	6	33.5
J. Faull	60	3	271	8	33.9

WICKET-KEEPER	PLAYED	CAUGHT	STUMPED
A. Wells	12	8	3

NOTABLE BATTING PERFORMANCES

PLAYER	OPPOSITION	SCORE
G. Webber	Neath	97*
J. Wells	Old Breconians	80

NOTABLE BOWLING PERFORMANCES

PLAYER	OPPOSITION	FIGURES
H. Rich	Llandovery College	4-11
G. Webber	King's Gloucester	4-24
B. Painter	Rougemont	4-28

CHRIST'S HOSPITAL

Horsham, West Sussex RH13 0JE

Tel: 01403 247738 Fax: 01403 247732
Email: hph@christs-hospital.org.uk

Master i/c Cricket: Howard Holdsworth   Coach: Les Lenham

2005 SEASON

Played: 16   Won: 10   Lost: 3   Drawn: 3

Captain: J. Mitra   Vice-captain: J. Maxwell

Team selected from: J. Mitra*, J. Maxwell*, J. Maddren*,
T. Sanderson*, M. Quest*, S. Millicheap*, W. Bex-Russell,
B. Bawtree-Jobson, T. Day, D. Westerhout, M. Bassett, B. Walker,
S. Montgomery, C. Collins, S. Parr, S. Goodwin-Day, F. Hardy,
A. Whittingham, T. Hayes.
Scorer: G. Janes

SUMMARY

The Christ's Hospital 1st XI achieved ten victories, equalling the number of successes by the record-breaking 2002 team. The side was ably led by the talented James Mitra, whose opportunities to shine with big scores were severely limited by chasing a number of small totals. James Maxwell was the leading run-scorer, but he did tend to get himself out when well set.

The leading all-rounder was the wholehearted James Maddren, whose batting improved enormously. He was the third highest wicket-taker behind two younger players - the hugely promising 16-year-old quickie, Michael Quest, who will tour South Africa with the Sussex Academy in December 2005, and the consistent slow left-armer, Sam Millicheap, who has also been training with Sussex.

The fielding and catching of the team has been excellent, with Tom Sanderson setting a fine example as wicket-keeper.

There were two notable victories. The first was against Eastbourne College, who we had not beaten for twenty-nine years! The other was over the MCC, who we had not beaten for twenty-four years! How fitting it was that the captain, James Mitra, should finish that match, the last of four and a half seasons in the XI, with a six over the sightscreen.

AVERAGES

BATSMAN	INNINGS	NOT OUT	RUNS	H. SCORE	AVERAGE
J. Mitra	13	5	380	92*	47.5
J. Maxwell	14	3	402	82*	36.6
J. Maddren	14	4	362	88*	36.2
T. Sanderson	12	2	220	62*	22.0
B. Walker	7	3	69	34	17.3
M. Bassett	6	0	98	58	16.3

BOWLER	OVERS	MAIDENS	RUNS	WICKETS	AVERAGE
S. Millicheap	125	31	361	30	12.0
M. Quest	124	16	356	27	13.2
B. Bawtree-Jobson	66	8	243	16	15.2
J. Maddren	118	18	395	22	18.0
W. Bex-Russell	77	7	294	12	24.5
T. Day	57	3	239	9	26.6

WICKET-KEEPER	PLAYED	CAUGHT	STUMPED
T. Sanderson	12	11	2
J. Maxwell	4	3	0

NOTABLE BATTING PERFORMANCES

PLAYER	OPPOSITION	SCORE
J. Mitra	Eastbourne College	92*
J. Maxwell	Eastbourne College	82*
J. Maddren	Sussex Martlets	88*
M. Bassett	Sussex Martlets	58
T. Sanderson	Worth	62*

NOTABLE BOWLING PERFORMANCES

PLAYER	OPPOSITION	FIGURES
S. Millicheap	QEH Bristol	6-8
S. Millicheap	Worth	5-15
J. Maddren	Old Blues	5-27
M. Quest	St. George's Weybridge	4-7

CLAYESMORE SCHOOL

Iwerne Minster, Blandford Forum, Dorset DT11 8NF

Tel: 01747 812122 Fax: 01747 813208
Email: hmsec@clayesmore.com

Master i/c Cricket: Daniel Rimmer   Coach: Paul Warron

2005 SEASON

Played: 11   Won: 3   Lost: 3   Drawn: 2   Abandoned: 3

Captain: J. Morton   Vice-captain: B. Merrell

Team selected from: J. Morton*, A. Stuart, B. Merrell*, L. Dyckhoff,
J. Truscott, G. White, D. Briggs, G. Howard, B. Noifeld, A. Simpson,
E. Old, L. Hopkinson, H. Rolph, C. Yau.

SUMMARY

In a summer plagued by what can only be described as malicious
weather, Clayesmore was forced to cancel four fixtures and abandon
three.

It was a rather mediocre season with the bat, with only three boys
(James Truscott, Ben Noifeld and the captain, Justin Morton) managing
to score fifties. The main strength of the side lay with its fielding and
bowling. The most impressive bowling performances came from Ben
Noifeld against XL Club and Luke Dyckhoff against MCC.

AVERAGES

BATSMAN	INNINGS	NOT OUT	RUNS	H. SCORE	AVERAGE
J. Truscott	8	3	329	74	65.8
J. Morton	11	0	282	74	25.6
A. Simpson	11	0	229	46	20.8

BOWLER	OVERS	MAIDENS	RUNS	WICKETS	AVERAGE
G. Howard	60.5	6	248	26	9.5
J. Morton	42.5	4	203	14	14.5
L. Dyckhoff	83.4	10	352	20	17.6
B. Merrell	54	7	326	12	27.2
C. Yau	54.4	4	287	10	28.7
B. Noifeld	85	6	451	12	37.6

WELCOME TO THE BUNBURYS!

by Dr David English MBE, founder of the Bunbury Cricket Club

To me, Bunbury is the very epitome of what life is all about. It has passion, emotion, excitement and tension, skill, determination, friendship, successes and disappointments, toughness, kindness and a commitment to a challenge.

U15 cricket captures the moment between childhood and manhood; the players are faintly worldly-wise but with the refreshing outlook of children. They are adolescent, perhaps having experienced their first shave but still peeking over the Coca-Cola cans and dreaming of playing for England. They play with a free spirit, without the fear of failure, and oblivious to the demons they'll have to tackle in later years. I tell the lads, 'Work hard, and you'll get success. The only time success comes before work is in the dictionary.'

The Bunbury ESCA Festival is unquestionably the most important Schools' Cricket week for U15s in this country. In the ECB's development of excellence programme it represents the pinnacle of a young cricketer's career and the opportunity to play for England. In fact, during the past thirty years, 95% of all our Test cricketers have been 'discovered' at this festival, including Gooch, Gower, Hussain, Stewart, Gatting, Botham, Atherton and even Gary Lineker, a fine cricketer! Furthermore, eight of the triumphant England Ashes team are Bunburys. The three that slipped the net are Strauss and Pieterson who were brought up in South Africa and Geraint Jones who was in Papua New Guinea. To see Freddy, Vaughany, Tres, Harmy and co excel in a glorious summer makes the Old Bunbarians even more precious.

The Bunbury ESCA Festival represents a 'Cricket-for-all Opportunity'. Whether a lad attends a state school or a public school, he will have the same chance to reach this festival. He or she will play for their school team, then their county and finally, after a further trial, represent their region. The four regions, North, South, West and Midlands converge on a different county each year where the forty-four best lads in England compete in a 'round robin' tournament. The selectors pick the best eleven who then represent England.

2002 saw the introduction of the Daily Telegraph Bunbury Scholarship, dedicated to the memory of Ben Hollioake who excelled in the 1992 Bunbury Festival. The U15 scholarship winners are judged on their performances throughout the season, culminating in their play in the Bunbury Festival. They then attend the ECB Academy at Loughborough thus underlining the Bunbury motto of giving the young 'The Roots to Grow and Wings to Fly'.

www.bunburycricket.com

CLIFTON COLLEGE

32 College Road, Clifton, Bristol BS8 3JH

Tel: 0117 315 7276 Fax: 0117 315 7275
Email: jbobby@clifton-college.avon.sch.uk

Master i/c Cricket: John Bobby   Coach: Paul Romaines

2005 SEASON

Played: 15   Won: 9   Lost: 3   Drawn: 2   Tied: 1

Captain: F. Dengu   Vice-captain: J. Innes

Team selected from: F. Dengu, J. Innes, O. Palmer, W. Greig, J. Virgo, A. Le Friec, J. Paull, T. Read, S. Lakin, J. Goody, J. Askew, J. Harris.
Scorer: Jenny Fong

SUMMARY

This was an excellent season for Clifton's 1st XI. A move towards playing a greater number of 50 over matches has certainly led to an abundance of exciting cricket, resulting in many more wins.

The strength of the side was an experienced and balanced bowling attack, coupled with six players who made valuable contributions with the bat throughout the season.

Fungai Dengu captained the team superbly and it will be a huge asset to next year's 1st XI that he will again lead the side.

The performance of the season was undoubtedly a brilliant 122* by Jamie Innes against King's Taunton.

A squad of sixteen players took part in a very successful Caribbean tour to St. Lucia and St. Vincent in July.

AVERAGES

BATSMAN	INNINGS	NOT OUT	RUNS	H. SCORE	AVERAGE
F. Dengu	14	5	457	87*	50.8
J. Innes	13	2	352	122*	32.0
W. Greig	10	1	251	58*	27.9
J. Virgo	10	3	166	41*	23.7
O. Palmer	14	0	266	44	19.0
J. Paull	12	1	175	52	15.9

BOWLER	OVERS	MAIDENS	RUNS	WICKETS	AVERAGE
W. Greig	124	11	445	25	17.8
J. Harris	45	5	236	13	18.2
J. Askew	67	7	235	12	19.6
T. Read	84	14	248	12	20.7
A. Le Friec	93	9	360	17	21.2
J. Innes	89	11	281	12	23.4

WICKET-KEEPER	PLAYED	CAUGHT	STUMPED
J. Goody	14	10	2

NOTABLE BATTING PERFORMANCES

PLAYER	OPPOSITION	SCORE
J. Innes	King's College Taunton	122*
F. Dengu	Queen's Taunton	87*

NOTABLE BOWLING PERFORMANCES

PLAYER	OPPOSITION	FIGURES
W. Greig	King Edward's Bath	7-3-18-5
T. Read	Old Cliftonian XI	8-3-12-4
J. Innes	King's Bruton	8-1-22-4

CRANBROOK GRAMMAR SCHOOL

Waterloo Road, Cranbrook TN17 3JD

Tel: 01580 711800 Fax: 01580 711828
Email: admin@cranbrook.kent.sch.uk

Master i/c Cricket: A.J. Presnell

2005 SEASON

Played: 17   Won: 6   Lost: 1   Drawn: 10

Captain: W. Goulstone   Vice-captain: E. Towner

Team selected from: W. Goulstone, J. Kain, E. Towner, D. Wickham, O. Morkel, T. Bateman, D. Avery, Z. Nathan, J. Baker, M. Daley, A. Wenman, R. Austin, R. Jackson.

SUMMARY

Cranbrook had a young side which found the going tough. The fielding was always of a high standard and the bowling tidy, but lacking in penetration.

The batting relied heavily on Jasper Kain who scored runs all season. Seven of the boys are back next season and with a good winter net session, the future is encouraging.

> *Did you know? . . .* The most wicket-keeping dismissals for England in a Test innings is the 7 taken by Bob Taylor against India at Bombay in 1979/80. Jack Russell holds the record of 11 in a whole Test match against South Africa in 1995/6.

AVERAGES

BATSMAN	INNINGS	NOT OUT	RUNS	H. SCORE	AVERAGE
J. Kain	17	1	557	158	34.8
E. Towner	15	1	399	67	28.5
W. Goulstone	14	2	274	43	22.8

BOWLER	OVERS	MAIDENS	RUNS	WICKETS	AVERAGE
O. Morkel	85.3	12	372	19	19.6
A. Wenman	85	19	253	12	21.1
M. Daley	77	8	334	15	22.3

WICKET-KEEPER	PLAYED	CAUGHT	STUMPED
R. Austin	10	6	0
Z. Nathan	7	4	1

NOTABLE BATTING PERFORMANCES

PLAYER	OPPOSITION	SCORE
J. Kain	Chatham GS	158
J. Kain	Mote CC	102*
J. Kain	Bethany	79
E. Towner	Eltham College	67

NOTABLE BOWLING PERFORMANCES

PLAYER	OPPOSITION	FIGURES
R. Jackson	Chatham GS	5-31

CRANLEIGH SCHOOL

Horseshoe Lane, Cranleigh, Surrey GU6 8QQ

Tel: 01483 273666 Fax: 01483 267398
Email: wnb@cranleigh.org

Master i/c Cricket: Neil Bennett   Coach: Stuart Welch

2005 SEASON

Played: 16   Won: 6   Lost: 3   Drawn: 7

Captain: A. Cope

Team selected from: A. Cope*, M. Crump*, S. Waters*, J. Haynes,
S. Meaker*, J. Jupp, M. Roper, H. Barson, J. Smith, B. Gilchrist,
N. Pritchard*, T. Rose, T. Crump, P. Roper.

SUMMARY

Before the season in England began, A. Cope (Surrey Academy) and
S. Meaker (England U16) had both been on tours to South Africa.
Unfortunately A. Cope was injured and had to miss the majority of the
season.

M. Crump and S. Waters formed a reliable opening partnership,
with Waters hitting consecutive centuries towards the end of the
season. J. Haynes, S. Meaker and B. Gilchrist made up a solid middle-
order.

The bowling attack saw Meaker and N. Pritchard opening, ably
supported by the medium pace of J. Jupp and M. Crump. The spin
department was shared between two of our youngsters, T. Crump and
M. Roper.

With only two of the squad leaving and A. Cope restored to fitness,
next season has a great deal of promise.

AVERAGES

BATSMAN	INNINGS	NOT OUT	RUNS	H. SCORE	AVERAGE
S. Waters	10	2	525	137*	65.6
J. Haynes	9	3	330	78	55.0
M. Crump	13	1	404	96*	33.7
S. Meaker	11	2	253	86	28.1
B. Gilchrist	10	1	245	86	27.2

BOWLER	OVERS	MAIDENS	RUNS	WICKETS	AVERAGE
M. Crump	122	20	419	22	19.0
T. Crump	66	8	229	12	19.1
S. Meaker	182	35	586	27	21.7
J. Jupp	85	14	260	11	23.6
N. Pritchard	167	26	573	24	23.9

WICKET-KEEPER	PLAYED	CAUGHT	STUMPED
M. Roper	19	17	3

NOTABLE BATTING PERFORMANCES

PLAYER	OPPOSITION	SCORE
S. Waters	St. Peter's York	137*
S. Waters	St. Peter's York	130*
M. Crump	Old Cranleighans	96*
S. Meaker	St. John's	86
B. Gilchrist	XL Club	86

CULFORD SCHOOL

Culford, Bury St. Edmunds, Suffolk IP28 6TX

Tel: 01284 728615 Fax: 01284 728631
Email: culfordschool@culford.co.uk

Master i/c Cricket: A. Marsh   Coach: Andrew Tweedie

2005 SEASON

Played: 12   Won: 3   Lost: 8   Drawn: 1

Captain: R. Petherick   Vice-captain: P. Shepperson

Team selected from: W. Williamson*, T. Osborn, P. Shepperson,
T. Turner, R. Petherick, M. Feczko*, T. Recaldin, J. Dennis,
J. Davey, T. Jonason, H. Ogunfowora, J. Lee,
J. Absolon, F. Ogunfowora.
Scorer: L. Kelly

SUMMARY

A young and inexperienced side, Culford improved as the season progressed. Two close defeats early in the season were due, more than anything, to us being unable to hold our nerve in tight situations.

In the 2006 season the batting should be relatively strong. The bowling lacked variety in 2005 and the search for a spinner is on. Nine of the side return for 2006.

Did you know? . . . Jim Laker's 19-90 for England against Australia at Manchester in 1956 are the best Test match bowling figures by any player. Tony Lock took the other wicket.

AVERAGES

BATSMAN	INNINGS	NOT OUT	RUNS	H. SCORE	AVERAGE
T. Osborn	11	-	365	106	33.2
W. Williamson	11	-	323	77	29.4
T. Turner	10	-	206	42	20.6
P. Shepperson	11	-	220	58	20.0
T. Recaldin	10	-	135	50	13.5
R. Petherick	12	-	137	36	11.4

BOWLER	OVERS	MAIDENS	RUNS	WICKETS	AVERAGE
J. Dennis	-	-	137	9	15.2
T. Turner	-	-	370	19	19.5
H. Ogunfowora	-	-	210	10	21.0
T. Osborn	-	-	401	12	33.4
W. Williamson	-	-	510	12	42.5

WICKET-KEEPER	PLAYED	CAUGHT	STUMPED
R. Petherick	-	-	-

NOTABLE BATTING PERFORMANCES

PLAYER	OPPOSITION	SCORE
T. Osborn	Gentlemen of Suffolk	106
T. Osborn	Woodbridge	95
W. Williamson	Gentlemen of Suffolk	77

NOTABLE BOWLING PERFORMANCES

PLAYER	OPPOSITION	FIGURES
W. Williamson	Norwich	5-75

DAUNTSEY'S SCHOOL

High Street, West Lavington, Devizes, Wilts SN10 4HF

Tel: 01380 814500 Fax: 01380 814501
Email: info@dauntseys.wilts.sch.uk

Master i/c Cricket: A.J. Palmer Coach: S.C. Cloete

2005 SEASON

Played: 16 Won: 9 Lost: 7

Captain: J. Wookey Vice-captain: T. Chadwick

Team selected from: J. Wookey, T. Hammond, C. Rivers, J. Lodwick,
T. Chadwick, T. Street, A. Penny*, R. Croucher, S. Palmer, R. Thomas,
W. Whyte*, C. Marshall, J. Vickery, T. Southernden, J. Grant,
A. Smith, O. Wilkinson, N. Westlake, C. Mann.
Scorer: M. Hodson

SUMMARY

A team of mainly lower sixth formers had the most victories in a regular season since 1995. They reached the quarter-finals of the Twenty20 Cup and finished equal fourth in the Bath and District Schools' League.

The batting was always positive, with run-rates often reaching seven an over. Only on a very few occasions did individuals convert good starts to substantial innings.

Alex Denny hit the ball very hard through the off-side. Fifteen-year-old Jon Lodwick (a West region player) started to fulfill some of his enormous potential as the season progressed.

In general, the bowling lacked sufficient control with far too many wides and no-balls delivered. Team spirit was strong, fielding energetic and with a tour of Grenada and Carriacou to look forward to in April, prospects are good for 2006.

AVERAGES

BATSMAN	INNINGS	NOT OUT	RUNS	H. SCORE	AVERAGE
A. Penny	16	1	378	53	25.2
J. Wookey	15	1	307	43*	21.9
J. Lodwick	14	2	248	60	20.7
R. Thomas	11	2	183	37	20.3
T. Chadwick	10	1	155	34	17.2
T. Street	12	3	153	70	17.0

BOWLER	OVERS	MAIDENS	RUNS	WICKETS	AVERAGE
J. Lodwick	75	8	296	22	13.5
W. Whyte	73	7	300	15	20.0
T. Street	68	9	255	11	23.2
A. Penny	74	14	347	13	26.7
S. Palmer	58	5	302	11	27.5

NOTABLE BATTING PERFORMANCES

PLAYER	OPPOSITION	SCORE
T. Street	Old Dauntseians	70
J. Lodwick	Beechen Cliff	60
A. Penny	Wiltshire Queries	53

NOTABLE BOWLING PERFORMANCES

PLAYER	OPPOSITION	FIGURES
J. Lodwick	Abingdon	4-14
J. Lodwick	King's Bruton	4-38

DENSTONE COLLEGE

Uttoxeter, Staffordshire ST14 5HN

Tel: 01889 590484 Fax: 01889 590744
Email: admissions@denstonecollege.org

Master i/c Cricket: S.J. Dean

2005 SEASON

Played: 15   Won: 9   Lost: 3   Drawn: 3

Captain: M. Gouldstone   Vice-captain: M. Ovens

Team selected from: M. Gouldstone, M. Ovens, J. Sharp, R. Rouse, A. Hopkins, G. McAloon, J. Parker, T. Morgan, G. Gill, J. Burnett, J. Young, B. Cheadle, H. Siddique.
Scorer: R. Hemingway

SUMMARY

Matt Gouldstone captained the side to nine victories - one of the best seasons for some time! On the back of a successful tour to South Africa at Easter, the spirit was high throughout the season.

The team performed well as a whole and Luke Cheadle proved a worthy addition to the squad. James Burnett scored his maiden century and completed notable scores in his last three innings. Matt Gouldstone made five more half-centuries to finish fourth in the all-time leading run-scorers for Denstone cricket. His twenty-four half-centuries in total is a new record. Tom Morgan scored two fifties, one a splendid effort against Repton.

Richard Rouse and Jon Sharp shouldered the bowling as a new ball pair, but others chipped in when needed. Gareth McAloon's 4-48 and Hamza Siddique's 5-24 spring to mind.

The games we lost were to Worksop, Repton and Melbourne HS. Next season will see another year of rebuilding as nine of the squad will be leaving.

AVERAGES

BATSMAN	INNINGS	NOT OUT	RUNS	H. SCORE	AVERAGE
M. Gouldstone	11	5	451	88*	75.2
J. Burnett	8	2	310	128*	51.7
B. Cheadle	14	3	379	86*	34.5
J. Parker	8	2	174	85	29.0
T. Morgan	10	2	204	64*	25.5
M. Ovens	9	1	150	39	18.8

BOWLER	OVERS	MAIDENS	RUNS	WICKETS	AVERAGE
R. Rouse	96.1	19	347	21	16.5
J. Sharp	121	18	451	21	21.5

WICKET-KEEPER	PLAYED	CAUGHT	STUMPED
A. Hopkins	13	7	5
G. McAloon	2	2	0

NOTABLE BATTING PERFORMANCES

PLAYER	OPPOSITION	SCORE
J. Burnett	Queen Mary's Walsall	128*
M. Gouldstone	MCC	88*
M. Gouldstone	Bromsgrove	87
B. Cheadle	Mount St. Mary's College	86*
J. Parker	Abbotsholme	85
J. Burnett	Bishop Vesey's	80*
J. Burnett	Bromsgrove	65
T. Morgan	Repton	64*

NOTABLE BOWLING PERFORMANCES

PLAYER	OPPOSITION	FIGURES
R. Rouse	Mount St. Mary's College	9-3-10-5
H. Siddique	Bishop Vesey's	6-1-24-5
J. Sharp	Wrekin College	6-0-29-4

DOLLAR ACADEMY

Dollar, Clacks, FK14 7DU

Tel: 01259 740572 Fax: 01259 742867
Email: foster.j@dollaracademy.org.uk

Master i/c Cricket: John Foster   Coach: Lee Spendlove

2005 SEASON

Played: 10   Won: 4   Lost: 6

Captain: N. Alston   Vice-captain: K. Barrow

Team selected from: N. Alston*, K. Barrow*, S. Tennant*, I. Tennant*, S. Brenkel, B. Auld, T. Allen, D. Witko, J. McPherson, A. Shedden, S. Jabbar, A. Bell-Scott, T. Barber-Fleming, M. Bremner, A. Tester.

SUMMARY

With only one of last year's XI returning, experience was at a premium, therefore it was reasonably satisfying to finish with four wins. Four matches were lost to the weather.

Victories against Strathallan, Edinburgh Academy and Stewart's Melville, together with encouraging performances versus Fettes and the MCC were the highlights of a transitional season, which saw six fourth form boys making their 1st XI debuts.

Billy Auld (wicket-keeper) played in every match, and Matthew Bremner (Scotland U15) and Angus Tester played in half the fixtures. Statistically, the side relied heavily on Korni Barrow and Nicholas Alston, but they were well supported by Iain Tennant and Sam Brenkel with the bat, and solid bowling performances from Dan Witko and Angus Tester. As the season progressed, Nicholas Alston matured as a captain and the batting of Korni Barrow improved.

With almost all the present squad returning, together with the successful 2005 Colts XI to select from, future prospects for Dollar cricket are encouraging.

AVERAGES

BATSMAN	INNINGS	NOT OUT	RUNS	H. SCORE	AVERAGE
K. Barrow	10	2	442	101*	55.3
N. Alston	10	2	216	65*	27.0

BOWLER	OVERS	MAIDENS	RUNS	WICKETS	AVERAGE
N. Alston	72.1	9	272	18	15.1
K. Barrow	71	9	276	18	15.3

WICKET-KEEPER	PLAYED	CAUGHT	STUMPED
B. Auld	10	11	4

NOTABLE BATTING PERFORMANCES

PLAYER	OPPOSITION	SCORE
K. Barrow	Rectors XI	101*
K. Barrow	Edinburgh Academy	81
K. Barrow	Stewart's Melville	61*
K. Barrow	Hutchesons' GS	66
N. Alston	Strathallan	65*

NOTABLE BOWLING PERFORMANCES

PLAYER	OPPOSITION	FIGURES
N. Alston	Hutchesons' GS	5-21
K. Barrow	Strathallan	4-17

DOWNSIDE SCHOOL

Stratton-on-the-Fosse, Radstock, Bath BA3 4RJ

Tel: 01761 235104 Fax: 01761 235105
Email: riago@downside.co.uk

Master i/c Cricket: Richard A. Iago

2005 SEASON

Played: 6   Won: 2   Lost: 3   Drawn: 1

Captain: O. Mellotte

Team selected from: E. Westlake, C. Gross, O. Mellotte*, H. Marland,
H. Monro, A. Knight, T. McClellan, J. Gatehouse, O. Lombard,
W. Harris*, C. Sweeney, T. Gross, D. Tracey.
Scorer: T. Thicknesse

SUMMARY

A young team, well led by Mellotte, played with great spirit and enthusiasm, producing some notable performances.

An outstanding second wicket partnership of 195, between Mellotte (102*) and Westlake (82) at Wycliffe, was the batting highlight. There were some promising contributions from Messrs Marland and Knight in the middle-order, but too often batsmen perished playing rashly when well set.

Monro, a very promising leg-spin bowler, all but carried the attack, setting up victory against the MCC. He generally exhibited good variety and an exemplary line and length.

Poor catching marred what were otherwise perfectly competent fielding displays, costing matches that should have been won. The notoriously short school season was decimated by the inclement weather, with four fixtures lost to rain.

The restoration of the pavilion and the experience gained this year by a young team augurs well for the future of Downside cricket.

AVERAGES

BATSMAN	INNINGS	NOT OUT	RUNS	H. SCORE	AVERAGE
O. Mellotte	6	1	225	102*	45.0
H. Monro	4	1	112	38	37.3
J. Gatehouse	4	1	85	32	28.3
H. Marland	5	0	126	41	25.2
E. Westlake	6	0	142	82	23.7

BOWLER	OVERS	MAIDENS	RUNS	WICKETS	AVERAGE
H. Monro	75	8	328	14	23.4
O. Mellotte	26.3	3	122	4	30.5
W. Harris	45.2	5	186	6	31.0
H. Marland	25	1	133	2	66.5

WICKET-KEEPER	PLAYED	CAUGHT	STUMPED
C. Gross	6	2	2

NOTABLE BATTING PERFORMANCES

PLAYER	OPPOSITION	SCORE
O. Mellotte	Wycliffe College	102*
E. Westlake	Wycliffe College	82
O. Mellotte	Emeriti CC	75

NOTABLE BOWLING PERFORMANCES

PLAYER	OPPOSITION	FIGURES
H. Monro	MCC	4-34

DR CHALLONER'S
GRAMMAR SCHOOL

Chesham Road, Amersham, Bucks HP6 5HA

Tel: 01494 787500 Fax: 01494 721862
Email: admin@challoners.com

Master i/c Cricket: D. Atkinson

2005 SEASON

Played: 11   Won: 4   Lost: 4   Abandoned: 3

Captain: H. Pegler   Vice-captain: M. Watson

Team selected from: H. Pegler*, M. Watson*, S. Litchfield*,
D. Bishop, T. Graham, M. Dunning, D. Cranfield-Thompson*,
J. Jutla*, A. Soni*, A. Ladha, S. Mubarak, J. Harmer, A. Martin,
O. Richards, D. Daly, S. McCubbin, C. Luddy, J. Rice.

SUMMARY

The first half of the season was disappointing. After losing two games to rain, defeats at RGS High Wycombe, St. George's Weybridge, Watford GS and Stowe were characterised by the team playing some good cricket, but never doing enough to pressurise the opposition.

After a break for exams and half-term, the team reappeared rejuvenated. The MCC match should always be the highlight of a school fixture list, and this year's game could not be bettered. The boys earned the unwavering admiration of the MCC side for their spirit, talent and determination. Jason Jutla and Tom Graham made early inroads to reduce MCC to 23-3. Matt Watson bowled a marathon spell of leg-spin and finished with figures of 2-66 from 21 overs. The MCC total of 182 was competitive, and Hywel Pegler and David Cranfield-Thompson ensured a good start to our reply with some sensible batting. At 75-1 everything looked promising, but a flurry of wickets reduced us to a precarious 80-5. However, Watson and Ollie Richards seized the initiative and put on 71 for the sixth wicket. Wickets and runs were then exchanged, before Mike Dunning and Jutla took the school past the MCC total with two wickets and two overs to spare. This was a fine game of cricket played in excellent spirit.

The last two games of the season were won. John Lyon were beaten only off the last ball, thanks to a spell of hostile fast bowling from James Harmer, who took 4 wickets in 4 overs without conceding a run. The final fixture, against the XL Club, was won by the batsmen. Pegler and Watson, opening together in their final game for the school, put on 88, and Pegler went on to score 79 as we successfully chased 174.

AVERAGES

BATSMAN	INNINGS	NOT OUT	RUNS	H. SCORE	AVERAGE
D. Cranfield-Thompson	8	1	236	76	33.7
H. Pegler	6	0	158	79	26.3
A. Soni	6	1	119	45	23.8
M. Watson	8	0	190	54	23.8
S. Litchfield	7	0	164	51	23.4

BOWLER	OVERS	MAIDENS	RUNS	WICKETS	AVERAGE
J. Harmer	23	7	75	7	10.7
M. Watson	78	11	262	11	23.8
J. Jutla	46	6	146	5	29.2

NOTABLE BATTING PERFORMANCES

PLAYER	OPPOSITION	SCORE
S. Litchfield	RGS High Wycombe	51
D. Cranfield-Thompson	Watford GS	76
M. Watson	MCC	45
H. Pegler	XL Club	79

NOTABLE BOWLING PERFORMANCES

PLAYER	OPPOSITION	FIGURES
J. Harmer	John Lyon	4-4-0-4

DUKE OF YORK'S
ROYAL MILITARY SCHOOL

Guston, Dover, Kent CT15 5EQ

Tel: 01304 245024 Fax: 01304 245019
Email: headmaster@doyrms.com

Master i/c Cricket: S. Salisbury   Coach: N.J. Dexter

2005 SEASON

Played: 12   Won: 6   Lost: 3   Drawn: 3

Captain: B. Inshaw

Team selected from: B. Inshaw*, R. Kaye*, J. Inshaw, J. Baber,
J. Blondell, T. Thurston, C. Thurston, R. Boulton, D. Malla*, S. Rana,
M. Roberts, P. Gurung, S. Hindley.

SUMMARY

The 1st XI had an entertaining summer, with some close finishes and the added excitement of a good run in the Kent Cup.

The captain, Ben Inshaw, and Richard Kaye both enjoyed their final season, having been in the XI together for four years. The team had a good spread of young talent and established players, and everyone made crucial contributions at critical times.

James Baber and Jamie Inshaw, both young batsmen, look to have a good future and should thrive next summer.

AVERAGES

BATSMAN	INNINGS	NOT OUT	RUNS	H. SCORE	AVERAGE
R. Kaye	12	4	392	110	49.0
B. Inshaw	11	0	298	58	27.1
J. Baber	11	0	257	43	23.4
S. Rana	12	0	225	58	18.8
J. Inshaw	11	0	155	39	14.1

BOWLER	OVERS	MAIDENS	RUNS	WICKETS	AVERAGE
R. Kaye	100	19	332	25	13.3
J. Inshaw	40.2	7	166	10	16.6
J. Blondell	68	12	244	12	20.3
D. Malla	58.4	6	287	11	26.1

CHANCE TO SHINE

by Nick Gandon, Director of the Cricket Foundation

As someone whose professional career up until two years ago was spent as a teacher within independent schools, I am pleased to contribute to the inaugural edition of *The Schools' Cricket Almanac*. The book records the achievements of cricket-playing schools. These are important since cricket is vital to the life of schools. Cricket matters. Of course all competitive sport matters, but for me – and millions like me – competitive cricket matters most.

It's not an exclusive claim but, like other team-games, cricket encourages challenge, teamwork and discipline. It provides competition and rivalry; it teaches us to meet with Kipling's two impostors in a measured way. Cricket demands collective and individual responsibility; it advances character; it stimulates guile as well as gristle. It's a vital force for learning and healthy living, for drawing people together from diverse backgrounds and creating a sense of belonging. Who needs government reports to understand that cricket and other team sports have vital parts to play in promoting positive values, respect and integration, in driving the Anti-Slob and Anti-Yob strategies?

Cricket matters - and it matters that young people, all young people, are given opportunities to play. Up until quite recently my professional concern had revolved around the 7% of young people that enjoy the benefits of private education. Now my greater concern is for the 93% that don't. Cricketing provision within the two educational sectors has been a chasm, as far apart as Brisbane is from Bristol. 'Cricket in schools is an oxymoron,' Michael Parkinson insisted recently in one of his Monday morning polemics in *The Daily Telegraph*. If cricket is measured in opportunities to play the game, then Mr Parkinson has a point.

Don't be misled by some of the statistics. According to our research, and despite the heroic endeavours of committed teachers working mostly in isolation and without adequate funding, fewer than 10% of state schools offer opportunities to boys and girls to take part in at least five organised matches each year. I suspect the entries within this almanac will support this contention.

Chance to Shine is the Cricket Foundation's campaign to regenerate competitive cricket in state schools. Launched in May 2005, it aims to generate £50 million with which to create sustainable cricket cultures within a third of all schools in England and Wales over ten years. We're under no illusion that our task will be easy, but we know what the challenges are and we know how to address them. In providing coaches engaged by good local clubs to deliver quality coaching and competition within groups of local schools, in funding equipment and facility improvement and in creating partnerships involving independent schools amongst others, we have a clear plan. Our pilot programmes undertaken in 2005 give us cause to be confident.

My mind is already taking me towards 2015, to the tenth anniversary of *The Schools' Cricket Almanac*. The London Olympics will have been and gone; Kevin Pietersen will be approaching retirement, the white hairs on his head perhaps no longer cosmetic. It is my fervent hope that the tenth edition will record the achievements of many more cricketing state schools because cricket matters - and it matters that all young people are given, through cricket, their chance to shine.

www.chancetoshine.org

DULWICH COLLEGE

London SE21 7LD

Tel: 020 8693 3601 Fax: 020 8693 3186
Email: cooperdj@dulwich.org.uk

Master i/c Cricket: John Cooper   Coach: Bill Athey

2005 SEASON

Played: 21   Won: 9   Lost: 4   Drawn: 8

Captain: T. Roy   Vice-captain: R. Brathwaite

Team selected from: T. Roy*, R. Brathwaite*, C. Southern*,
S. Mahgani*, D. Diamond, R. Chahar, K. Siuakumaran, B. Precious*,
F. Bucknell*, J. Lawrence, W. Charnley*, M. Kafle*, D. Ranatunga,
A. Brawn, J. Tedaldi, M. Goodwin.
Scorer: T. O'Reilly

SUMMARY

This was another impressive season on what is a very strong circuit.
The losses to Free Foresters, Harrow, Taunton and Westville were not
too disappointing. We enjoyed many excellent wins, especially the
Tonbridge game when we finished nine down chasing 129. It was our
first win over them since 1974. However, there were too many draws
when chasing relatively low scores.

Ruel Brathwaite and Rama Chahar were the pick of the bowlers and
Rama Chahar, Tommy Roy and Dhyan Ranatunga were the best
batsmen. The side should be pleased with their achievements, but
disappointed that they did not progress further than the quarter-finals
of the Twenty20 competition.

AVERAGES

BATSMAN	INNINGS	NOT OUT	RUNS	H. SCORE	AVERAGE
T. Roy	19	4	688	90	45.9
R. Chahar	16	3	489	121	37.6
K. Siuakumaran	18	4	424	56	30.3
M. Kafle	14	0	375	77	26.8
D. Ranatunga	19	0	482	81	25.4
B. Precious	14	3	238	56*	21.6

BOWLER	OVERS	MAIDENS	RUNS	WICKETS	AVERAGE
R. Brathwaite	122	33	347	28	12.4
R. Chahar	199.1	22	600	37	16.2
B. Precious	126.5	19	475	22	21.6
M. Goodwin	58	11	245	11	22.3
K. Siuakumaran	191.4	26	818	27	30.3

WICKET-KEEPER	PLAYED	CAUGHT	STUMPED
D. Ranatunga	16	26	8
J. Tedaldi	4	7	1

NOTABLE BATTING PERFORMANCES

PLAYER	OPPOSITION	SCORE
R. Chahar	King's College Wimbledon	121
R. Chahar	Knox GS (Australia)	105*
T. Roy	Knox GS (Australia)	90
D. Ranatunga	Knox GS (Australia)	81

NOTABLE BOWLING PERFORMANCES

PLAYER	OPPOSITION	FIGURES
R. Brathwaite	Brighton College	16-3-29-6
R. Chahar	Haileybury	12-0-35-6
B. Precious	Chigwell	6.2-4-4-5
K. Siuakumaran	Tonbridge	9.2-0-23-4

DURHAM SCHOOL

Durham City DH1 4SZ

Tel: 0191 386 4783   Fax: 0191 383 1025
Email: enquiries@durhamschool.co.uk

Master i/c Cricket: P. Gerard   Coach: M. Fishwick

2005 SEASON

Played: 16   Won: 9   Lost: 3   Drawn: 4

Captain: P. Dias   Vice-captain: P. Muchall

Team selected from: P. Dias*, P. Muchall*, W. Dias, R. Fairlamb,
J. Hutton, A. Morton, G. Pratt, S. Rae, A. Stevenson, O. Steadman,
S. Tiffin*, M. Turns, H. Whalley.

Scorer: R. Davison

SUMMARY

Durham had another excellent season under new Australian coach
Michael Fishwick. Established players Paul Muchall and Stuart Tiffin
topped the averages and were selected for HMC teams.

Captain Patrick Dias engendered a fine team spirit and work ethic,
bowling the most overs and taking the most wickets.

Important contributions were made by Arnie Stevenson, Gareth
Pratt, Adam Morton, Will Dias and wicket-keeper Hugh Whalley.

Youngsters John Hutton (15), Oliver Steadman (13) and Michael
Turns (14) made impressive debuts and became regular 1st XI players
in a side that defeated, amongst others, strong teams from the MCC,
Durham Pilgrims and the Imran Khan XI.

Michael Turns has since been selected for the England U15 squad.

AVERAGES

BATSMAN	INNINGS	NOT OUT	RUNS	H. SCORE	AVERAGE
S. Tiffin	16	7	671	103*	74.6
P. Muchall	14	4	683	160*	68.3
O. Steadman	12	1	353	98	32.1
J. Hutton	7	5	44	18	22.0
P. Dias	14	3	191	55	17.4

BOWLER	OVERS	MAIDENS	RUNS	WICKETS	AVERAGE
P. Muchall	84	23	236	21	11.2
J. Hutton	108	27	325	22	14.8
S. Tiffin	129	39	406	26	15.6
M. Turns	53	11	175	11	15.9
G. Pratt	70	14	250	13	19.2
A. Stevenson	61	4	272	14	19.4
P. Dias	155	27	609	31	19.6

NOTABLE BATTING PERFORMANCES

PLAYER	OPPOSITION	SCORE
P. Muchall	Durham Pilgrims	100*
S. Tiffin	Durham Pilgrims	103
P. Muchall	Imran Khan XI	130
O. Steadman	Ampleforth College	98
P. Muchall	Glenalmond	160*
S. Tiffin	Sunshine Coast GS (Australia)	103*
S. Tiffin	MCC	70*

NOTABLE BOWLING PERFORMANCES

PLAYER	OPPOSITION	FIGURES
J. Hutton	King's Tynemouth	4-1
G. Pratt	Pocklington	4-14
P. Dias	Imran Khan XI	5-29
P. Muchall	Imran Khan XI	5-62
P. Muchall	Glenalmond	6-43
P. Dias	Sunshine Coast GS (Australia)	4-25
S. Tiffin	MCC	4-26

EASTBOURNE COLLEGE

Old Wish Road, Eastbourne, East Sussex BN21 4JX

Tel: 01323 452320 Fax: 01323 452327
Email: hmsec@eastbourne-college.co.uk

Master i/c Cricket: N.L. Wheeler   Coach: R.C. Bromley

2005 SEASON

Played: 16   Won: 8   Lost: 6   Drawn: 2

Captain: C. Chisholm   Vice-captain: E. Miller

Team selected from: C. Chisholm*, E. Miller, J. Newton*,
G. Chapman, O. Priestman, C. Hinchliffe, A. Stewart, P. Bradford,
L. Munro, F. Florry, G. Newton, M. Sands, J. Sibrec.

SUMMARY

A tough tour to Australia in December 2004 revealed the strengths and weaknesses of this untried team. Only Chad Chisholm remained from the unbeaten side of 2004 and he was by far the outstanding player of the year. His 149* versus Epsom was a brilliant innings on a pitch that no other player could master.

304-5 (50 overs) against Hurstpierpoint was a high point, as was a losing finals place in the new Twenty20 Langdale Cup format for Sussex independent schools.

Chad Chisholm's 7-27 was by far the best bowling of the season. Young players from the U16 XI, notably Charlie Hinchliffe, Ollie Priestman and Angus Stewart, should help in producing quality cricket as ever at Eastbourne.

Richard Bromley, the former deputy headmaster and master in charge of cricket at Christ's College Christchurch gave the team a disciplined, efficient and fun flair as professional.

AVERAGES

BATSMAN	INNINGS	NOT OUT	RUNS	H. SCORE	AVERAGE
C. Chisholm	12	1	444	149*	40.4
C. Hinchliffe	13	2	390	107	35.5
P. Bradford	7	3	120	55	30.0
J. Newton	10	2	229	47	28.6
O. Priestman	15	0	326	79	21.7
G. Chapman	8	2	112	40	18.7

BOWLER	OVERS	MAIDENS	RUNS	WICKETS	AVERAGE
C. Chisholm	111	26	320	28	11.4
G. Chapman	40	5	153	12	12.7
A. Stewart	27	3	118	8	14.7
J. Newton	100	15	309	15	20.6
E. Miller	46	6	201	8	25.1
O. Priestman	76	8	285	11	25.9

WICKET-KEEPER	PLAYED	CAUGHT	STUMPED
C. Hinchliffe	14	24	2

NOTABLE BATTING PERFORMANCES

PLAYER	OPPOSITION	SCORE
C. Chisholm	Epsom College	149*
C. Hinchliffe	Hurstpierpoint College	107

NOTABLE BOWLING PERFORMANCES

PLAYER	OPPOSITION	FIGURES
C. Chisholm	Sussex Martlets	16-11-27-7

Top Left: Khalid Sawas (King's Macclesfield) 904 runs at 60.3
Top Right: James Brooklyn (The Leys) 35 wickets at 10.2
Bottom Left: Daniel Woods (The Manchester GS) 42 wickets at 12.8
Bottom Right: Robbie Williams (Marlborough College) 32 wickets at 8.6

ELIZABETH COLLEGE

St. Peter Port, Guernsey, Channel Islands GY1 2PY

Tel: 01481 726544 Fax: 01481 714839
Email: mkinder@elizcoll.org

Master i/c Cricket: M.E. Kinder   Coach: A. Bannerjee

2005 SEASON

Played: 17   Won: 11   Lost: 5   Tied: 1

Captain: J. Nussbaumer   Vice-captain: S. De La Rue

Team selected from: J. Nussbaumer*, P. Le Hegarat*, R. Allen*,
B. Ferbrache*, S. De La Rue*, J. Wilkes-Green, J. Warr*, J. Clark,
F. Calderwood, M. Copeland, L. Nussbaumer*, T. Le Tissier*,
C. Whitworth, O. Dowding, J. Byrne, M. Creber, A. Robin,
T. Ravenscroft, M. Chilton, C. Dravers, D. Landles, R. Angliss.

SUMMARY

Due to the demands of the timetable and academic pressures, we no longer play mid-week cricket and have very little practice sessions. But we do enjoy our cricket! Recently in Guernsey, Denis Rogers, ACB Chairman, stated that there are no problems with school cricket and you should always be positive. I will remember that for a long time!

The overall record indicates our progress made during the season and shows the attempts made to play positively at all times. The cricket played at home was competitive, but only of 40 overs. All six games were won and the College became champions of the Weekend League Division One. The OEs were defeated by one wicket and captain Jamie Nussbaumer scored 107* against old rivals Victoria College Jersey, in a five wicket victory. This was the first Elizabeth century against Victoria since 1989.

It was a pity that the festival, due to be held in Guernsey in 2005, was decimated by withdrawls. However, Hampton and Merchant Taylors' visited the Island and a three team festival was well received.

The season was dominated by captain Jamie Nussbaumer and featured, in the festival, U13 cricketer Tim Ravenscroft, of Guernsey, Hampshire and the West of England.

AVERAGES

BATSMAN	INNINGS	NOT OUT	RUNS	H. SCORE	AVERAGE
S. De La Rue	6	2	140	61*	35.0
J. Nussbaumer	13	2	286	107*	26.0
P. Le Hegarat	13	1	307	67*	25.6
J. Wilkes-Green	7	1	139	43*	23.2
R. Allen	11	2	176	63*	19.6
L. Ferbrache	13	1	218	73*	18.2

BOWLER	OVERS	MAIDENS	RUNS	WICKETS	AVERAGE
T. Le Tissier	35	3	130	11	11.8
J. Byrne	38.1	4	201	13	15.5
L. Nussbaumer	79.3	2	351	20	17.6
J. Warr	51	6	213	8	26.6
S. De La Rue	72	7	311	11	28.3
O. Dowding	95	12	353	12	29.4

WICKET-KEEPER	PLAYED	CAUGHT	STUMPED
J. Nussbaumer	14	8	4

NOTABLE BATTING PERFORMANCES

PLAYER	OPPOSITION	SCORE
J. Nussbaumer	Victoria College Jersey	107*
B. Ferbrache	Wanderers	73*
P. Le Hegarat	Sparsholt College	67*
R. Allen	Wanderers	63*
S. De La Rue	GICC	61*

NOTABLE BOWLING PERFORMANCES

PLAYER	OPPOSITION	FIGURES
T. Le Tissier	Rovers	5-16
J. Byrne	Merchant Taylors'	5-60

ELLESMERE COLLEGE

Ellesmere, Shropshire SY12 9ES

Tel: 01691 622321 Fax: 01691 623286
Email: haypj@ellesmere.com

Master i/c Cricket: P.J. Hayes   Coach: C.C. Cawcutt

2005 SEASON

Played: 11   Won: 4   Lost: 1   Drawn: 6

Captain: N. James   Vice-captain: C. Coates

Team selected from: N. James*, C. Coates*, A. Choudhary*,
P. Cudmore*, W. Hockenhull*, P. Jain*, S. Bannister, W. Blackwell,
P. Daborn, J. Thompson, J. Upton, A. Whittle.

SUMMARY

A young side made an excellent start to the season and in the first six matches recorded wins against Birkenhead, Ormskirk, Rydal Penrhos and Newcastle-under-Lyme.

The season ended with three of the last four matches brought to an early end by rain. The only defeat came in the last match when, in the final over, Bloxham squeezed home by three wickets.

Centuries were scored by captain Nicholas James (121) against the Old Ellesmerians, and William Hockenhull (109*) against Rydal Penrhos.

While the batting was dependent largely on the success of Nicholas James, all the bowlers played their part and wickets were shared around. Patrick Cudmore was the only bowler to take five wickets in the match against Wrekin.

In addition to the all day matches, Ellesmere also entered the National Independent Schools' Twenty20 competition for the first time and hosted the final round group matches on the only hot and sunny day in the first half of term. The day was a great success, even though Ellesmere lost their three matches all by the narrowest margins - one wicket with scores level, one wicket in the final over and finally by six runs.

AVERAGES

BATSMAN	INNINGS	NOT OUT	RUNS	H. SCORE	AVERAGE
N. James	11	2	537	121	59.7
C. Coates	10	2	197	66	24.6
W. Hockenhull	11	1	226	109*	22.6
P. Jain	7	2	103	50	20.6
P. Cudmore	8	1	128	53	18.3
J. Upton	11	0	153	44	13.9

BOWLER	OVERS	MAIDENS	RUNS	WICKETS	AVERAGE
P. Cudmore	97.2	24	246	20	12.3
P. Daborn	74.4	15	219	13	16.8
A. Whittle	43.2	6	175	7	25.0
P. Jain	95.3	22	275	11	25.0
J. Upton	57	5	247	9	27.4
J. Thompson	55	9	206	7	29.4

WICKET-KEEPER	PLAYED	CAUGHT	STUMPED
N. James	4	3	2
W. Hockenhull	7	5	0

NOTABLE BATTING PERFORMANCES

PLAYER	OPPOSITION	SCORE
N. James	Old Ellesmerians	121
W. Hockenhull	Rydal Penrhos	109*
N. James	Ormskirk	95
N. James	Birkenhead	79*

NOTABLE BOWLING PERFORMANCES

PLAYER	OPPOSITION	FIGURES
P. Cudmore	Wrekin College	5-57

ENFIELD GRAMMAR SCHOOL

Market Place, Enfield, Middlesex EN2 6LN

Tel: 020 8363 1095 Fax: 020 8342 1805
Email: enfgrammar@aol.com

Master i/c Cricket: M. Alder

2005 SEASON

Played: 17   Won: 5   Lost: 4   Drawn: 8

Captain: T. Ludlam   Vice-captain: J. MacDonald

SUMMARY

A large squad has made selection for all the sides, from 1st XI to 4th XI, easy and competitive. Six bowlers have taken more than ten wickets each this year, which has meant we have bowled many sides out. Six batsmen have also scored more than 150 runs, so the team has not only been able to chase totals set by the opposition, but also make large first innings totals.

Two losses at the very start of the season, against UCS and Forest on wet wickets, were disappointing. Throughout June the side went undefeated until the last two games of the month.

The match against John Lyon gave them belief that games could be won from poor situations. After setting the opponents just 140 to win, a seemingly hopeless situation saw them add just 8 runs for 8 wickets enabling us to win by 4 runs. From that point, the side were always competitive and best of all, a good team spirit developed.

One of the highlights of the season came against the MCC, with the 1st XI recording its second best ever result. Despite restricting the MCC to 45-5, they managed to set a formidable 242-8 declared. The school batted steadily and with 20 overs to go, they were nicely placed on 128-2. Confident batting then left the school needing one run to win off the last ball, but unfortunately a wicket was lost and we recorded a draw.

The 1st XI beat West Thames in the Middlesex Cup in a thrilling final. Batting first, we scored 183-4 off 35 overs and then bowled out the opposition for 120 runs.

The side was well marshalled by captain Tom Ludlam and vice-captain James MacDonald. Twenty boys played for the 1st XI at some point this summer and competition will intensify next year.

AVERAGES

BATSMAN	INNINGS	NOT OUT	RUNS	H. SCORE	AVERAGE
J. Plumb	17	5	531	74	44.3
S. Levy	12	0	408	84	34.0
K. Bachus-Brown	8	1	163	57	23.3
A. Perera	13	3	202	72	20.2
T. Ludlam	13	0	204	64	15.7
N. Jackson	14	2	167	53	13.9

BOWLER	OVERS	MAIDENS	RUNS	WICKETS	AVERAGE
N. Jackson	47	4	178	12	14.8
D. Jackson	78	12	236	14	16.9
A. Barrell	114	10	397	18	22.1
S. Levy	78	4	378	16	23.6
A. Perera	64	2	330	12	27.5
J. MacDonald	134	8	507	15	33.8

Did you know? . . . The first Test match took place between England and Australia in 1877 at Melbourne. Australia won by 45 runs in front of a crowd that at one time reached 12,000. One of England's excuses for the defeat was that their only wicket-keeper had been left in police custody in New Zealand after a brawl. A second Test was quickly arranged which England won by 4 wickets.

FELSTED SCHOOL

Felsted, Essex CM6 3LL

Tel: 01371 822600   Fax: 01371 822607
Email: hms@felsted.org

Master i/c Cricket: C.S. Knightley   Coach: N.J. Lockhart

2005 SEASON

Played: 17   Won: 12   Drawn: 5

Captain: J. Buttleman   Vice-captain: C. Huntington

Team selected from: C. Huntington, M. Surry, N. Harrison,
G. Phillips, A. Pheloung, F. Blackwell, M. Drain, J. Wall,
H. Bevitt-Smith, J. Buttleman, S. Weller, D. Pheloung, S. Burrett.

Scorer: Flavia Birch

SUMMARY

Having started off with the difficult task of maintaining the records set in 2004, the side completed a remarkable season by retaining the Twenty20 National Schools Competition and remaining unbeaten. The last two years have seen the side win thirty-six and draw ten of their fixtures. The attacking style of our cricket was a credit to the players, led by Joseph Buttleman who departs to Durham University after two years at the helm.

The pattern in 2005 was to bat first and set a difficult, but achievable, target for our opposition and give the side time to bowl them out. It was a mainly successful tactic, helped by the masterful leg-spin bowling of 16-year-old Daniel Pheloung, who finished his first complete season with a record-breaking 62 wickets in all competitions. This was a record that had stood since 1976 by Derek Pringle.

The batsmen who set the tone in the games were 16-year-old Matthew Surry and Christopher Huntington, who has gone on to represent Essex 2nd XI after being capped by the HMC U18 England Schools XI against Sri Lanka U19 this summer. Joseph Buttleman, injured from bowling duties, scored well and his hundred against the MCC was a great innings. Nicholas Harrison had his most successful season in the side with wickets and runs, and the promising Mark Drain and Samuel Weller will return hungry for more success.

The 2005 season will be remembered for the whole team putting their hand up when needed and the school wishes the five leavers great success in the future. The side will tour Australia again in 2006/7 and the young players will have a challenge to maintain the success of Felsted cricket.

AVERAGES

BATSMAN	INNINGS	NOT OUT	RUNS	H. SCORE	AVERAGE
M. Surry	16	5	769	125*	69.9
C. Huntington	16	2	778	133*	55.6
J. Buttleman	14	2	596	103	49.7
S. Burrett	11	3	273	88	34.1
N. Harrison	10	5	169	50*	33.8
F. Blackwell	12	3	260	96	28.9

BOWLER	OVERS	MAIDENS	RUNS	WICKETS	AVERAGE
D. Pheloung	193.5	43	597	49	12.2
S. Weller	80	11	301	21	14.3
N. Harrison	151.2	38	382	21	18.2
C. Huntington	39	1	171	9	19.0
J. Buttleman	31	8	102	5	20.4
M. Drain	119.3	28	316	14	22.6

WICKET-KEEPER	PLAYED	CAUGHT	STUMPED
F. Blackwell	17	13	11

Felsted after winning the Independent Schools' Twenty20 Final at Edgbaston.
Standing (left to right): N. Lockhart, C. Huntington, M. Surry, N. Harrison,
G. Phillips, A. Pheloung, F. Blackwell, C. Knightley
Kneeling: M. Drain, J. Wall (12th man), H. Bevitt-Smith, J. Buttleman*,
S. Weller, D. Pheloung. *Photo by C.R.S. Lee*

FETTES COLLEGE

Carrington Road, Edinburgh EH4 1QX

Tel: 0131 332 2281 Fax: 0131 332 3081
Email: cs.thomson@fettes.com

Master i/c Cricket: C.S. Thomson   Coach: A.B. Russell

2005 SEASON

Played: 15   Won: 9   Lost: 4   Drawn: 2

Captain: S. Maclennan   Vice-captain: D. Philip

Team selected from: L. Bax, M. Bax, H. Boisseau*, R. Forsyth*,
A. Fyffe, O. Hunt, D. Keith, C. Kinloch, S. Maclennan*, A. Murdoch,
E. Philip, D. Philip*, M. Pickles, J. Rann.
Scorer: Y. Bashenko

SUMMARY

This was a pleasing season which saw a number of boys moving towards realising their potential. There were undoubted benefits gained from the thirteen day pre-season tour to South Africa in March and April. This was evident in much of the cricket which the boys played.

There were a number of highs, including the 224-5 notched in just 30 overs against Stewart's Melville. However, the 108 run victory over Monkton Combe in the last game of the season was the most complete performance of the summer, as Monkton were bowled out for 142 in reply to Fettes' 250.

Scotland U17 skipper Scott Maclennan showed good understanding and tactical awareness in his first summer as captain of the side. He also led from the front with his batting, amassing 463 runs at 46.3, while Oliver Hunt, with 27 wickets, and Harry Boisseau, with 25 wickets, were the pick of the bowlers.

AVERAGES

BATSMAN	INNINGS	NOT OUT	RUNS	H. SCORE	AVERAGE
S. Maclennan	12	2	463	89	46.3
D. Philip	14	4	308	101*	30.8
R. Forsyth	14	1	387	126*	29.8
O. Hunt	13	0	291	60	22.4
A. Fyffe	11	2	147	43	16.3
M. Pickles	6	0	84	52	14.0

BOWLER	OVERS	MAIDENS	RUNS	WICKETS	AVERAGE
M. Bax	11	1	37	5	7.4
O. Hunt	91	13	311	27	11.5
H. Boisseau	101.1	16	304	25	12.2
A. Murdoch	12.3	3	45	3	15.0
D. Philip	110.1	21	316	21	15.0
C. Kinloch	29	7	90	5	18.0

NOTABLE BATTING PERFORMANCES

PLAYER	OPPOSITION	SCORE
R. Forsyth	Lothian Schools	126*
D. Philip	Stewart's Melville	101*
S. Maclennan	Monkton Combe	89
S. Maclennan	XL Club	75*
S. Maclennan	MCC	68
S. Maclennan	Strathallan	64
O. Hunt	Stewart's Melville	60

NOTABLE BOWLING PERFORMANCES

PLAYER	OPPOSITION	FIGURES
H. Boisseau	Dollar Academy	5-22
H. Boisseau	Edinburgh Academy	4-33
D. Philip	Loretto	4-34
O. Hunt	Edinburgh Academy	4-36
D. Keith	Monkton Combe	3-13
O. Hunt	Merchiston Castle	3-16
H. Boisseau	Monkton Combe	3-18

Ashes' Captain's Innings by Jack Russell, showing the moment when Michael Vaughan reached 100 at Old Trafford
(Reproduced by kind permission of the Jack Russell Gallery)

ASHES SUMMER

by Jack Russell MBE, FRSA

The weather forecasters promised an Indian summer but I think most would agree it turned into an Australian one. What a Test series! What a contest! People who never normally follow cricket became devotees almost overnight.

After a disappointing start, losing the first Test match at Lord's, the England team moved up a gear with a nail-biting win in the last over at Edgbaston to square the series. From then on it continued to be 'edge of the seat' stuff for the spectators. Every game went to the wire as the advantage swung to and fro between the teams.

There were so many breathtaking performances by players on both sides that to single out special moments would be difficult, but if I had to, it would probably come down to two. Firstly at Trent Bridge, when Ashley Giles scored the winning runs to put us one game ahead of the Aussies, and secondly, in the fifth and final Test at The Oval, when Kevin Pietersen scored a magnificent century to bring the Ashes home to England for the first time in eighteen years.

I am currently slaving away in my studio trying to capture some scenes and atmosphere from this magnificent series, in what will surely go down in history as one of England's greatest victories over our old adversity. The finished paintings are on show at my art gallery in Chipping Sodbury and limited edition Giclée prints are available of some of them.

Jack Russell Gallery, 41 High Street, Chipping Sodbury,
South Gloucestershire BS37 6BA Telephone 01454 329583
www.jackrussell.co.uk

Jack Russell painting at Old Trafford during the third Test match

FOREST SCHOOL

College Place, Snaresbrook, London E17 3PY

Tel: 020 8520 1744 Fax: 020 8520 3656
Email: warden@forest.org.uk

Master i/c Cricket and Coach: Stuart Turner

2005 SEASON

Played: 18   Won: 12   Lost: 2   Drawn: 4

Captain: C. Swainland   Vice-captain: G. Whorlow

Team selected from: C. Swainland*, G. Whorlow*, A. Palmer*,
A. Ryatt*, E. Murphy*, T. Monk*, E. Connell, J. Yeo, D. Hawkes,
S. Bains, J. Waller, H. Sayeed, S. Baldwin.
Scorer: Mrs J. Hawkes

SUMMARY

As you can see by our playing record, this was an excellent season, due to a good team effort with everybody making contributions along the way.

Leading from the front, Chris Swainland and Gordon Whorlow, both in their last year and Essex CCC academy boys, were wonderful examples to everyone. They will be sorely missed.

Things move on though and we have some talented cricketers coming through in the lower age groups - many of them playing for Essex CCC XIs.

There is a great deal of pride in Forest cricket having produced England players Nasser Hussain and James Foster. Things certainly bode well for the future of cricket here.

AVERAGES

BATSMAN	INNINGS	NOT OUT	RUNS	H. SCORE	AVERAGE
G. Whorlow	14	5	626	109*	69.6
A. Ryatt	13	5	297	107*	37.1
A. Palmer	16	0	533	87	33.3
E. Murphy	14	3	296	63	26.9
C. Swainland	13	1	307	68	25.6

BOWLER	OVERS	MAIDENS	RUNS	WICKETS	AVERAGE
A. Ryatt	157.1	36	504	31	16.3
S. Bains	74	15	275	16	17.2
D. Hawkes	97.4	19	358	19	18.8
E. Connell	99.4	15	400	19	21.1
G. Whorlow	84.5	19	303	13	23.3

WICKET-KEEPER	PLAYED	CAUGHT	STUMPED
C. Swainland	14	14	2

NOTABLE BATTING PERFORMANCES

PLAYER	OPPOSITION	SCORE
A. Ryatt	Coopers Coburn	107*
G. Whorlow	Chigwell	109*

NOTABLE BOWLING PERFORMANCES

PLAYER	OPPOSITION	FIGURES
S. Bains	Bancroft's	5-14

FRAMLINGHAM COLLEGE

College Road, Framlingham, Suffolk IP13 9EY

Tel: 01728 723789 Fax: 01728 724546
Email: registrar@framcollege.co.uk

Master i/c Cricket: M.J. Marvell   Coach: M.D. Robinson

2005 SEASON

Played: 13   Won: 5   Lost: 1   Drawn: 7

Captain: A. Wybar   Vice-captain: R. Newton

Team selected from: A. Wybar*, R. Newton*, P. Clarke*, B. Davies*,
H. Bush, T. Sallis, W. Poole, H. Dunham, B. Mark, S. Abubakar,
O. Woodgate, O. Poole, N. Lawson, O. Boon.
Scorer: C. Magnay

SUMMARY

Tom Sallis' well-paced century on the last day of term was enough to ensure that the side remained unbeaten on the domestic circuit. Their only defeat was at the hands of Prince Alfred College Adelaide.

The rest of the season was dominated by the batting of 15-year-old Robert Newton, whose twelve innings included five centuries at an average of 94.7.

Peter Clarke was the leading all-rounder in the team, mixing pace and aggression with admirable control, to ensure that opponents rarely had the opportunity to realistically chase totals. In his first season as captain, John Wybar was handicapped by losing the toss on all but one occasion.

With no leavers this year and a tour to Sri Lanka to look forward to, the omens are good.

AVERAGES

BATSMAN	INNINGS	NOT OUT	RUNS	H. SCORE	AVERAGE
R. Newton	12	2	947	153	94.7
T. Sallis	7	3	220	100*	55.0
P. Clarke	11	4	229	53	32.7
A. Wybar	12	1	318	59*	28.9
H. Dunham	8	2	105	43*	17.5
H. Bush	12	0	189	31*	15.8

BOWLER	OVERS	MAIDENS	RUNS	WICKETS	AVERAGE
P. Clarke	95	21	272	15	18.1
S. Abubakar	42.4	8	166	7	23.7
H. Bush	61	2	300	12	25.0
B. Davies	99.4	21	336	12	28.0
H. Dunham	60	5	281	9	31.2
B. Mark	27	1	169	5	33.8

WICKET-KEEPER	PLAYED	CAUGHT	STUMPED
T. Sallis	7	4	1
A. Wybar	3	5	0

NOTABLE BATTING PERFORMANCES

PLAYER	OPPOSITION	SCORE
R. Newton	Ipswich	108
R. Newton	Brentwood	113*
R. Newton	RGS Colchester	112*
R. Newton	Royal Hospital	153
R. Newton	Culford	124
T. Sallis	Old Framlinghamians	100*

NOTABLE BOWLING PERFORMANCES

PLAYER	OPPOSITION	FIGURES
S. Abubakar	Woodbridge	4-17
P. Clarke	Woodbridge	3-18
P. Clarke	Norwich	3-20
B. Davies	Brentwood	3-26
H. Bush	Brentwood	3-31
H. Dunham	Old Framlinghamians	3-35
P. Clarke	Gentlemen of Essex	3-37

GIGGLESWICK SCHOOL

Settle, North Yorkshire BD24 0DE

Tel: 01729 893135 Fax: 01729 893168
Email: sjwilliams@giggleswick.org.uk

Master i/c Cricket: S. Williams
Coaches: M. Greatbach and P. Humphries

2005 SEASON

Played: 16   Won: 4   Lost: 12

Captain: A. Canaway   Vice-captain: E. Stamper

Team selected from: E. Stamper, H. Wilman, R. Bousfield, N. Thursby,
S. Illingworth, I. Jenkinson, C. Dean, Y. Shimizu*, E. Tame,
A. Canaway*, M. Woolnough, M. Gemmell, G. Dunston.

Scorer: J. Tavernor

SUMMARY

Well led by Alistair Canaway, this year's 1st XI was very young, with only two upper sixth boys in the team. Having Mark Greatbach (ex-New Zealand opening batsman) involved, the team received some excellent coaching. Victories were few, but highlights of the season were impressive wins over Stonyhurst, a Headmaster's XI, Silcoates and Kirkham GS.

Ross Bousfield was always sharp as wicket-keeper and narrowly missed out on a hundred against Silcoates. Yuma Shimizu, from Japan, proved to be an excellent swing bowler, taking 21 wickets with an average of 14.5.

With only two boys leaving the team, next year should be more successful.

AVERAGES

BATSMAN	INNINGS	NOT OUT	RUNS	H. SCORE	AVERAGE
R. Bousfield	15	0	270	92	18.0
S. Illingworth	15	2	207	55	15.9
A. Canaway	13	0	202	60	15.5
E. Stamper	16	0	212	30	13.3

BOWLER	OVERS	MAIDENS	RUNS	WICKETS	AVERAGE
Y. Shimizu	114	26	304	21	14.5
H. Wilman	59	5	245	14	17.5
N. Thursby	81	5	394	15	26.3
S. Illingworth	91	9	408	15	27.2

WICKET-KEEPER	PLAYED	CAUGHT	STUMPED
R. Bousfield	15	10	0

NOTABLE BATTING PERFORMANCES

PLAYER	OPPOSITION	SCORE
N. Thursby	Old Giggleswickians	59*
S. Illingworth	King's Parramatta (Australia)	55
A. Canaway	Woodhouse Grove	60
R. Bousfield	Silcoates	92

NOTABLE BOWLING PERFORMANCES

PLAYER	OPPOSITION	FIGURES
Y. Shimizu	Stonyhurst College	11-2-11-4
S. Illingworth	Stonyhurst College	12-1-34-4
E. Stamper	Clitheroe GS	9-0-35-3
Y. Shimizu	Silcoates	8-2-17-4

THE GLASGOW ACADEMY

Colebrook Street, Glasgow G12 8HE

Tel: 0141 334 8558 Fax: 0141 337 3473
Email: enquiries@theglasgowacademy.org.uk

Master i/c Cricket: A.G. Lyall   Coach: V. Hariharan

2005 SEASON

Played: 8   Won: 3   Lost: 2   Drawn: 1   Abandoned: 2

Captain: N. Dowers   Vice-captain: S. Bannerman

Team selected from: N. Dowers, S. Bannerman, J. Duckworth,
J. Young, F. Marchetti, I. Smart, R. Paton, T. Fleming
R. Kelso, R. Beattie, A. Crawford, A. Kraszewski, R. Sood,
A. MacLauchlan, S. Young.

SUMMARY

Having been awarded the Henry Grierson trophy in 2004 by the XL Club, it certainly was a big ask to expect this year's team to perform at the same level as in the past couple of years. It should also be noted that some of our star players had left the school. But what transpired during the season was something of which the team could be justly proud.

While we had a few closely fought matches, there is no doubt that the highlight was the game against Hutchesons' GS. The Academy boys had to chase a huge score of 237 runs in 40 overs on a big outfield, which in school cricket would be considered virtually impossible to beat. However, the Glasgow Academy boys created history by believing in themselves and scoring runs at every possible opportunity. There was some quite unbelievable running between the wickets which enabled us to win the match in the last over with just two balls to spare! It was probably the best school cricket match that I have seen played for many years.

AVERAGES

BATSMAN	INNINGS	NOT OUT	RUNS	H. SCORE	AVERAGE
N. Dowers	6	0	167	85	27.8
S. Bannerman	6	0	156	53	26.0
R. Kelso	6	0	106	48	17.7
R. Beattie	6	0	82	25	13.7
R. Paton	6	1	58	28	11.6
A. MacLauchlan	6	1	56	21	11.2

BOWLER	OVERS	MAIDENS	RUNS	WICKETS	AVERAGE
N. Dowers	6	0	30	2	15.0
A. Crawford	19	2	77	5	15.4
R. Sood	9.2	0	62	3	20.7
S. Bannerman	39.4	7	160	7	22.9
R. Paton	40	2	171	7	24.4
T. Fleming	43	3	159	6	26.5

WICKET-KEEPER	PLAYED	CAUGHT	STUMPED
J. Duckworth	6	2	1

NOTABLE BATTING PERFORMANCES

PLAYER	OPPOSITION	SCORE
N. Dowers	Hutchesons' GS	85

Did you know? . . . The most Tests played by an Englishman is the 133 matches in which Alec Stewart represented his country.

GORDONSTOUN SCHOOL

Elgin, Moray, Scotland IV30 5RF

Tel: 01343 837829 Fax: 01343 837808
Email: rufeyj@gordonstoun.org.uk

Master i/c Cricket: James Rufey

2005 SEASON

Played: 13   Won: 3   Lost: 6   Drawn: 4

Captain: G. Falconer   Vice-captain: S. Sharma

Team selected from: O. Tillard, G. Falconer, S. Sharma, L. Broekman, N. Latham, K. Manby, G. Paterson, H. Radford, G. Beaumont, I. Burton, W. Smith, J. Heard, G. Heard, J. Oak, W. Eastcroft, G. Wadhwani, A. Wadhwani.

SUMMARY

This was an indifferent season for a youthful Gordonstoun team. With regards to the batting, Graeme Falconer was the outstanding performer, hitting several scores over fifty. Other batsmen to record notable scores were Nick Latham, Gregor Paterson and Luke Broekman.

The bowling was a consistent aspect of the side with Hugo Radford, Will Smith and Graeme Falconer all having good seasons.

The season started well with a good victory against Aberdeen University. It ended with a festival featuring St. Phillip's College Alice Springs, which included a Twenty20 game. Gordonstoun finished with a tour to schools in southern England. We look forward to a good season next year as most of the side will still be here.

AVERAGES

BATSMAN	INNINGS	NOT OUT	RUNS	H. SCORE	AVERAGE
G. Falconer	10	1	458	88	50.9

BOWLER	OVERS	MAIDENS	RUNS	WICKETS	AVERAGE
H. Radford	84	8	385	13	29.6
W. Smith	60	5	219	9	24.3
G. Falconer	106.4	20	260	20	13.0

NOTABLE BATTING PERFORMANCES

PLAYER	OPPOSITION	SCORE
G. Falconer	St. Albans	88
N. Latham	Aberdeen University	53
G. Falconer	XL Club	65
G. Falconer	Aberdeenshire	73*

NOTABLE BOWLING PERFORMANCES

PLAYER	OPPOSITION	FIGURES
G. Falconer	Glenalmond	5-15

GRESHAM'S SCHOOL

Cromer Road, Holt, Norfolk NR25 6EA

Tel: 01263 713271 Fax: 01263 712028
Email: registrar@greshams-school.co.uk

Master i/c Cricket: Alan Ponder Coach: Younis Ahmed

2005 SEASON

Played: 16 Won: 6 Lost: 5 Drawn: 5

Captain: M. Lintott Vice-captains: C. Ponder and F. Flower

Team selected from: M. Lintott*, F. Flower*, A. Clark, S. Foster, C. Ponder*, N. Hannington, O. Boesen, A. Campbell, B. Jones, B. Williams, O. Elsbury, A. King*, T. Hawes, B. Pienaar.

SUMMARY

With a very young side, this was a most encouraging season and results were better than expected. Opening bat and off-spinner, Felix Flower, was absolutely outstanding. He scored more runs in a season than any other Gresham's batsman, made the highest individual score and already has more runs than any Gresham's batsman with still a season to go. His off-spin also improved greatly, taking seven wickets in a match twice.

Charlie Ponder was a chirpy and consistent wicket-keeper, also making useful runs, and Sam Foster (son of Neil, ex-Essex and England) is a promising all-rounder. Two of the defeats came against very strong overseas teams and in the match of the season, we only lost to Oundle off the last ball of the match, with nine wickets down.

AVERAGES

BATSMAN	INNINGS	NOT OUT	RUNS	H. SCORE	AVERAGE
F. Flower	15	1	943	171	67.4
C. Ponder	15	1	340	63	24.3
S. Foster	16	2	332	62*	23.7
A. Clark	15	0	295	51	19.7
M. Lintott	14	4	146	31*	14.6

BOWLER	OVERS	MAIDENS	RUNS	WICKETS	AVERAGE
F. Flower	205.4	31	645	33	19.6
A. King	90.3	7	384	16	24.0
S. Foster	127	14	394	15	26.3
T. Hawes	80	10	296	8	37.0
O. Elsbury	84	14	357	9	39.7

WICKET-KEEPER	PLAYED	CAUGHT	STUMPED
C. Ponder	16	11	5

NOTABLE BATTING PERFORMANCES

PLAYER	OPPOSITION	SCORE
F. Flower	Oundle	135
F. Flower	Oakham	121
F. Flower	Old Greshamians	171
F. Flower	Wisbech	125
F. Flower	Norwich	93
C. Ponder	Oakham	63
S. Foster	Framlingham College	62*

NOTABLE BOWLING PERFORMANCES

PLAYER	OPPOSITION	FIGURES
F. Flower	Framlingham College	18-5-35-7
F. Flower	West Norfolk CC	20-6-52-7
F. Flower	Oundle	16-1-61-5

HABERDASHERS' ASKE'S BOYS' SCHOOL

Butterfly Lane, Elstree, Hertfordshire WD6 3AF

Tel: 020 8266 1700 Fax: 020 8266 1800

Email: charlwood_s@habsboys.org.uk

Master i/c Cricket: S.D. Charlwood   Coach: B.R. Mahoney

2005 SEASON

Played: 22   Won: 15   Lost: 6   Drawn: 1

Captain: E. Clements   Vice-captain: M. Gray

Team selected from: E. Clements*, R. Pandya*, G. Baker*,
R. Clements*, S. Patel*, A. Soni, M. Trunkwala, A. Cook,
H. Nosworthy, M. Gray, H. Majeethia, O. Lee,
L. Ruthirapathy, K. Morjaria.
Scorer: G. Schey

SUMMARY

Despite some disappointing defeats, notably to local rivals Merchant Taylors' and again to Exeter, 2005 has been a good year for the XI with arguably the highest number of victories in one season. An MCC side was defeated for only the second time in nearly twenty years and we also achieved wins against UCS, Berkhamsted, St. Albans, Bishop's Stortford HS and Watford GS. We also won the Aldenham Twenty20 Cup.

Edward Clements has led the side with distinction. His younger brother, Robert, has been outstanding with both bat and ball. His century against Berkhamsted was a particular highlight and the best individual score since 1992. Another talented cricketer, Gavin Baker, also performed well throughout the season, scoring seven half-centuries in addition to bowling several penetrative spells with the new ball.

Overall, however, this was a good team performance with all members of the side contributing. Opener Rishi Pandya was consistent throughout, while all-rounder Sheilen Patel produced evidence on several occasions of his undoubted ability. Alex Cook's glovework was reliable and 14-year-old all-rounder Ajay Soni showed much promise.

The annual Devon Tour, with all matches played under sunny skies for a change, was most enjoyable. Thanks in particular to the sterling efforts of Doug Yeabsley, the squad can now look forward to spending Christmas and the New Year in Hong Kong and Malaysia. Incidentally, the school was delighted to host the Hong Kong CC on its short tour of the UK this summer, and we look forward to renewing acquaintances in December.

AVERAGES

BATSMAN	INNINGS	NOT OUT	RUNS	H. SCORE	AVERAGE
R. Clements	18	4	726	133	51.9
G. Baker	19	3	671	87	41.9
R. Pandya	18	3	383	62*	25.5
S. Patel	17	1	336	67	21.0
E. Clements	17	0	347	52	20.4
M. Trunkwala	18	6	210	49	17.5

BOWLER	OVERS	MAIDENS	RUNS	WICKETS	AVERAGE
R. Clements	158	30	484	32	15.1
G. Baker	148.1	21	496	27	18.4
E. Clements	135	17	539	28	19.2
S. Patel	71.2	10	280	14	20.0
A. Soni	61	6	271	13	20.8
H. Nosworthy	53.5	4	226	8	28.2

WICKET-KEEPER	PLAYED	CAUGHT	STUMPED
A. Cook	13	8	0
K. Morjaria	8	6	1

NOTABLE BATTING PERFORMANCES

PLAYER	OPPOSITION	SCORE
R. Clements	Berkhamsted	133
R. Clements	Glenwood HS (South Africa)	97*
G. Baker	Bishop's Stortford HS	87
G. Baker	Bancroft's	83
R. Clements	Merchant Taylors'	87
G. Baker	Old Haberdashers' CC	70*
R. Pandya	Old Haberdashers' CC	62*

NOTABLE BOWLING PERFORMANCES

PLAYER	OPPOSITION	FIGURES
R. Clements	Exeter CC	8-1-27-6
E. Clements	St. Albans	8-0-30-6
R. Clements	University College	12-3-20-4
A. Soni	Watford GS	5-1-10-3
S. Patel	Queen Elizabeth's Barnet	7-1-12-3
S. Patel	D.I. Yeabsley's XI	10-3-19-3
G. Baker	St. Albans	8-0-21-3

HAILEYBURY

Hertford, Herts SG13 7NU

Tel: 01992 462507 Fax: 01992 470663
Email: cricket@haileybury.com

Master i/c Cricket: C.E. Igolen-Robinson   Coach: G.P. Howarth OBE

2005 SEASON

Played: 15   Won: 3   Lost: 9   Drawn: 2   Tied: 1

Captain: T. Stewart   Vice-captain: W. Sheldon

Team selected from: J. Scarborough, R. Noach*, D. Wilson,
T. Stewart*, D. Gregory, B. Stewart, S. Sehmbey, R. Carter,
G. Martindale, W. Sheldon, E. Rayfield*, L. Mason*, J. Pain,
R. Swaminathan, R. Macpherson-Smith, D. Bresciani, T. Hollington,
J. Anthony, S. Thurgood.
Scorer: J. Rhodes

SUMMARY

2005 started with purposeful winter coaching with the addition to the staff of Michael Cawdron, formerly of Gloucestershire CCC and Northamptonshire CCC. Another lift was the agreement of Alec Stewart OBE to be patron of Haileybury cricket.

In April, the XL Club provided the XI with their first test. Chasing a target of 169, openers Ross Noach and Ben Stewart put on over a hundred runs. The job was finished off by Graham Martindale and Rhys Carter. At Oundle, the side performed somewhere near its potential. Oundle batted first and were dismissed for 190, with 3 wickets each for Luke Mason, Will Sheldon and Ben Stewart. The Haileybury top order batted well and Ross Noach carried his bat with 69*, but we ended 20 runs short. The St. Albans opener, bowling with gale force winds in his back, produced a 'snorter' first ball that saw Ross Noach back in the pavilion. Captain Tom Stewart was bowled by a delivery coinciding with the simultaneous blowing over of the sight screen. James Scarborough scored a maiden half-century and we set St. Albans 185 to win, but the game ended in a draw.

Against MCC our opponents batted first, setting the XI 219 to win. Despite being 93-6, James Scarborough (63), David Gregory (53) and Sheldon helped us to victory for the third year in a row.

Against Uppingham, excellent batting from most of the top order, including James Scarborough (56*) and debutant U15 David Wilson (44), enabled us to post an impressive 271-6. Uppingham were finally dismissed for 258 (Mason 4-59).

Entertaining Australia's Toowoomba GS, we made 204-8 in our 45 overs. Toowoomba started well, but with two overs remaining, the tourists needed 11 runs to win with 2 wickets left. Ben Stewart bowled the penultimate over - a single and a 2 coming from the first 4 balls. He then bowled a no-ball that was struck for 6 and Toowoomba were left with the last over in which to score 1 run to win. The scores were dead level at 204-8 each and Ed Rayfield bowled a maiden to force the most uncommon of results - a tie, and a write up in *The Times*.

AVERAGES

BATSMAN	INNINGS	NOT OUT	RUNS	H. SCORE	AVERAGE
J. Scarborough	8	2	221	63	36.8
R. Noach	15	1	370	69*	26.4
D. Wilson	6	0	137	46	22.8
T. Stewart	12	0	241	76	20.1
D. Gregory	11	1	196	53	19.6
B. Stewart	11	0	202	60	18.4

BOWLER	OVERS	MAIDENS	RUNS	WICKETS	AVERAGE
B. Stewart	81	14	319	13	24.5
L. Mason	92.1	12	371	15	24.7
W. Sheldon	100	8	410	16	25.6
E. Rayfield	113.5	13	474	15	31.6
R. Carter	148.2	19	550	14	39.3

NOTABLE BATTING PERFORMANCES

PLAYER	OPPOSITION	SCORE
T. Stewart	Dulwich College	76
R. Noach	Oundle	69*
S. Sehmbey	Haileybury Hermits	72
J. Scarborough	MCC	63
B. Stewart	XL Club	60
R. Carter	Toowoomba GS (Australia)	59*

NOTABLE BOWLING PERFORMANCES

PLAYER	OPPOSITION	FIGURES
L. Mason	Uppingham	4-59
B. Stewart	Toowoomba GS (Australia)	4-47
E. Rayfield	Cheltenham College	5-65
W. Sheldon	St. Albans	3-21
R. Carter	Haileybury Hermits	3-28
E. Rayfield	Marlborough College	3-34
L. Mason	Oundle	3-38

HAMPTON SCHOOL

Hanworth Road, Hampton, Middlesex TW12 3HD

Tel: 020 8979 5526 Fax: 020 8941 7368
Email: staff@hampton.richmond.sch.uk

Master i/c Cricket: E.M. Wesson   Coach: C. Harrison

2005 SEASON

Played: 15   Won: 9   Lost: 3   Drawn: 3

Captain: R. Brown

Team selected from: R. Brown, S. Riley, T. Roland-Jones, A. Ansari, A. Lightman, T. Handel, N. Jupp, A. O'Mahoney, S. Jewell, R. Allen, M. Samways, J. Stevenson, S. Stevenson.

Scorer: J. Brewer

SUMMARY

The highlight of the season was a good run in the National Independent Schools' Twenty20 tournament. The team deservedly reached the final at Edgbaston, only to lose by 10 runs to Felsted in a match shortened by rain.

Otherwise, this 1st XI achieved its potential sporadically. Runs were plentiful but wickets, and real pressure in the field, harder to come by. The players who stood out were the upper sixth formers, opening bowler Stuart Riley and off-spinner and skipper Richard Brown, who contributed 40 out of the 91 wickets taken with the ball.

AVERAGES

BATSMAN	INNINGS	NOT OUT	RUNS	H. SCORE	AVERAGE
A. Ansari	11	5	426	100*	71.0
N. Jupp	12	4	390	70*	48.8
T. Roland-Jones	14	0	563	125	40.2
A. Lightman	12	1	438	90	39.8
A. O'Mahoney	7	1	159	65	26.5
T. Handel	13	2	278	50	25.3

BOWLER	OVERS	MAIDENS	RUNS	WICKETS	AVERAGE
S. Riley	132.1	22	393	27	14.6
S. Jewell	70	11	261	13	20.1
A. Ansari	71.5	9	283	14	20.2
R. Brown	81.5	7	291	13	22.4
T. Roland-Jones	67.3	8	274	12	22.8
M. Samways	95	13	357	12	29.7

WICKET-KEEPER	PLAYED	CAUGHT	STUMPED
N. Jupp	10	9	5
A. O'Mahoney	5	3	3

NOTABLE BATTING PERFORMANCES

PLAYER	OPPOSITION	SCORE
A. Ansari	Trinity	100*
T. Roland-Jones	John Fisher	125

NOTABLE BOWLING PERFORMANCES

PLAYER	OPPOSITION	FIGURES
R. Brown	Reigate GS	5-24
S. Riley	Elizabeth College	5-19

HARROW SCHOOL

High Street, Harrow on the Hill, Middlesex HA1 3HP

Tel: 020 8872 8000 Fax: 020 8423 3112
Email: harrow@harrowschool.org.uk

Master i/c Cricket: S.J. Halliday   Coach: S.A. Jones

2005 SEASON

Played: 17   Won: 13   Drawn: 4

Captain: C. Travers   Vice-captain: S. Crawley

Team selected from: C. Travers*, S. Crawley*, W. Spencer*,
S. Northeast*, M. Habib*, R. Querl*, I. Jenkins*, G. Harper*,
C. Pelham*, G. Matthey*, T. Coaker*.

Scorers: Mrs J. Harper and O. Cohen

SUMMARY

Harrow enjoyed a fantastic season, winning thirteen of their seventeen games and remaining unbeaten. The highlight was the seven wicket victory over Eton at Lord's, but they also won the Cowdrey Cup for the second successive year (a league involving Eton, Wellington, Tonbridge and Charterhouse). Brighton were beaten at Hove and there were close finishes against Charterhouse (1 wicket), Bedford (2 wickets) and Tonbridge (2 wickets), showing the true character in the team.

All team members contributed significantly, however Glenn Querl and Will Spencer were outstanding all-rounders. Mumtaz Habib and Chris Travers were not far behind. The batting had real depth, with all of the top eight making significant runs. Sam Northeast was the most consistent.

The bowling was disciplined and varied. The fielding was excellent, led by the immaculate Giles Matthey behind the stumps. Chris Travers was an inspirational and astute captain.

In December 2005, the Harrow School 1st XI were judged
The Daily Telegraph School Team of the Year.

AVERAGES

BATSMAN	INNINGS	NOT OUT	RUNS	H. SCORE	AVERAGE
S. Northeast	15	3	627	101*	52.3
R. Querl	13	5	415	100*	51.9
M. Habib	14	3	422	81	38.4
W. Spencer	17	0	550	81	32.4
S. Crawley	13	4	282	54*	31.3
C. Travers	17	1	389	124	24.3

BOWLER	OVERS	MAIDENS	RUNS	WICKETS	AVERAGE
R. Querl	125	35	299	27	11.1
M. Habib	81	19	210	12	17.5
C. Travers	88	9	335	19	17.6
W. Spencer	160	20	580	30	19.3
T. Coaker	109	18	336	13	25.8
G. Harper	126	22	370	13	28.5

WICKET-KEEPER	PLAYED	CAUGHT	STUMPED
G. Matthey	15	11	2

NOTABLE BATTING PERFORMANCES

PLAYER	OPPOSITION	SCORE
C. Travers	Malvern College	124
S. Northeast	Pretoria (South Africa)	101*
R. Querl	Radley College	100*
S. Northeast	Dulwich College	88
S. Northeast	Brighton College	84
M. Habib	Wellington College	81
W. Spencer	St. Edward's	81

NOTABLE BOWLING PERFORMANCES

PLAYER	OPPOSITION	FIGURES
W. Spencer	Bradfield College	4-14
R. Querl	Eton College	4-26
G. Harper	Radley College	4-31
T. Coaker	I Zingari	4-47
W. Spencer	Bedford	4-21
W. Spencer	Oakham	4-62

THE HARVEY GRAMMAR SCHOOL

Cheriton Road, Folkestone, Kent CT19 5JY

Tel: 01303 252131 Fax: 01303 220721
Email: pjharding@harveygs.kent.sch.uk

Master i/c Cricket: P.J. Harding   Coach: N. Bristow

2005 SEASON

Played: 15   Won: 8   Lost: 5   Drawn: 2

Captain: B. Washer   Vice-captain: B. Vincent

Team selected from: B. Washer*, K. Mann*, B. Vincent*, S. Butler, T. Squire, C. Hemphrey, P. Thornton-Smith, M. Davey, W. Dennis, R. Harrison, R. Johnston, B. Allon, J. Vincent, J. Squire.

SUMMARY

The 1st XI won the County Cup by defeating Eltham College in the final, having amassed a record score of 282. Harvey has won the competition more times than any other school in Kent.

Good teamwork, rather than individual brilliance, characterised the season. This state grammar school maintains a high-quality fixture list with regular Saturday matches. In 2006 we will again be taking the 1st XI to Barbados.

Did you know? . . . M.J.C. Allom is the only player to have taken a hat trick on Test debut for England, doing so in 1929/30 against New Zealand at Christchurch. He actually took four wickets in five balls.

AVERAGES

BATSMAN	INNINGS	NOT OUT	RUNS	H. SCORE	AVERAGE
B. Washer	7	1	199	105*	33.2
T. Squire	12	1	283	85	25.7
M. Davey	8	0	181	75	22.6
K. Mann	11	1	222	47*	22.2
C. Hemphrey	8	0	159	129	19.9
S. Butler	12	0	152	49	12.7

BOWLER	OVERS	MAIDENS	RUNS	WICKETS	AVERAGE
P. Thornton-Smith	66	9	229	12	19.1
T. Squire	77	7	290	13	22.3

WICKET-KEEPER	PLAYED	CAUGHT	STUMPED
K. Mann	13	11	0

NOTABLE BATTING PERFORMANCES

PLAYER	OPPOSITION	SCORE
C. Hemphrey	Bethany	129
B. Washer	Duke of York's RMS	105*
T. Squire	Eltham College	85

NOTABLE BOWLING PERFORMANCES

PLAYER	OPPOSITION	FIGURES
P. Thornton-Smith	Bethany	4-14
T. Squire	Chatham House	3-8

HURSTPIERPOINT COLLEGE

Hassocks, West Sussex BN6 9JS

Tel: 01273 833636 Fax: 01273 835257
Email: registrar@hppc.co.uk

Master i/c Cricket: C.W. Gray   Coach: M. Scott

2005 SEASON

Played: 19   Won: 1   Lost: 12   Drawn: 6

Captain: C. Viggor   Vice-captain: T. Voller

Team selected from: C. Viggor*, T. Voller*, T. Bishop*, T. Brown*, O. Pearce*, T. Poole, S. Voller, M. Layzell, T. Gogarty, T. Deck, W. Sexton, D. Hudson, A. Deck, A. Pearce.

SUMMARY

This was a poor season, not helped by long-term illness and injury to our opening bowlers. With only one win, against Worth, this was scant reward for a difficult season.

The team never found a balanced bowling attack, despite the odd individual successes. The batting was stronger and numbers one to eight all made half-centuries. Tim Bishop was the leading player with 572 runs and 28 wickets.

Seven boys return next year when things should return to normality.

AVERAGES

BATSMAN	INNINGS	NOT OUT	RUNS	H. SCORE	AVERAGE
T. Bishop	17	2	572	103*	38.1
C. Viggor	16	0	413	129	25.8
O. Pearce	16	2	351	50	25.1
T. Poole	15	3	276	73	23.0
S. Voller	16	0	322	81	20.1

BOWLER	OVERS	MAIDENS	RUNS	WICKETS	AVERAGE
T. Poole	70	9	298	13	22.9
T. Bishop	183.3	28	728	28	26.0
T. Brown	152	26	747	26	28.7
M. Layzell	128	24	585	18	32.5

WICKET-KEEPER	PLAYED	CAUGHT	STUMPED
T. Voller	14	9	5

NOTABLE BATTING PERFORMANCES

PLAYER	OPPOSITION	SCORE
C. Viggor	XL Club	129
T. Bishop	Old Johnians	103*
T. Bishop	Worth	100

NOTABLE BOWLING PERFORMANCES

PLAYER	OPPOSITION	FIGURES
T. Brown	Ellesmere College	6-45
T. Bishop	St. George's Weybridge	6-27

IPSWICH SCHOOL

25 Henley Road, Ipswich IP1 3SG

Tel: 01473 408300 Fax: 01473 400058
Email: registrar@ipswich.suffolk.sch.uk

Master i/c Cricket: A.K. Golding   Coach: R.E. East

2005 SEASON

Played: 15   Won: 3   Lost: 7   Drawn: 4   Abandoned: 1

Captain: D. Crame

Team selected from: D. Crame*, O. Bowditch, P. Brooks, A. Burton,
B. Connelly, T. Davey, E. Driver*, A. Gravell, J. Holden,
P. Messent, G. Pinner, E. Pope, D. Sargeant, H. Thomas,
M. Treharne*, N. Runnacles.

SUMMARY

This was a difficult season. The 1st XI was inexperienced and although playing some good cricket in patches, they struggled to maintain their performances over long periods. We recorded encouraging wins against Woodbridge and Norwich at the start of the season and Edinburgh Academy at the end.

Dominic Crame led the side ably, and used his bowling resources well, setting sensible fields. His opening partnership with Tom Davey was productive on several occasions, including a dynamic stand of 90 in 14 overs against King's School Macclesfield and 120 against Edinburgh Academy. If Tom Davey can build upon his scoring this year, he will be a highly productive opener for the side next season.

Disappointingly, the middle order did not score the runs expected, but in Peter Brooks, Ed Pope, David Sargeant and Phillip Messent the team have players of increased experience for next year. George Pinner played the innings of the season, scoring a rapid 92 against a strong Brentwood attack. David Sargeant kept wicket well for the side, showing considerable skill and technique in dealing with some occasionally wayward throwing. Brooks played several aggressive innings which promise much for next year.

Ed Pope of Year 10 led the bowlers with 40 wickets, followed by Mark Treharne with 15. The remaining bowlers struggled a little on the true Ivry Street pitch, but Anthony Burton, James Holden, Ben Connelly, Peter Brooks and Nick Runnacles all return next year. Although the results were a little disappointing, with many players still available next season things should improve.

AVERAGES

BATSMAN	INNINGS	NOT OUT	RUNS	H. SCORE	AVERAGE
T. Davey	15	0	452	76	30.1
D. Crame	14	0	283	45	20.2
E. Pope	14	4	196	45	19.6
P. Brooks	11	0	204	50	18.5
G. Pinner	12	0	193	92	16.1

BOWLER	OVERS	MAIDENS	RUNS	WICKETS	AVERAGE
E. Pope	146	23	536	40	13.4
N. Runnacles	60	11	212	11	19.3
M. Treharne	84	15	360	15	24.0
A. Burton	85	12	301	10	30.1

NOTABLE BATTING PERFORMANCES

PLAYER	OPPOSITION	SCORE
G. Pinner	Brentwood	92

NOTABLE BOWLING PERFORMANCES

PLAYER	OPPOSITION	FIGURES
E. Pope	Norwich	6-75

JOHN LYON SCHOOL

Middle Road, Harrow, Middlesex HA2 0HN

Tel: 020 8872 8404 Fax: 020 8872 8455
Email: staff.parker@johnlyon.org

Master i/c Cricket: Ian Parker
Coaches: Angus Fraser and Ian Blanchett

2005 SEASON

Played: 16 Won: 5 Lost: 8 Drawn: 3

Captain: N. Rughani Vice-captain: K. Desai

Team selected from: N. Rughani*, K. Desai*, G. Dhami, A. Gill,
R. Joshi, S. Juma*, A. Murthy, P. Patel, S. Quraishy, N. Ruparelia*,
R. Seth, V. Seth, K. Toor*.

SUMMARY

The 1st XI had a rather mixed season. In the opening game we
recorded a draw at Hampton, and then achieved good victories over
Aldenham and Berkhamsted, when there was a very tense finish.
Berkhamsted needed 4 to win off 2 overs, with 4 wickets in hand -
John Lyon won by 1 run. We were defeated in the next match versus
Enfield in similar circumstances. John Lyon needed 10 to win in 3
overs, with 5 wickets in hand, but failed to reach the target.

A defeat against Haberdashers' was followed by victory over Mill
Hill in a Twenty20 game (due to weather) with Kabir Toor scoring
102*. A 10 wicket victory over St. Benedict's was followed by a draw
at Westminster. John Lyon declared on 206-4 (Toor 122*) with
Westminster reaching 174-9. There were defeats against Harrow, MCC
and an Old Boys side.

U15 player Kabir Toor was selected for Middlesex U17 and scored
209 versus Wiltshire. He was also selected for England U15 and scored
123 against Guyana U16.

AVERAGES

BATSMAN	INNINGS	NOT OUT	RUNS	H. SCORE	AVERAGE
K. Toor	15	4	718	122*	65.3
G. Dhami	7	1	210	65	35.0
N. Ruparelia	15	1	238	71	17.0

BOWLER	OVERS	MAIDENS	RUNS	WICKETS	AVERAGE
N. Rughani	111.3	21	409	21	19.5
K. Toor	171	16	652	31	21.0
N. Ruparelia	94	13	387	18	21.5
K. Desai	63.2	10	228	10	22.8

WICKET-KEEPER	PLAYED	CAUGHT	STUMPED
S. Juma	14	8	8
R. Joshi	2	2	0

NOTABLE BATTING PERFORMANCES

PLAYER	OPPOSITION	SCORE
K. Toor	Westminster	122*
K. Toor	Mill Hill	102*
N. Ruparelia	Aldenham	71
K. Toor	St. Benedict's	82*

NOTABLE BOWLING PERFORMANCES

PLAYER	OPPOSITION	FIGURES
N. Rughani	Aldenham	4-7
N. Ruparelia	Enfield	4-14
K. Toor	Queen Elizabeth's Barnet	4-26

THE JUDD SCHOOL

Brook Street, Tonbridge, Kent TN9 2PN

Tel: 01732 770880 Fax: 01732 771661
Email: david.joseph@judd.kent.sch.uk

Master i/c Cricket and Coach: D.W. Joseph

2005 SEASON

Played: 18   Won: 10   Lost: 6   Drawn: 1   Tied: 1

Captain: J. Southwart   Vice-captain: J. Baldwin

Team selected from: J. Baldwin*, O. Renton*, J. Southwart*,
A. Owens*, S. Marshall*, W. Mahoney*, C. Raveney*,
M. Boardman*, I. Smith*, S. Lewis, A. Dowson, T. Probert*,
C. Curran*, J. Whitehead, J. Nimho.

Scorer: Ms J. Cole

SUMMARY

2005 was Judd 1st XI's best season for a number of years. Narrowly losing the Kent U19 league final and another close defeat in the U19 Kent Cup semi-final showed the progression the team has made.

Throughout the season the players were well lead by captain Joe Southwart, who was ably assisted by vice-captain Jamie Baldwin. What is encouraging is that many of the key performers are returning next year. Jamie Baldwin, who scored 512 runs and took 28 wickets; Oscar Renton, 438 runs and 14 wickets; Chris Raveney who took 30 wickets and Matthew Boardman with 20 dismissals will form the core of next season's 1st XI.

High points of the season were Jamie Baldwin's 99* against Eltham College and Alex Owens' hat trick against Skinners'. The team are already looking forward to next season and their pre-season tour of Barbados.

AVERAGES

BATSMAN	INNINGS	NOT OUT	RUNS	H. SCORE	AVERAGE
J. Baldwin	18	1	512	99*	30.1
O. Renton	17	2	438	84*	29.2
A. Owens	14	3	213	50	19.4
J. Southwart	16	2	269	58*	19.2
S. Marshall	13	2	185	42*	16.8
W. Mahoney	14	0	180	36	12.9

BOWLER	OVERS	MAIDENS	RUNS	WICKETS	AVERAGE
C. Raveney	90.2	28	323	30	10.8
J. Baldwin	98	14	323	28	11.5
I. Smith	78.1	9	228	19	12.0
J. Southwart	48.2	6	204	15	13.6
O. Renton	62.1	9	229	14	16.4
A. Owens	74.5	5	311	15	20.7

WICKET-KEEPER	PLAYED	CAUGHT	STUMPED
M. Boardman	15	16	4

NOTABLE BATTING PERFORMANCES

PLAYER	OPPOSITION	SCORE
J. Baldwin	Eltham College	99*
O. Renton	Sir Joseph Williamson's	84*
O. Renton	Eltham College	78*
O. Renton	Eltham College	70
J. Baldwin	Cranbrook	69
J. Baldwin	Sevenoaks	64
J. Southwart	King's Rochester	58*

NOTABLE BOWLING PERFORMANCES

PLAYER	OPPOSITION	FIGURES
J. Southwart	Chislehurst & Sidcup GS	5-28
C. Raveney	Eltham College	4-28
J. Baldwin	Wallington GS	4-25
I. Smith	Enfield GS	3-27
A. Owens	Bethany	3-7
T. Probert	Bethany	3-14
O. Renton	Sir Joseph Williamson's	3-22

150 YEARS OF OUNDLE SCHOOL CRICKET

by Andrew Radd, Oundle School Archivist

One thing leads to another, as they say. Planning celebrations to mark 150 years of cricket at Oundle, master-in-charge John Wake discovered that the game had actually figured in the life of the school for rather longer.

The match against Uppingham in August 1855 was reckoned to be the earliest of which an account survives. But it didn't take too much digging in local newspapers and the school's own archives to take the story back as far as 1830, when Oundle suffered a slightly embarrassing defeat at the hands of 'eleven young gentlemen' from the nearby village of King's Cliffe.

So was the school celebrating a 150th or a 175th anniversary when Oundelians past and present, and their guests, gathered for a memorable Anniversary Dinner in the Great Hall last June? No-one seemed to mind too much.

Great figures from Oundle's cricketing past were recalled and honoured, not least Henry St John Reade, headmaster from 1876 to 1883 and a notable player in his own right, who did much to encourage the game at the school and in Northamptonshire as a whole, serving on the first committee of the newly-organised county club from 1878. Luckily for future researchers, he also founded 'The Laxtonian' magazine, which explains why detailed year-by-year records date from Reade's time.

So far, forty-two Oundelians have appeared in first-class cricket, from John Morley Lee (later honorary Canon at Winchester Cathedral) in 1845 to Mark Phythian for Durham UCCE last season. In between came the likes of Arthur Sutthery, eminent Victorian; Reggie Ingle and Frank Greenwood, captain of Somerset and Yorkshire respectively in the 1930s; father and son Mike Mills (Warwickshire) and Peter Mills (Northamptonshire), who both led out Cambridge University at Lord's, and the present-day Essex opener Will Jefferson.

All this is not to mention a 'walk-on' part for W.G. Grace, father of an Oundle master, who scored his 200th century in all cricket at the school in 1901. The Champion would have nodded with approval at the exploits of the 2004 side, skippered by Cameron Wake, which registered a record fifteen victories. The team was undefeated and also carried off the Silk Trophy for the first time.

This maintained Oundle's position as one of the top ten cricketing schools in the country. According to *Wisden*, Oundle is one of only a handful of schools that have posted over one hundred victories in the last decade and only two schools have achieved more wins than Oundle during this period. Among recent successes, the 1st XI has totalled forty-eight wins in the past four seasons, and over the past thirteen years, successive 1st XI sides have won 144 matches, with only thirty-six defeats.

As the old school song has it – 'Oundle, long may she flourish, wax and grow great in the land!'

W.G. Grace scores his 200th century, Oundle 1901

KIMBOLTON SCHOOL

Kimbolton, Huntingdon, Cambs PE28 0EA

Tel: 01480 860505 Fax: 01480 860386
Email: a_lawless@kimbolton.biblio.net

Master i/c Cricket: A.S. Lawless

2005 SEASON

Played: 20   Won: 4   Lost: 14   Drawn: 2

Captain: O. Huggins   Vice-captain: D. Payne

Team selected from: O. Huggins*, D. Payne*, C. May*, P. Sarkies,
W. Mackay, S. Lambert, A. Parker*, W. Briggs*, H. Gillam*,
S. Roberts, C. Abington, N. Brandler*, M. Fitter*,
D. Thurmott, J. Spink, R. Howcroft*, R. Miller*,
M. Townsend, N. Borkett, J. Hunter.

Scorers: R. Butler and R. Brodie

AVERAGES

NOTABLE BATTING PERFORMANCES

PLAYER	OPPOSITION	SCORE
D. Payne	King's Peterborough	92*
O. Huggins	King's Peterborough	104
O. Huggins	Monmouth	132

NOTABLE BOWLING PERFORMANCES

PLAYER	OPPOSITION	FIGURES
A. Parker	Old Kimboltonians	13-3-53-5
P. Sarkies	Oakham	10-1-41-4

Leaders
in the field

Sponsors of the
C&G Cheltenham Cricket Festival
and C&G Trophy

C&G Cheltenham & Gloucester

Cheltenham & Gloucester plc Registered Office: Barnett Way, Gloucester GL4 3RL. Registered
in England and Wales No. 2299428.

KING EDWARD VII
AND QUEEN MARY SCHOOL

Clifton Drive, Lytham St Annes, Lancashire FY8 1DT

Tel: 01253 784100 Fax: 01253 731623
Email: jal@keqms.co.uk

Master i/c Cricket and Coach: J. Liggett

2005 SEASON

Played: 22 Won: 12 Lost: 4 Drawn: 6

Captain: P. Jackson Vice-captain: N. Jones

Team selected from: J. Atherton*, S. Ormsby*, N. Jones*, N. Little,
T. Shillito*, P. Jackson*, J. Whittam*, J. Dearden, D. Tufft*,
M. Dorans, A. Hassan, G. Joliffe, A. Cole*.

Scorer: Mrs S. Atherton

SUMMARY

We had an excellent season with twelve victories. The school recorded their first ever win over the MCC, by three wickets. The team's strength was the batting line-up, with all players capable of scoring runs.

James Atherton was the leading run-scorer, after doing the same last year. He still has another year to go. Nick Jones set a school wicket-taking record with 42 at an average of 13.1. He also just failed to make 500 runs.

In the game against Bolton School, James Atherton scored 96 in an opening partnership of 130 in seventy-five minutes. In one over he managed to score 27 runs (4 sixes, a 2 and a single). This was matched by S. Ormsby against Stockport GS.

The team was ably led by captain Peter Jackson and in his absence, Nick Jones. Only two of the players featured in the averages will be returning next year.

AVERAGES

BATSMAN	INNINGS	NOT OUT	RUNS	H. SCORE	AVERAGE
A. Hassan	11	4	291	68	41.6
J. Atherton	21	3	713	96	39.6
N. Jones	17	3	492	73*	35.1
P. Jackson	13	3	270	82	27.0
D. Tufft	20	3	353	70*	20.8
S. Ormsby	21	2	353	76	18.6

BOWLER	OVERS	MAIDENS	RUNS	WICKETS	AVERAGE
N. Jones	182	49	552	42	13.1
A. Hassan	98	14	284	17	16.7
P. Jackson	137	36	376	22	17.1
J. Atherton	115	18	426	21	20.3
J. Whittam	129	15	492	17	28.9
M. Dorans	86	7	385	12	32.1

WICKET-KEEPER	PLAYED	CAUGHT	STUMPED
A. Cole	13	20	0

NOTABLE BATTING PERFORMANCES

PLAYER	OPPOSITION	SCORE
J. Atherton	Lancaster Royal	89
J. Atherton	Bolton	96
P. Jackson	St. Francis Xavier's College	82

NOTABLE BOWLING PERFORMANCES

PLAYER	OPPOSITION	FIGURES
N. Jones	Stockport GS	5-34
P. Jackson	Lancaster Royal GS	4-14
M. Dorans	Kirkham	3-8
J. Atherton	Arnold	4-29

THE HARVEY GRAMMAR SCHOOL

by Phil Harding, Deputy Headmaster

Cricket at The Harvey Grammar School dates back to 1865, when the school lost its first match by an innings and 107 runs, having been dismissed for 5 and 8. From that inauspicious start, the game has developed into a major school activity that currently involves fielding six teams, each with regular fixtures on Saturdays and in midweek.

In 1920, a fifteen-year-old by the name of Les Ames scored a century for the Harvey 1st XI against Dover County School. He subsequently went on to become, in the words of Sir Don Bradman, 'the greatest wicket-keeper/batsman of all time'. The Harvey's cricket pavilion, opened in 1997 by Colin Cowdrey and funded by the Old Harveians Association, is dedicated to his memory. On 3rd December 2005, the school marked the 100th anniversary of the birth of its most famous cricketing son with a special dinner.

The current programme of cricket, very extensive for a state school, maintains a long tradition. The annual 1st XI tours to the West Country, a feature of that programme for over twenty years, have now been replaced by a tour every three years to Barbados, the next in 2006. Annual games against The XL Club and MCC on the County Ground at Folkestone are also an important part of that programme, and in the MCC game in 2004, fourteen-year-old Charles Hemphrey, a member of the Kent CCC Academy, scored a century – the youngest player to do so for the school 1st XI since Les Ames eighty-four years earlier.

The Harvey is justly proud of its record of cricketing success, and has won the Sir Dawnay Lemon Cup (the County Cup for school 1st XIs in Kent) on a record nine occasions. In defeating Eltham College in the 2005 Final, the Harvey set a new scoring record for the competition, with a score of 284 in 50 overs.

The school enjoys a strong and mutually beneficial relationship with the senior clubs in the area, all of which have a strong contingent of former Harvey pupils amongst their membership. With its new designation as a Specialist Sports College, and the 'hub' school for sport in the area, the Harvey is well placed to further enhance its excellent cricketing reputation.

Opposite - The Les Ames Pavilion was opened in July 1997 by Sir Colin Cowdrey (he was enobled as Lord Cowdrey the following day). The Harvey played an Invitation XI led by Mike Denness, former captain of Kent and England. *(Photo by Vic Seymour)*

KING EDWARD VI COLLEGE STOURBRIDGE

Stourbridge, West Midlands DY8 1TD

Tel: 01384 398100 Fax: 01384 398123
Email: reception@kedst.ac.uk

Masters i/c Cricket: Mark Ryan and Richard Williams
Coach: Mark Ryan

2005 SEASON

Played: 10   Won: 6   Lost: 4

Captain: M. Patel

Team selected from: M. Patel, R. Jones, D. Wood, A. Price, J. Afzal, E. Jones, M. Fradgley, R. Powell, C. Bayley, N. Tranter, C. James, S. Ahmed, K. Ahmed, A. Krishna.

SUMMARY

A highly successful season, considering that our two best players were frequently away on county and senior club duty. Given the constant demand to play limited-overs matches and ECB bowling directives, it is increasingly impossible for players to score hugely and take large numbers of wickets. Nevertheless, there were plenty of highlights as shown in the averages.

The side was admirably organised off the field and wonderfully encouraged on the field by Mitesh Patel. Enthusiasm abounded, especially remarkable as it was necessary to call up reserves when the bane of examinations (too many too often) forced us to dig deep.

AVERAGES

BATSMAN	INNINGS	NOT OUT	RUNS	H. SCORE	AVERAGE
M. Patel	9	0	419	104	46.6
M. Fradgley	6	0	195	64	32.5
J. Afzal	8	1	201	96*	28.7
A. Price	7	0	158	53	22.6

BOWLER	OVERS	MAIDENS	RUNS	WICKETS	AVERAGE
J. Afzal	54.2	3	225	15	15.0
M. Fradgley	43.3	6	157	9	17.4
C. Bayley	40.2	9	159	9	17.7
M. Patel	25	2	129	6	21.5
N. Tranter	59	6	249	10	24.9

NOTABLE BATTING PERFORMANCES

PLAYER	OPPOSITION	SCORE
M. Patel	XL Club	104
J. Afzal	Bishop Vesey's GS	96*

NOTABLE BOWLING PERFORMANCES

PLAYER	OPPOSITION	FIGURES
J. Afzal	XL Club	6-22
C. Bayley	South Bromsgrove HS	5-17

Did you know? . . . The slowest century for England in Test match cricket took 488 minutes. It was made by P.E. Richardson at Johannesburg in the 1956/7 series.

Top: Harrow enjoyed an unbeaten season, winning thirteen of their seventeen games
Bottom Left: Patrick Foster (Oundle) 46 wickets at 12.1
Bottom Middle: Luke Harvey (Repton) 627 runs and 37 wickets
Bottom Right: Michael Wakefield (Reed's) 630 runs and 29 wickets

Above: Paul Borrington and James Blackwell broke a school record with their unbeaten 314 run partnership (Repton)

Top Left: Brothers Greg (139*) and Daniel Wood (139*) featured in an undefeated opening partnership of 300 for QEGS Wakefield
Bottom Left: James Sharland (Monkton Combe) 26 dismissals
Bottom Right: Neil Pinner is the youngest centurion in the school's history (RGS Worcester)

KING EDWARD'S SCHOOL BIRMINGHAM

Edgbaston Park Road, Birmingham B15 2UA

Tel: 0121 472 1672 Fax: 0121 415 4327
Email: mds@kes.bham.sch.uk

Master i/c Cricket: M.D. Stead Coach: D. Collins

2005 SEASON

Played: 21 Won: 6 Lost: 9 Drawn: 5 Tied: 1

Captain: N. Chase

Team selected from: N. Chase*, J. Metcalfe*, D. Neale, A. Gatrad,
P. Neale, T. Burn, W. Arnold, S. Patel, H. Hussain, J. Botha*,
L. Virdee, Z. Khan, V. Banerjee, A. Prinja, K. Iyer, P. Grewal, R. Hall,
H. Bhogal, S. Gateley, A. Shanghavi.

Scorer: A. Townsend

SUMMARY

After three excellent years, 2005 was a transitional season when the opportunity to blood several younger players was taken. The results reflect the performances and were probably what was expected.

Captain Nick Chase led from the front, scoring 594 runs and taking 31 wickets with his left-arm spin. He was well supported by senior players James Metcalfe (367 runs and 23 wickets), Adam Gatrad (309 runs) and Jon Botha (15 wickets). Lower sixth formers Dan Neale, with 526 runs including a century, and Sam Patel, with 21 wickets, also did well.

Fifteen-year-old wicket-keeper Phillip Neale is highly promising and his batting is improving quickly. The 2006 season is again likely to be difficult, but with several talented U15 and U14 players eager for their chance, the future looks reasonably bright.

AVERAGES

BATSMAN	INNINGS	NOT OUT	RUNS	H. SCORE	AVERAGE
N. Chase	19	1	594	73	33.0
D. Neale	19	1	526	101	29.2
J. Metcalfe	16	1	367	49	24.5
A. Gatrad	18	2	309	61	19.3
P. Neale	11	2	168	52	18.7
W. Arnold	15	6	164	38*	18.2

BOWLER	OVERS	MAIDENS	RUNS	WICKETS	AVERAGE
J. Metcalfe	113	16	414	23	18.0
N. Chase	198	48	576	31	18.6
S. Patel	132	17	467	21	22.2
J. Botha	109	23	372	15	24.8
D. Neale	82	7	347	9	38.6

WICKET KEEPER	PLAYED	CAUGHT	STUMPED
P. Neale	12	6	3
L. Virdee	11	7	2

NOTABLE BATTING PERFORMANCES

PLAYER	OPPOSITION	SCORE
D. Neale	Nottingham HS	101
N. Chase	Prince Henry's Evesham	73
A. Gatrad	Solihull HS	61
P. Neale	King's Worcester	52

NOTABLE BOWLING PERFORMANCES

PLAYER	OPPOSITION	FIGURES
J. Metcalfe	Kestrels	6-2-15-5
N. Chase	Old Swinford Hospital	11-4-21-5
S. Patel	MCC	18-2-58-7

Top Left: Henry Grant (St. George's College) 408 runs and 44 wickets
Top Right: Jonathan Bairstow (St. Peter's York) 478 runs and 21 wickets
Bottom Left: Tom Hanman (Sir Joseph Williamson's) 21 wickets at 7.7
Bottom Right: Graeme White (Stowe) 732 runs and 55 wickets

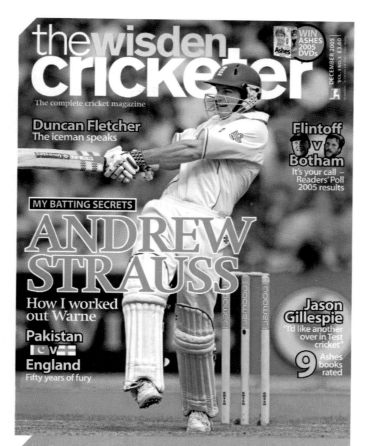

the**wisden**
cricketer

The complete cricket magazine

WIN ASHES 2005 DVDs

DECEMBER 2005 · VOL 3 NO. 3 £3.60

Duncan Fletcher
The iceman speaks

Flintoff v **Botham**
It's your call –
Readers' Poll
2005 results

MY BATTING SECRETS

ANDREW STRAUSS

How I worked
out Warne

Pakistan
v
England
Fifty years of fury

Jason Gillespie
"I'd like another over in Test cricket"

9 Ashes books rated

the complete
cricket magazine

KING'S COLLEGE TAUNTON

South Road, Taunton TA1 3LA

Tel: 01823 328200 Fax: 01823 328207
Email: reception@kings-taunton.co.uk

Master i/c Cricket: P.A. Dossett   Coach: D. Breakwell

2005 SEASON

Played: 11   Won: 5   Lost: 4   Drawn: 2

Captain: C. Lenygon   Vice-captain: A. Trollope

Team selected from: O. Attinger*, A. Penn, T. Elphinstone*,
C. Lenygon*, K. Kohli, R. Kilbride, W. Finch, H. Bowditch*,
A. Trollope*, I. Jeanes*, C. Langdon, J. Buttler, W. Webster,
J. Williams*, M. Dusting.

SUMMARY

An inexperienced side was well led by Charles Lenygon and played
some excellent cricket. The highlight for most was the victory over the
Royal Marines. Chasing 253 for victory, King's recovered from 104-6
to win in the last over.

Having bowled out Millfield for 208, King's reached 69-0 at tea,
before the rain ruined what would have been a great game. Blundell's
and King's Bruton were beaten, but losses were sustained at the hands
of Taunton and Sherborne.

Tom Elphinstone led the batting effort and was well supported by
colts Hanson Bowditch and Alex Penn, as well as the captain. The top
five in the averages are all available again in 2006, so things look
promising for next season.

Old hands Anthony Trollope and Ian Jeanes led the bowling effort,
but off-spinner John Williams was very consistent and the pace of
Chris Langdon caused opposition batsmen some problems at the end of
the season. With a tour to South Africa next Easter and a number of
promising youngsters coming through, the future looks bright.

AVERAGES

BATSMAN	INNINGS	NOT OUT	RUNS	H. SCORE	AVERAGE
T. Elphinstone	10	2	325	80	40.6
J. Buttler	4	1	101	40	33.7
C. Lenygon	8	1	218	63	31.1
H. Bowditch	8	1	190	78	27.1
A. Penn	7	1	157	70	26.2
O. Attinger	10	2	206	59	25.8

BOWLER	OVERS	MAIDENS	RUNS	WICKETS	AVERAGE
C. Lenygon	62	14	166	14	11.9
J. Williams	76	14	249	15	16.6
I. Jeanes	79	8	311	15	20.7
A. Trollope	84	8	361	13	27.8
C. Langdon	43	6	216	6	36.0

WICKET-KEEPER	PLAYED	CAUGHT	STUMPED
H. Bowditch	11	8	2

NOTABLE BATTING PERFORMANCES

PLAYER	OPPOSITION	SCORE
T. Elphinstone	Royal Marines CC	80
H. Bowditch	XL Club	78
A. Penn	XL Club	70

NOTABLE BOWLING PERFORMANCES

PLAYER	OPPOSITION	FIGURES
J. Williams	OA Club	9-3-27-5
W. Webster	Blundell's	4-1-14-4

THE KING'S SCHOOL CANTERBURY

Canterbury, Kent CT1 2ES

Tel: 01227 595501 Fax: 01227 595595
Email: rcw@kings-school.co.uk

Master i/c Cricket: R. White   Coach: A. Ealham

2005 SEASON

Played: 16   Won: 10   Lost: 4   Drawn: 2

Captain: W. Bruce

Team selected from: T. Boucher*, W. Bruce*, G. Chilcott, P. Dixey*,
M. Gwyer, C. Harvey, A. Holmes, D. Johnston*, S. Middleton,
H. Simmons, G. Sweetman*, O. Tennant, L. Thorne*.

Scorer: C. Heslop

SUMMARY

King's enjoyed one of their best seasons for several years. After a disappointing start, when the quality of cricket was affected by the damp pitch conditions, the XI recorded a run of ten wins in thirteen games.

The side was superbly led by William Bruce and his individual performances with both bat and ball were outstanding. He was given great support by England wicket-keeper Paul Dixey and opening bowler Dan Johnston, in particular.

Notable performances included an opening stand of 190 by William and Paul against St. Lawrence College and an unbroken second wicket stand of 118, out of 206-4, between William (150*) and Graham Sweetman, to beat Highgate. There was also a magnificent team effort in chasing 247 to win against Haileybury, featuring a century by Paul; a ten wicket win, chasing 134 against Cranbrook and then finally Will's 5-29 and 81* in the nine wicket victory against Kent U16.

AVERAGES

BATSMAN	INNINGS	NOT OUT	RUNS	H. SCORE	AVERAGE
P. Dixey	10	4	393	128*	65.5
W. Bruce	15	4	702	150*	63.8
T. Boucher	13	4	286	51*	31.8
G. Sweetman	14	2	359	59*	29.9
A. Holmes	7	2	97	26	19.4
C. Harvey	7	1	116	54*	19.3

BOWLER	OVERS	MAIDENS	RUNS	WICKETS	AVERAGE
W. Bruce	162	33	468	33	14.2
D. Johnston	158.3	28	509	32	15.9
G. Chilcott	31	6	83	5	16.6
H. Simmons	26	4	103	6	17.2
T. Boucher	19.5	4	73	4	18.2
O. Tennant	102.1	25	238	12	19.8

WICKET-KEEPER	PLAYED	CAUGHT	STUMPED
P. Dixey	10	4	5
S. Middleton	6	4	4

NOTABLE BATTING PERFORMANCES

PLAYER	OPPOSITION	SCORE
W. Bruce	Trinity	150*
P. Dixey	Haileybury	128*
W. Bruce	Sevenoaks	102
P. Dixey	St. Lawrence College	89
W. Bruce	St. Lawrence College	82
W. Bruce	Kent U16	81*
W. Bruce	Cranbrook	77*

NOTABLE BOWLING PERFORMANCES

PLAYER	OPPOSITION	FIGURES
W. Bruce	Kent U16	5-29
D. Johnston	Cranbrook	5-35
W. Bruce	Highgate	4-24
D. Johnston	Whitgift	4-26
D. Johnston	Trinity	4-29
W. Bruce	Whitgift	4-45
O. Tennant	Sevenoaks	3-15

THE KING'S SCHOOL ELY

Ely, Cambridgeshire CB7 4DB

Tel: 01353 660706 Fax: 01353 667485
Email: johnmarshall@kings-ely.cambs.sch.uk

Masters i/c Cricket: John Marshall and Kevin Daniel
Coach: John Stannard

2005 SEASON

Played: 14   Won: 4   Lost: 8   Drawn: 2

Captain: H. Sperling   Vice-captain: J. Payne

Team selected from: T. Baker, A. Broadhurst, G. Eddy, T. Howgego,
D. Kneeshaw, O. Lucraft, R. Mahendra, D. Muil, J. Payne*, S. Pearce,
R. Ransom*, H. Sperling*, A. Vincent*, E. Waites.

SUMMARY

Overall the season was a little disappointing, but there were some very good team and individual performances. The captain, Harry Sperling, enjoyed a memorable season, breaking the school batting aggregate record with 812 runs and scoring three undefeated centuries. His innings of 141* in a seven wicket victory over the MCC was the highlight of the season. MCC declared on 252-5 (George Eddy 3-55) before Sperling and Andrew Vincent (59) shared a partnership of 170 for the second wicket, establishing a foundation for a win with two overs to spare.

Other victories were obtained against Royal Hospital, St Edmund's College and Old Eleans.

Sperling dominated the batting throughout the season. Although the other leading batsmen all made good scores, they were not consistent.

The bowling attack was led by Tommy Howgego and George Eddy, who both enjoyed encouraging debut seasons. A number of young players showed promise when given their opportunities, and their experience in 2005 will be invaluable when they establish their positions next year.

AVERAGES

BATSMAN	INNINGS	NOT OUT	RUNS	H. SCORE	AVERAGE
H. Sperling	14	4	812	141*	81.2
A. Vincent	14	0	333	88	23.8
R. Ransom	12	1	219	39	19.9
T. Howgego	10	2	154	50*	19.3
J. Payne	12	0	225	77	18.8

BOWLER	OVERS	MAIDENS	RUNS	WICKETS	AVERAGE
H. Sperling	41.1	5	187	10	18.7
D. Kneeshaw	21	0	132	7	18.9
T. Howgego	87	25	295	13	22.7
G. Eddy	89.1	9	432	17	25.4

WICKET-KEEPER	PLAYED	CAUGHT	STUMPED
J. Payne	12	14	2

NOTABLE BATTING PERFORMANCES

PLAYER	OPPOSITION	SCORE
H. Sperling	MCC	141*
H. Sperling	St. Edmund's College	118*
H. Sperling	Kimbolton	103*
H. Sperling	Old Eleans	93*
A. Vincent	St. Edmund's College	88
J. Payne	Gibraltar U19	77
J. Payne	Old Eleans	69

NOTABLE BOWLING PERFORMANCES

PLAYER	OPPOSITION	FIGURES
G. Eddy	Royal Hospital	4-22
R. Ransom	Old Eleans	4-24
E. Waites	Kimbolton	4-64

THE KING'S SCHOOL MACCLESFIELD

Westminster Road, Macclesfield, Cheshire SK10 1DA

Tel: 01625 260000 Fax: 01625 260022
Email: mail@kingsmac.co.uk

Master i/c Cricket and Coach: Stephen Moores

2005 SEASON

Played: 20   Won: 9   Lost: 8   Drawn: 3

Captain: T. Parfett-Manning   Vice-captain: J. Lee

Team selected from: T. Parfett-Manning*, K. Sawas*, E. Purdom*, J. Lee*, N. Barker*, A. McGeorge*, T. McKvenny*, J.D. Barratt*, J.P. Barratt*, J. Done, S. Parks, C. Robinson, A. Kimber, O. Jones.

SUMMARY

The 1st XI had a season of highs and lows. We were bowled out for 86 by Wrekin but dismissed Lancaster for the same score later in the season. King's chased 255 against Sedburgh, but failed in chasing 130 against Bangor GS the following day.

Khalid Sawas (904 runs at 60.3 including 4 centuries), Tom Parfett-Manning (678 runs at 45.2) and Elliot Purdom (736 runs at 46) all excelled with the bat. Leg-spinner Jonathan Barratt led the wicket-takers with 35 at 18.1.

The team enjoyed good wins versus Lancaster, Sedburgh and Ipswich, but there were heavy defeats at the hands of Wrekin, Manchester GS, Brighton College, MCC and the Old Boys.

AVERAGES

BATSMAN	INNINGS	NOT OUT	RUNS	H. SCORE	AVERAGE
K. Sawas	20	5	904	122*	60.3
E. Purdom	19	3	736	150*	46.0
T. Parfett-Manning	18	3	678	130	45.2
J.D. Barratt	12	1	241	63	21.9

BOWLER	OVERS	MAIDENS	RUNS	WICKETS	AVERAGE
N. Barker	90.2	17	331	21	15.8
J. Lee	167	40	443	26	17.0
J.P. Barratt	151.3	25	633	35	18.1
T. Parfett-Manning	60.2	5	255	10	25.5

WICKET-KEEPER	PLAYED	CAUGHT	STUMPED
A. McGeorge	16	7	6
J. Done	14	2	1

NOTABLE BATTING PERFORMANCES

PLAYER	OPPOSITION	SCORE
E. Purdom	King's Chester	150*
K. Sawas	Cheadle Hulme	104*
K. Sawas	Merchant Taylors'	102*
K. Sawas	Birkenhead	122*
K. Sawas	KEQMS Lytham	103*
E. Purdom	KEQMS Lytham	88
T. Parfett-Manning	Rossall	130

NOTABLE BOWLING PERFORMANCES

PLAYER	OPPOSITION	FIGURES
J.D. Barratt	Merchant Taylors'	7-12
J.P. Barratt	Newcastle-under-Lyme	7-19
J.P. Barratt	MCC	6-54
N. Barker	Sedburgh	5-60
J.P. Barratt	Rossall	6-46

THE KING'S SCHOOL TYNEMOUTH

Huntington Place, Tynemouth NE30 4RF

Tel: 0191 258 5995 Fax: 0191 296 3826
Email: admissions@kings-tynemouth.co.uk

Master i/c Cricket: P.J. Nicholson   Coach: N. Quinn

2005 SEASON

Played: 8   Won: 2   Lost: 4   Drawn: 2

Captain: B. Telfer   Vice-captain: S. Khanna

Team selected from: B. Telfer*, P. Morse*, J. Coates, S. Khanna,
J. Davidson, P. Clark, S. Orrick, R. Handa, A. Iftikhar, J. Graham,
W. Sharp, N. Bagher, N. Jones, P. McCleod, W. Smith, M. Fearon,
T. Walker, L. Johnson, J. Walter.

SUMMARY

A pre-season injury to captain Bryan Telfer restricted him to just the
final match of the season. It was a disappointing finish to a five season
1st XI career.

Sumeet Khanna was captain in Telfer's absence and the side made
an encouraging start, beating the Old Boys and Yarm School, whilst
drawing with Royal Belfast Academy and RGS Newcastle. However, it
proved a false dawn and the four remaining fixtures were lost.

Philip Morse, a tall left-handed bat made a superb 130* againt RGS
Newcastle and claimed match-winning figures of 6-23 versus Yarm. He
was the outstanding player. Too many others made promising starts,
but failed to deliver heavy runs. U15 spinner R. Handa claimed 6-46 in
the defeat at Barnard Castle. Only Morse and Telfer leave in 2005.

AVERAGES

BATSMAN	INNINGS	NOT OUT	RUNS	H. SCORE	AVERAGE
P. Morse	6	1	199	130*	39.8
J. Coates	7	1	126	40	21.0
S. Khanna	7	0	138	38	19.7
J. Davidson	4	3	13	5*	13.0
P. Clark	3	1	23	16	11.5
S. Orrick	6	2	37	14*	9.3

BOWLER	OVERS	MAIDENS	RUNS	WICKETS	AVERAGE
P. Morse	51.4	13	143	14	10.2
R. Handa	32	6	120	7	17.1
A. Iftikhar	52.3	16	123	7	17.6
J. Davidson	14	1	37	2	18.5
N. Jones	8	1	40	2	20.0
L. Johnson	5	2	20	1	20.0

WICKET-KEEPER	PLAYED	CAUGHT	STUMPED
P. McCleod	6	3	2

NOTABLE BATTING PERFORMANCES

PLAYER	OPPOSITION	SCORE
P. Morse	RGS Newcastle	130*

NOTABLE BOWLING PERFORMANCES

PLAYER	OPPOSITION	FIGURES
P. Morse	Yarm	9-2-23-6
R. Handa	Barnard Castle	14-4-46-6

THE LEYS SCHOOL

Cambridge CB2 2AD

Tel: 01223 508900 Fax: 01223 505333
Email: office@theleys.cambs.sch.uk

Master i/c Cricket: A.R.C. Batterham   Coach: J. Coleman

2005 SEASON

Played: 13   Won: 7   Lost: 4   Drawn: 2

Captain: T. Hoy   Vice-captain: W. Heald

Team selected from: T. Hoy*, W. Heald, N. Bolton*, J. Brooklyn*,
Z. King, E. Jessop, R. Woolley, D. Rice, A. Sewell, G. Price,
J. O'Brien, A. Eve, A. Smethers, P. Dennis. Scorer: Emily Charkham

SUMMARY

An excellent set of results which exceeded all expectations. The side
was inspired by a close sixth form group whose role in maximising the
potential of the younger players was crucial. Brooklyn's contribution
with the ball was the key to so many wins and the team's ability to
chase runs was effectively led by skipper Hoy. Rice and Sewell, both
15 years old, helped to underpin the team's success by their consistent
form throughout the season.

BATSMAN	INNINGS	NOT OUT	RUNS	H. SCORE	AVERAGE
T. Hoy	13	2	451	104	41.0
D. Rice	13	3	408	86*	40.8
A. Sewell	13	1	347	92	28.9
N. Bolton	13	2	327	77	29.7

BOWLER	OVERS	MAIDENS	RUNS	WICKETS	AVERAGE
J. Brooklyn	126	27	358	35	10.2

WICKET-KEEPER	PLAYED	CAUGHT	STUMPED
N. Bolton	13	12	5

NOTABLE BATTING PERFORMANCES

PLAYER	OPPOSITION	SCORE
T. Hoy	Gresham's	104
A. Sewell	Bedford Modern	92

NOTABLE BOWLING PERFORMANCES

PLAYER	OPPOSITION	FIGURES
J. Brooklyn	Gresham's	6-9
J. Brooklyn	Royal Hospital	6-26
J. Brooklyn	Mill Hill	5-15

LLANDOVERY COLLEGE

Llandovery, Carmarthenshire SA20 0EE

Tel: 01550 723000 Fax: 01550 723002
Email: mail@llandoverycollege.com

Master i/c Cricket and Coach: J.C.O. Thomas

2005 SEASON

Played: 5   Lost: 5

Captain: E. Phillips   Vice-captain: T. Kiel

Team selected from: A. Al-Ajooz*, P. Bradley*, E. Phillips, T. Keil,
A. Kouderis, R. Frame, M. Miller, J. Edwards, R. Jones*, L. Griffiths*,
J. Perkins, D. Davies, T. Gould, M. Squirrell*, J. Thorley, S. Thomas.
Scorer: T. Dewland

SUMMARY

A disappointing season was dominated by bad weather early on. The
first game of the season was played in May. Four matches were rained
off and outside practice on the square was very limited. Despite the
poor run of results, there were some notable performances and two of
the matches were lost by only 14 and 27 runs. Next season bodes well
with some fine younger players coming through.

BATSMAN	INNINGS	NOT OUT	RUNS	H. SCORE	AVERAGE
E. Phillips	5	0	222	110	44.4
M. Squirrell	4	2	36	27	18.0
L. Griffiths	4	0	50	28	12.5

BOWLER	OVERS	MAIDENS	RUNS	WICKETS	AVERAGE
E. Phillips	15	0	70	6	11.7

NOTABLE BATTING PERFORMANCES

PLAYER	OPPOSITION	SCORE
E. Phillips	Rougemont	65
E. Phillips	Hartridge	110

NOTABLE BOWLING PERFORMANCES

PLAYER	OPPOSITION	FIGURES
E. Phillips	Rougemont	2-17
E. Phillips	Old Llandoverians	2-7

MALVERN COLLEGE

Malvern, Worcs WR14 3DF

Tel: 01684 581565   Fax: 01684 581617
Email: enquiry@malcol.org

Master i/c Cricket: A.J. Murtagh   Coach: R.W. Tolchard

2005 SEASON

Played: 15   Won: 4   Lost: 5   Drawn: 4   Abandoned: 2

Captain: O. Powell   Vice-captain: R. Price

Team selected from: O. Powell*, R. Price*, T. Chappell*, M. King*,
C. Griffiths*, C. Wright*, R. Remington*, O. Sloane*, J. Hughes*,
C. Lunn*, E. Smith*, C. Gifford*, C. Elsden, T. Fuller,
S. Vaughan, A. Brierley.

Scorer: Miss E. Davy

SUMMARY

Malvern has hitherto enjoyed a halcyon period of half-a-dozen years of talented players and unparalleled success. By contrast, this season was always going to be one of retrenchment. Considering it was a young and untested side (all but two colours will be returning next year), they performed rather better than was expected. Two significant highlights were a thumping win against Wesley College, on tour from Melbourne, and a comprehensive dismantling of a strong Charterhouse side in the final game of the season.

Oliver Powell, the captain, scored the only century all term (100* versus Wesley College), with Tom Chappell, Mike King and Charles Griffiths scoring useful runs in the middle order.

Our strength in bowling lay with our spinners. Our top bowler, Robert Price, was sadly confined to only 36 overs in the season through injury, but Griffiths (17) and King (28) shouldered the burden.

AVERAGES

BATSMAN	INNINGS	NOT OUT	RUNS	H. SCORE	AVERAGE
O. Powell	15	3	415	100*	34.6
T. Chappell	14	1	326	74	25.1
C. Griffiths	14	2	287	75*	23.9
M. King	14	1	255	40*	19.6
C. Wright	12	4	156	37*	19.5
R. Remington	14	1	189	32*	14.5

BOWLER	OVERS	MAIDENS	RUNS	WICKETS	AVERAGE
M. King	166	21	403	28	14.4
E. Smith	53	9	163	10	16.3
R. Price	36	8	131	7	18.7
C. Griffiths	122	19	321	17	18.9
O. Powell	52	5	239	9	26.5
C. Gifford	68	4	212	5	42.5

WICKET-KEEPER	PLAYED	CAUGHT	STUMPED
R. Remington	14	5	4

NOTABLE BATTING PERFORMANCES

PLAYER	OPPOSITION	SCORE
O. Powell	Wesley College (Australia)	100*
C. Griffiths	King Edwards's Birmingham	75*
T. Chappell	Charterhouse	74

NOTABLE BOWLING PERFORMANCES

PLAYER	OPPOSITION	FIGURES
C. Griffiths	Wesley College (Australia)	7-15
M. King	Charterhouse	6-62
O. Powell	Dean Close	4-28

THE MANCHESTER GRAMMAR SCHOOL

Old Hall Lane, Manchester M13 0XT

Tel: 0161 224 7201 Fax: 0161 257 2446

Email: d.moss@mgs.org

Master i/c Cricket: David Moss

2005 SEASON

Played: 15   Won: 9   Drawn: 6

Captain: N. Reid

Team selected from: N. Reid*, N. Anderson, I. Azam, M. David, A. Gilman*, M. Krishnan*, D. Leeming*, T. Murray, C. Reid, D. Rudolf, O. Wildig, R. Wingate-Saul*, D. Woods*, I. Zahid*.

Scorer: E. James

SUMMARY

This 1st XI was one of the best in recent times. To go unbeaten is increasingly difficult when there are more overs matches now. The above record is even more impressive when it is recognised that three of the drawn matches were rain intervened. Captain Nick Reid led by example and created a team ethic that demanded the highest standards, being rewarded with some excellent cricket. The weather in April and May was very mixed and three Saturday fixtures were lost, but after half term the weather improved. Problems remain with the pitch - it is now three years since it was re-laid and although there has been marginal improvement, it is a worry that it still plays very slow and low.

A successful side needs good balance in all departments of the game. The batting was especially secure. The opening pair, David Leeming and Nick Reid, were exceptional. David's 'purple patch' came in mid-season with unbeaten hundreds against MCC, Arnold and King's Macclesfield, interspersed with 91* against Bolton School. The century against the MCC came in a storybook ending to the match and he scored the winning run from the last ball to complete his hundred. Nick scored consistently, especially after half-term, to ensure the team got off to a positive start. However, the great strength of batting lay in its depth. The most improved player was Tim Murray. He gained confidence from a match-winnning innings against Worksop College and his driving was always delightful. Rupert Wingate-Saul was again a consistent performer but never quite went on to that very big score. Imran Azam missed a lot of the season, initially through exam worries and then through injury. Madhu Krishnan, returning from a wrist injury that had kept him out all of last season, took his chance with enthusiasm, always batting according to the demands of the game and setting a wonderful example in the field. In the same way, Nick Anderson, coming in down the order, showed he was able to move the game on when required - his explosive 31 from 10 balls at Macclesfield set up the declaration.

The bowling also had strength and depth. Central to this was left-arm spinner Daniel Woods, who continued to bowl with skill and control. With the help of the Lancashire Academy he has remodelled his action. He was again leading wicket taker with 42 wickets. The decision to promote Charles Reid from the U14 XI meant there were spin options. Charles bowls off-spin and later in the season he came into his own, taking six wickets against Loughborough. In fact on the dry wickets slow left-arm spinner David Rudolf (U15) was also included and had considerable success. Opening bowlers Nick Anderson and Imran Zahid may have preferred to play on quicker wickets away from MGS but they frequently took early wickets to ensure that opposition sides were kept in check. Nick took four wickets on three occasions and Imran had the happy knack of removing key opposition players. Inclusion of additional spinners meant that third seamer Nick Reid had less work than last year, but he always bowled with great accuracy.

Alex Gilman as wicket-keeper was the focus of the fielding. Although fielding is an area that can easily be neglected, this year the catching and ground-fielding were excellent. Five regular players will be leaving this year but there are several good players competing for their places. Pre-season preparation that will include a Caribbean tour should be interesting next year. Ethan James proved a valuable asset as 1st XI scorer and Elliot Shiers deputised when he was unavailable. I am most grateful for their efforts, which are all too easily taken for granted.

AVERAGES

BATSMAN	INNINGS	NOT OUT	RUNS	H. SCORE	AVERAGE
D. Leeming	15	5	635	114*	63.5
N. Reid	13	1	485	81	40.4
T. Murray	13	0	325	65	25.0
M. Krishnan	11	3	182	34	22.8
I. Azam	7	0	152	44	21.7
N. Anderson	11	2	190	47	21.1

BOWLER	OVERS	MAIDENS	RUNS	WICKETS	AVERAGE
D. Woods	226.5	62	537	42	12.8
D. Rudolf	53	14	143	11	13.0
N. Anderson	127.2	22	362	22	16.5
I. Zahid	89.5	16	244	12	20.3
C. Reid	135.1	30	372	18	20.7

MARLBOROUGH COLLEGE

Marlborough, Wiltshire SN8 1PA

Tel: 01672 892200 Fax: 01672 892207
Email: general.enquiries@marlboroughcollege.org

Master i/c Cricket: N.E.B. Briers   Coach: R.E.M. Ratcliffe

2005 SEASON

Played: 13   Won: 8   Lost: 4   Drawn: 1

Captain: A. Montagu-Pollock

Team selected from: A. Montagu-Pollock, E. Kilbee, G. Adair,
N. Ossrich, R. Williams, H. Simonds, T. Morton, T. Graham,
O. Bishop, H. Wallers, P. Stoop.

Scorer: M. Bennett

SUMMARY

Marlborough beat the MCC for the first time in nearly twenty years and Wellington for the first time in twenty-six years. There were also wins against Cheltenham, Haileybury, St. Edward's, Free Foresters and the Old Marlburians. The weather curtailed the traditional two-day Colours Match against Rugby, but the 150th anniversary of this game proved to be an excellent occasion.

Robbie Williams has been an outstanding fast bowler in his four years in the 1st XI (108 wickets - average 9.9); his hat trick against St. Edward's and his six wicket haul against the Free Foresters were memorable. At the end of term he signed his first professional summer contract with Middlesex County Cricket Club.

AVERAGES

BATSMAN	INNINGS	NOT OUT	RUNS	H. SCORE	AVERAGE
G. Adair	11	2	361	67	40.1
E. Kilbee	13	2	331	79*	30.1
R. Williams	11	2	257	74*	28.6
A. Montagu-Pollock	13	1	166	71*	13.8

BOWLER	OVERS	MAIDENS	RUNS	WICKETS	AVERAGE
R. Williams	123.2	35	276	32	8.6
H. Simonds	98.2	16	329	19	17.3
T. Graham	126.4	19	366	20	18.3

WICKET-KEEPER	PLAYED	CAUGHT	STUMPED
H. Wallers	13	12	4

NOTABLE BATTING PERFORMANCES

PLAYER	OPPOSITION	SCORE
E. Kilbee	Free Foresters	79*
G. Adair	Cheltenham College	67
R. Williams	MCC	74*
A. Montagu-Pollock	Free Foresters	71*

NOTABLE BOWLING PERFORMANCES

PLAYER	OPPOSITION	FIGURES
R. Williams	Free Foresters	6-25
R. Williams	Old Marlburians	5-30
R. Williams	St. Edward's	5-19

MILLFIELD SCHOOL

Butleigh Road, Street, Somerset BA16 0YD

Tel: 01458 442291 Fax: 01458 447276
Email: office@millfieldschool.com

Master i/c Cricket: R.M. Ellison   Coach: M.R. Davis.

2005 SEASON

1st XI - Played: 9   Won: 4   Lost: 4   Drawn: 1
The XI - Played: 13   Won: 11   Drawn: 2

Captain: R. Hamilton-Brown   Vice-captain: S. Parry

Teams selected from: R. Hamilton-Brown*, S. Parry*, O. Taylor*,
R. Lett*, R. Reid, H. Santa-Olalla*, T. Maynard, J. Fear, M. Waller,
C. Miller, D. Muralitharan, K. Powell, K. John, A. Nielson, T. Parker,
A. Roberts, J. Bisgrove, B. Middleton, J. Barrowman, A. Wheater,
A. Barrowman, M. Andrews. Scorer: T. Leggett

SUMMARY

The 1st XI had an average season. Victories were secured against
Blundell's, King's Bruton, Canford and Incogniti. Excellent matches
against Sherborne and Free Foresters were in the balance until the last
over. The 1st XI were comprised of many colts who had successfully
won the Lord's Taverners U15 competition in 2004. The fixtures were
designed to develop and educate them as cricketers and it was
generally considered to be a success.

1st XI AVERAGES

BATSMAN	INNINGS	NOT OUT	RUNS	H. SCORE	AVERAGE
J. Fear	5	0	217	129	43.4
T. Parker	6	1	202	71	40.4
K. John	8	1	261	66	37.3
J. Barrowman	7	1	194	69*	32.3
K. Powell	6	0	147	63	24.5

BOWLER	OVERS	MAIDENS	RUNS	WICKETS	AVERAGE
A. Roberts	39	5	149	10	14.9
D. Muralitharan	43.1	5	173	11	15.7

WICKET-KEEPER	PLAYED	CAUGHT	STUMPED
K. John	8	9	2

For the first time in the school's history, Millfield played two 1st XIs. The XI, the premier side, played county academy sides and strong club teams. The only English schools played were Eton and Tonbridge. Victories against Exeter University and Worcestershire, Glamorgan and Gloucestershire Academy sides were achieved. Wins against Bishop's Cape Town, Prince Alfred's Adelaide and SERC, a collection of schools from Johannesburg, sealed a highly successful season. Drawn games were played against the MCC and Gloucester Gypsies.

The strength of the XI was the batting. Seven hundreds were scored and three batsmen averaged over 70. The ability of players to score big runs undefeated showed a high degree of maturity.

THE XI AVERAGES

BATSMAN	INNINGS	NOT OUT	RUNS	H. SCORE	AVERAGE
R. Lett	8	2	506	119	84.3
T. Maynard	9	3	463	118*	77.2
R. Reid	10	4	421	150*	70.2
R. Hamilton-Brown	13	2	536	168*	48.7
J. Fear	10	3	267	106*	38.1
S. Parry	14	0	531	94	37.9

BOWLER	OVERS	MAIDENS	RUNS	WICKETS	AVERAGE
R. Hamilton-Brown	101.1	11	437	22	19.9
O. Taylor	109.4	4	436	19	22.9
M. Waller	99	4	351	15	23.4

WICKET-KEEPER	PLAYED	CAUGHT	STUMPED
H. Santa-Olalla	12	14	3

NOTABLE BATTING PERFORMANCES

PLAYER	OPPOSITION	SCORE
R. Hamilton-Brown	Tonbridge	168*
R. Reid	Old Millfieldians	150*
R. Lett	Eton College	119
R. Lett	Worcestershire Academy	117*
T. Maynard	SERC (South Africa)	118*
T. Maynard	Tonbridge	107*
J. Fear	SERC (South Africa)	106*

NOTABLE BOWLING PERFORMANCES

PLAYER	OPPOSITION	FIGURES
R. Hamilton-Brown	Eton College	5-31
D. Muralitharan	Old Millfieldians	5-27
R. Reid	Bishop's (South Africa)	5-55

MONKTON COMBE SCHOOL

Monkton Combe, Bath BA2 7HG

Tel: 01225 721185 Fax: 01225 723930
Email: wickenspr@monkton.org.uk

Master i/c Cricket: Paul Wickens
Coaches: Norman Button and Mike Abington

2005 SEASON

Played: 13 Won: 7 Lost: 6

Captain: J. Geake Vice-captain: R. Neil

Team selected from: J. Geake*, R. Neil*, S. Creed*, J. Sharland,
H. Searight, B. Morley, J. Nish, N. Spear, R. Martin, J. Blair,
T. Lawson, A. Shipp, J. Newport, S. Dewes.

SUMMARY

A season that exceeded expectations culminated in the XI winning the
Bath Schools' League for the first time, without losing a game. The
outstanding league batsman was R. Neil, whilst T. Lawson won the
bowling honours. A young side bowled and fielded competently and
Neil and S. Creed enjoyed 'purple patches' with the bat.

Results in other fixtures were not as good, but with all of the
players, bar one, returning next year, prospects remain good.

It has been enjoyable for the coaches at Monkton Combe to work
with a team that has more than fulfilled its potential - it doesn't happen
very often!

AVERAGES

BATSMAN	INNINGS	NOT OUT	RUNS	H. SCORE	AVERAGE
R. Neil	13	3	519	88	51.9
S. Creed	12	3	314	101*	34.9
J. Sharland	12	1	169	41*	15.4
H. Searight	5	1	56	23	14.0
B. Morley	6	5	14	10*	14.0
J. Nish	10	0	132	26	13.2

BOWLER	OVERS	MAIDENS	RUNS	WICKETS	AVERAGE
S. Creed	37	12	101	8	12.6
T. Lawson	82	12	297	23	12.9
N. Spear	30	5	133	9	14.8
J. Geake	105	21	342	23	14.9
R. Martin	34	1	134	8	16.7
J. Nish	75	7	250	13	19.2

WICKET-KEEPER	PLAYED	CAUGHT	STUMPED
J. Sharland	12	22	4

NOTABLE BATTING PERFORMANCES

PLAYER	OPPOSITION	SCORE
S. Creed	King Edward's	101*
R. Neil	MCC	88

NOTABLE BOWLING PERFORMANCES

PLAYER	OPPOSITION	FIGURES
J. Nish	Dauntsey's	4-27
J. Geake	Fettes	4-66

NEWCASTLE-UNDER-LYME SCHOOL

Mount Pleasant, Newcastle-under-Lyme, Staffordshire ST5 1DB

Tel: 01782 631197 Fax: 01782 632582
Email: info@nuls.org.uk

Master i/c Cricket: B.W. Aston   Coach: A. Hill

2005 SEASON

Played: 11   Won: 1   Lost: 3   Drawn: 7

Captain: G. Glenn   Vice-captain: F. Hussain

Team selected from: W. Bailey, M. Burgess, J. Burgess*,
S. Christmas*, G. Glenn*, R. Glenn, F. Hussain*, O. Hussain,
M. Jones, H. Leath*, A. Markshall, H. Moghadam,
B. Robson, R. Timewell.

SUMMARY

Although it could not boast a strong side, the 1st XI was often competitive and enjoyed its season. J. Burgess (one fifth of his overs were maidens) made himself into an economic opening bowler. Both vice-captain F. Hussain and S. Christmas proved themselves inspiring ground fieldsmen.

Batting at number five in every match, wicket-keeper H. Leath posted an average of 60.2. Even though he never scored a half-century, his average was the fourth highest in the school's history.

Did you know? . . . At Durban in 1938/9, H. Verity bowled 766 deliveries in a Test match. It remains the highest number for an England player in Test cricket.

AVERAGES

BATSMAN	INNINGS	NOT OUT	RUNS	H. SCORE	AVERAGE
H. Leath	10	4	361	49*	60.2
F. Hussain	10	1	197	46	21.9
A. Marshall	10	0	203	45	20.3

BOWLER	OVERS	MAIDENS	RUNS	WICKETS	AVERAGE
S. Christmas	76	10	284	17	16.7
F. Hussain	85	6	292	14	20.9
G. Glenn	106	12	412	16	25.7
J. Burgess	106	20	377	10	37.7

WICKET-KEEPER	PLAYED	CAUGHT	STUMPED
H. Leath	11	3	3

NOTABLE BATTING PERFORMANCES

PLAYER	OPPOSITION	SCORE
M. Burgess	Queen Mary's GS	64
G. Glenn	XL Club	50
H. Leath	Mount St. Mary's College	48
H. Leath	Ellesmere College	49*
H. Leath	Old Boys	49

NOTABLE BOWLING PERFORMANCES

PLAYER	OPPOSITION	FIGURES
S. Christmas	Old Boys	5-28
F. Hussain	Ellesmere College	5-53
J. Burgess	Queen Mary's GS	4-19

NORWICH SCHOOL

70 The Close, Norwich NR1 4DD

Tel: 01603 623194 Fax: 01603 627036
Email: tday@norwich-school.org.uk

Master i/c Cricket: Tim Day
Coaches: Rodney Bunting and Richard Sims

2005 SEASON

Played: 11   Won: 2   Lost: 8   Drawn: 1

Captain: M. Kelly   Vice-captain: P. Wilkins

Team selected from: M. Kelly*, P. Wilkins, J. Hill, S. Crook,
M. Strickland, T. Double*, A. Russell*, A. Lister, J. Cumby, C. Eades,
T. Watkin, C. Barkley, D. Treglown, T. Feary, M. Smith, J. Christopher.

Scorer: M. Campbell

SUMMARY

The 1st XI had a poor season in terms of raw results, although one of
the two victories was achieved against the mighty MCC - the first for
more than twenty years. Some of the losses were by very small
margins and several players developed considerably as cricketers -
notably Tom Double with the bat and Alastair Russell with the ball.
James Christopher, a rare leg-spinner, took five wickets on his debut
versus Ipswich. Otherwise, the team were noticeably dependent on
captain Matthew Kelly.

School professional, in addition to Rodney Bunting (ex-Sussex),
was Richard Sims, one of the Zimbabwean rebels led by Heath Streak.

AVERAGES

BATSMAN	INNINGS	NOT OUT	RUNS	H. SCORE	AVERAGE
M. Kelly	10	0	288	74	28.8
A. Lister	10	3	146	35*	20.9
T. Double	11	1	191	82*	19.1
A. Russell	10	1	162	32	18.0
P. Wilkins	9	0	158	42	17.6
S. Crook	10	0	142	70	14.2

BOWLER	OVERS	MAIDENS	RUNS	WICKETS	AVERAGE
C. Barkley	51	2	287	14	20.5
A. Russell	86.2	8	422	17	24.8
A. Lister	60	11	287	10	28.7
M. Kelly	44.4	7	236	8	29.5

WICKET-KEEPER	PLAYED	CAUGHT	STUMPED
J. Cumby	9	10	1
J. Hill	2	3	0

NOTABLE BATTING PERFORMANCES

PLAYER	OPPOSITION	SCORE
T. Double	Framlingham College	82*
M. Kelly	Wymondham	74
M. Kelly	Culford	72
S. Crook	Ipswich	70

NOTABLE BOWLING PERFORMANCES

PLAYER	OPPOSITION	FIGURES
A. Russell	Culford	5-28
C. Barkley	MCC	5-28
J. Christopher	Ipswich	5-46

OAKHAM SCHOOL

Chapel Close, Oakham, Rutland LE15 6FN

Tel: 01572 758500 Fax: 01572 758818
Email: fch@oakham.rutland.sch.uk

Master i/c Cricket: F.C. Hayes   Coach: D.S. Steele

2005 SEASON

Played: 17   Won: 6   Lost: 4   Drawn: 7

Captain: S. Bevin   Vice-captain: M. Collier

Team selected from: S. Bevin*, G. Sapal*, M. Collier*, S. Wills,
C. Morgan, S. Kelly, Y. Tariq, A. Selmes, B. Bayley, J. Marsh,
J. Padley, A. Wyatt, F. Taylor, R. Grundy, M. Denney, T. Rooney,
W. Bunn, J. White, M. Martin.

Scorer: R. Williamson

SUMMARY

By recent standards this was a very moderate year, as was the weather, with two matches cancelled and two others abandoned as a draw through rain.

No less than nineteen players appeared through the season as a result of injury and examination absence. Only Y. Tariq scored more than 500 runs, and of the fourteen bowlers used, only two achieved an average of more than one wicket a match. M. Collier was the leading wicket-taker with 33 victims. The performance of 15-year-old wicket-keeper and opening batsman, C. Morgan (420 runs and 21 dismissals), was commendable.

AVERAGES

BATSMAN	INNINGS	NOT OUT	RUNS	H. SCORE	AVERAGE
Y. Tariq	17	2	593	115	39.5
B. Bayley	13	6	230	56	32.9
C. Morgan	13	0	420	99	32.3
S. Bevin	16	3	420	66	32.3
G. Sapal	17	2	452	81	30.1
S. Wills	16	4	341	62	28.4

BOWLER	OVERS	MAIDENS	RUNS	WICKETS	AVERAGE
M. Collier	147.5	33	566	33	17.2
S. Kelly	123.4	24	424	21	20.2
G. Sapal	112	16	497	15	33.1
Y. Tariq	101	18	377	11	34.3

WICKET-KEEPER	PLAYED	CAUGHT	STUMPED
C. Morgan	13	17	4

NOTABLE BATTING PERFORMANCES

PLAYER	OPPOSITION	SCORE
Y. Tariq	Gresham's	115
C. Morgan	Worksop College	99
G. Sapal	Holcot	81
S. Bevin	Kimbolton	66
G. Sapal	Repton	65
S. Wills	Holcot	62
B. Bayley	Harrow	56

NOTABLE BOWLING PERFORMANCES

PLAYER	OPPOSITION	FIGURES
M. Collier	Kimbolton	4-6
M. Collier	MCC	4-27
S. Kelly	Gentlemen of Leicestershire	4-22
S. Kelly	Worksop College	3-35
A. Selmes	Worksop College	3-12
G. Sapal	Harrow	3-76

THE ORATORY SCHOOL

Woodcote, Nr Reading, Berkshire RG8 0PJ

Tel: 01491 683521 Fax: 01491 680020
Email: enquiries@oratory.co.uk

Master i/c Cricket: P.L. Tomlinson   Coach: I.P. Jordan

2005 SEASON

Played: 18   Won: 8   Lost: 6   Drawn: 4

Captain: R. Ashton   Vice-captain: W. Macdonald

Team selected from: D. Housego, B. Howell, M. Roberts,
W. Macdonald*, R. Ashton*, S. Boughton*, C. Stockings, A. Gray,
J. Woodward, T. Fenn, J. Marriott, A. Pearce, A. Nash, D. Cole.

SUMMARY

The season promised much, but the statistics suggest that performances and results did not always meet these expectations. Our batting line-up of D. Housego, B. Howell and M. Roberts should have guaranteed us more wins, but the openers were not as prolific as last year, when fourth formers. This, combined with the lack of a genuine 'quickie', meant that a number of tight games did not go our way. Many of our defeats came from winning positions and this lack of consistency throughout the season cost us dear.

Exam schedules meant that a number of Twenty20 games, featuring weakened teams, took place and provided great entertainment. Will Macdonald, with his slow off-spin, was the pick of the bowlers and David Cole burst onto the scene in the second half of the season. Richard Ashton captained the XI very well during the season and he and Sam Boughton were the only upper sixth boys to leave the XI at the end of the season.

Prospects for next year look good with Simon Steel joining us from the West Indies. Benny Howell went on to have a very busy season, playing for Hampshire 2nd XI and Danny Housego did likewise with Middlesex 2nd XI.

AVERAGES

BATSMAN	INNINGS	NOT OUT	RUNS	H. SCORE	AVERAGE
B. Howell	14	4	733	114	73.3
D. Housego	14	1	576	122*	44.3
M. Roberts	15	0	464	96	30.9
W. Macdonald	15	3	281	80	23.4
A. Pearce	12	3	208	62*	23.1
R. Ashton	15	2	283	50	21.8

BOWLER	OVERS	MAIDENS	RUNS	WICKETS	AVERAGE
C. Stockings	19	2	71	8	8.9
D. Cole	53	5	218	18	12.1
S. Boughton	75	10	280	16	17.5
J. Woodward	50	5	215	10	21.5
W. Macdonald	130	16	433	20	21.6
R. Ashton	46	2	221	9	24.6

NOTABLE BATTING PERFORMANCES

PLAYER	OPPOSITION	SCORE
D. Housego	Abingdon	122*
B. Howell	Pangbourne	100
B. Howell	St. Edward's	114
B. Howell	Greenflies	98
B. Howell	Abingdon	82*
D. Housego	Bradfield College	91
M. Roberts	MCC	96

NOTABLE BOWLING PERFORMANCES

PLAYER	OPPOSITION	FIGURES
D. Cole	Pretoria HS (South Africa)	4-0-15-4
S. Boughton	Harrow 'A'	7-3-15-4
J. Woodward	Cokethorpe	6-0-42-4
D. Housego	Berkshire Gentlemen	10-2-28-4
W. Macdonald	Eton 'A'	11-3-24-3
W. Macdonald	Pretoria HS (South Africa)	3.5-0-15-3

OUNDLE SCHOOL

Great Hall, New Street, Oundle PE8 4GH

Tel: 01832 277113 Fax: 01832 277119
Email: jrw@oundle.northants.sch.uk

Master i/c Cricket: J.R. Wake   Coach: V. d. Merwe Genis

2005 SEASON

Played: 22   Won: 8   Lost: 6   Drawn: 8

Captain: P. Foster   Vice-captain: M. Outar

Team selected from: P. Auld, M. Outar, G. Smith, J. Austin,
P. Foster, T. Wentworth-Waites, J. Grigson, T. Elborne,
H. Millington, F. Hodgson, J. Hodgkinson, H. Tonks, G. Krempels,
J. Holmes, S. Hicks.

SUMMARY

The 2005 season was the 150th anniversary of Oundle's first recorded inter-school game, played against Uppingham in 1855.

A young and inexperienced side did well to win eight games. The XI relied heavily on the batting of Michael Outar, Peter Auld and Greg Smith, who all scored over 600 runs at an average of more than 30. Captain Patrick Foster (ECB Academy) was the leading bowler (46 wickets at 12.1). He led by example, giving the side a rare, attacking cutting-edge with his mixture of seamers and outswingers. He was selected for ECB Schools against Combined Services and played for Northamptonshire 2nd XI.

AVERAGES

BATSMAN	INNINGS	NOT OUT	RUNS	H. SCORE	AVERAGE
M. Outar	22	5	627	100*	36.9
G. Smith	21	3	644	104	35.8
P. Auld	22	2	609	110	30.5
J. Austin	13	5	229	43*	28.6
P. Foster	14	1	246	38	18.9
G. Krempels	13	0	208	52	16.0

BOWLER	OVERS	MAIDENS	RUNS	WICKETS	AVERAGE
P. Foster	202.4	52	555	46	12.1
M. Outar	99.4	10	387	17	22.8
P. Auld	137.5	20	486	20	24.3
J. Austin	148	17	491	20	24.6
T. Wentworth-Waites	106.5	17	412	13	31.7

WICKET-KEEPER	PLAYED	CAUGHT	STUMPED
F. Hodgson	22	20	4

NOTABLE BATTING PERFORMANCES

PLAYER	OPPOSITION	SCORE
P. Auld	Kimbolton	104
G. Smith	Uppingham	110
M. Oukar	Bedford	100*

NOTABLE BOWLING PERFORMANCES

PLAYER	OPPOSITION	FIGURES
P. Foster	Shrewsbury	5-20
P. Foster	Oundle Rovers	5-12

THE PERSE SCHOOL

Hills Road, Cambridge CB2 2QF

Tel: 01223 403800 Fax: 01223 403810
Email: office@perse.co.uk

Master i/c Cricket: Ed Wiseman   Coach: Doug Collard

2005 SEASON

Played: 14   Won: 11   Lost: 1   Drawn: 2

Captain: W. Hammond

Team selected from: R. Hesketh*, J. Coe*, E. Pearson*, A. Brookes,
C. Rogers, S. Powell*, D. Howells*, W. Hammond*, R. Bourne,
A. Nathan*, A. Fullarton*, M. Weston, C. Ackroyd.

Scorer: J. Johnson

SUMMARY

The 2005 season was one of the best in the school's history. The 1st XI
retained both the County U19 Cup and the locally contested Leys-
Perse trophy.

The best individual performances for the 1st XI came from Richard
Hesketh with the bat, setting a school 1st XI record of 175 against
Wisbech in the County Cup final. He also scored a match-winning 99*
against Gresham's. Duncan Howells, Alex Fullarton and Richard
Hesketh all took five wickets in a match, with Duncan's 5-41 versus
Kimbolton being the season's best return.

Richard Hesketh, Duncan Howells and the captain, Will Hammond,
were awarded their 1st XI Pelican colours. Andrew Brookes, Adu
Nathan, Edward Pearson, James Coe, Sam Powell and Alex Fullarton
received their 1st XI colours.

The season continued into the holidays, with The Perse senior team
participating in the Sir Garfield Sobers International Schools' Cricket
Tournament in Barbados, West Indies.

AVERAGES

BATSMAN	INNINGS	NOT OUT	RUNS	H. SCORE	AVERAGE
A. Brookes	12	6	284	90*	47.3
R. Hesketh	15	1	656	175	46.9
C. Pearson	14	6	373	72	46.6
J. Coe	13	2	410	86	37.3

BOWLER	OVERS	MAIDENS	RUNS	WICKETS	AVERAGE
A. Fullarton	139.1	19	431	31	13.9
S. Powell	95.2	22	241	15	16.1
A. Nathan	122	24	378	21	18.0
R. Hesketh	66.2	9	261	12	21.7
D. Howells	169.1	24	531	24	22.1

WICKET-KEEPER	PLAYED	CAUGHT	STUMPED
W. Hammond	14	20	6

NOTABLE BATTING PERFORMANCES

PLAYER	OPPOSITION	SCORE
R. Hesketh	Wisbech	175
A. Brookes	Bishop's Stortford HS	90*
R. Hesketh	Gresham's	99*

NOTABLE BOWLING PERFORMANCES

PLAYER	OPPOSITION	FIGURES
D. Howells	Kimbolton	5-41
R. Hesketh	Norwich	5-45
A. Fullarton	Chigwell	5-58

QUEEN ELIZABETH GRAMMAR SCHOOL

154 Northgate, Wakefield WF1 3QX

Tel: 01924 373943 Fax: 01924 231603
Email: admissions@qegsss.org.uk

Master i/c Cricket: T. Barker   Coach: D. Ford

2005 SEASON

Played: 10   Won: 3   Lost: 5   Drawn: 2

Captain: D. Wood   Vice-captain: R. Sugden

Team selected from: D. Wood*, G. Wood, R. Sugden, E. White,
C. Kurwie, G. Fowler, N. Bramley, G. Dobson, R. Anderson,
B. Busfield, T. Chadwick, D. Sharp, P. Aveyard, A. Nixon, D. Addala.
Scorer: P. Dean

SUMMARY

The 1st XI had a mixed season. There were some good wins and outstanding individual successes, but we seemed unable to put together a consistent innings sequence.

Daniel Wood set three new school records over the season. He hit 174 against Silcoates, scored a total of 634 runs in the regular season and together with his brother, Greg, scored 300-0 against Leeds GS. This was a new school record partnership and also quite unique to have two brothers involved - both scoring 139*!

Daniel has had five seasons with the 1st XI, averaging nearly 40 and 16-year-old Greg has achieved every honour in the game for his age-group, culminating in his selection for England U19. Daniel has also played for the ECB. These achievements have slightly overshadowed the team's, but other notable highlights were team performances in beating Silcoates and Bradford GS, together with good winning draws against Leeds GS and Woodhouse Grove.

AVERAGES

BATSMAN	INNINGS	NOT OUT	RUNS	H. SCORE	AVERAGE
D. Wood	10	3	634	174	90.6
G. Wood	6	1	338	139*	67.6
C. Kurwie	7	2	107	28	21.4
E. White	8	0	119	32	14.9
R. Sugden	9	1	112	53	14.0
G. Fowler	5	1	50	22	12.5

BOWLER	OVERS	MAIDENS	RUNS	WICKETS	AVERAGE
R. Anderson	66.4	15	209	14	14.9
D. Wood	85	22	213	14	15.2
D. Sharp	47.1	4	193	12	16.1
G. Wood	57	12	181	9	20.1
G. Dobson	71	13	242	12	20.2
N. Bramley	58	10	239	7	34.1

WICKET-KEEPER	PLAYED	CAUGHT	STUMPED
G. Fowler	11	12	3

NOTABLE BATTING PERFORMANCES

PLAYER	OPPOSITION	SCORE
D. Wood	Silcoates	174
D. Wood	Leeds GS	139*
G. Wood	Leeds GS	139*
D. Wood	Old Savilians	81*
D. Wood	Bradford GS	75*
G. Wood	Woodhouse Grove	69
G. Wood	Bradford GS	60

NOTABLE BOWLING PERFORMANCES

PLAYER	OPPOSITION	FIGURES
R. Anderson	Leeds GS	4-10
B. Busfield	Old Savilians	4-22
D. Wood	RGS Lancaster	4-49
D. Wood	MCC	3-14
N. Bramley	RGS Lancaster	3-22
G. Dobson	Leeds GS	3-22
G. Dobson	Silcoates	3-27

QUEEN'S COLLEGE

Trull Road, Taunton TA1 4QS

Tel: 01823 272559 Fax: 01823 338430
Email: andrew_free@queenscollege.org.uk

Master i/c Cricket: A.S. Free   Coach: D.R. Bates

2005 SEASON

Played: 14   Won: 6   Lost: 6   Drawn: 2

Captain: R. Catchpole

Team selected from: R. Catchpole*, R. Dickins, O. Stewart*,
A. Dodden*, A. Bull*, S. Stewart*, C. Ridout, B. Orr, P. Baker,
F. Campbell-Wilson, O. Scaife, S. Hicks*.
Scorer: A. Knight

SUMMARY

The 1st XI have had a frustrating season, where momentum was difficult to generate due to poor weather and the pressures of exams. They should have won more games, and indeed they certainly should have scored more runs and batted with greater thought at times. Good wins over Exeter, Queen Elizabeth's Hospital, Wellington, Wellsway and Old Queenians were achieved, but the game of the season was probably the one wicket defeat to Taunton.

Richard Catchpole led the side with great skill and by excellent example and his clean hitting was certainly a memorable feature of the season. He was well supported by the all-round talents of Oliver Stewart, Robert Dickins, Simon Hicks and Simon Stewart, and by Andrew Dodden who had a fantastic season with the bat, scoring 636 runs in total. His opening stands of 233 with Oliver Stewart against the XL Club, and 211 against the Old Queenians with Charles Ridout were particular highlights.

A special mention should go to Alex Bull who has kept wicket with great skill and enthusiasm for the past three seasons - he has been the focal point of some very fine fielding displays. For the most part, this was a thoroughly enjoyable season.

AVERAGES

BATSMAN	INNINGS	NOT OUT	RUNS	H. SCORE	AVERAGE
A. Dodden	14	2	636	144	53.0
C. Ridout	10	1	314	96	34.9
S. Stewart	11	2	259	52	28.8
O. Stewart	13	2	305	70*	27.7
R. Catchpole	12	1	298	86	27.1
R. Dickens	11	1	145	39	14.5

BOWLER	OVERS	MAIDENS	RUNS	WICKETS	AVERAGE
S. Stewart	72	12	262	14	18.7
S. Hicks	92	16	314	16	19.6
O. Stewart	105	12	393	20	19.6
R. Catchpole	74.1	11	273	12	22.7
O. Scaife	53.3	7	229	10	22.9
B. Orr	71	7	282	11	25.6

WICKET-KEEPER	PLAYED	CAUGHT	STUMPED
A. Bull	-	-	-

NOTABLE BATTING PERFORMANCES

PLAYER	OPPOSITION	SCORE
A. Dodden	XL Club	144
R. Catchpole	Taunton	86
O. Stewart	XL Club	70*
C. Ridout	Old Queenians	96
A. Dodden	Old Queenians	91
S. Stewart	Taunton	52

NOTABLE BOWLING PERFORMANCES

PLAYER	OPPOSITION	FIGURES
O. Stewart	Taunton	5-42
B. Orr	Head's XI	4-59

RADLEY COLLEGE

Abingdon, Oxon OX14 2HR

Tel: 01235 543000 Fax: 01235 543106
Email: ajth@radley.org.uk

Master i/c Cricket: A.J.T. Halliday   Coach: A.R. Wagner

2005 SEASON

Played: 12   Won: 2   Lost: 5   Drawn: 5

Captain: C. Duffell   Vice-captains: T. Everitt and F. Qureshi

Team selected from: C. Duffell*, T. Everitt*, F. Qureshi*, F. Moynan*, R. Haddon*, E. Nineham*, J. North, A. Ruston, G. Cave, M. Evans, T. Bellamy, T. Maxwell, T. McPhail, F. Morrisson.

SUMMARY

Despite a successful pre-season tour to South Africa, the Radley XI did not enjoy a particularly productive season. This was not for a lack of individual or collective intent, but more a combination of stronger opposition and missed opportunities.

The captain, Duffell, kept wicket beautifully and his performances behind the stumps provided the highlights in an otherwise frustrating season.

Did you know? . . . The record number of ducks in Tests for England is 20 and is held by former captain and opening batsman Michael Atherton.

AVERAGES

BATSMAN	INNINGS	NOT OUT	RUNS	H. SCORE	AVERAGE
F. Qureshi	9	1	360	100*	45.0
C. Duffell	11	0	367	95	33.4
F. Moynan	10	2	180	64	22.5
T. Everitt	10	0	182	51	18.2

BOWLER	OVERS	MAIDENS	RUNS	WICKETS	AVERAGE
R. Haddon	126	25	396	23	17.2
G. Cave	67	15	222	10	22.2
M. Evans	84	12	332	13	25.5
E. Nineham	97	23	349	11	31.7

WICKET-KEEPER	PLAYED	CAUGHT	STUMPED
C. Duffell	-	-	-

NOTABLE BATTING PERFORMANCES

PLAYER	OPPOSITION	SCORE
F. Qureshi	Eton College	100*
C. Duffell	Radley Rangers	95

NOTABLE BOWLING PERFORMANCES

PLAYER	OPPOSITION	FIGURES
R. Haddon	Cheltenham College	5-17

RATCLIFFE COLLEGE

Fosseway, Ratcliffe-on-the-Wreake, Leics LE7 4SG

Tel: 01509 817000 Fax: 01509 817004
Email: phyed@ratcliffe.leics.sch.uk

Master i/c Cricket: R.M. Hughes   Coach: M.J. Deane

2005 SEASON

Played: 11   Won: 1   Lost: 9   Drawn: 1

Captain: J. Simpson   Vice-captain: P. Irvine

Team selected from: J. Simpson*, P. Irvine*, J. Grant*, S. Smith,
J. Northover, R. Cox, T.W. Smith, L. Fenton, S. Jivanji, F. Bainbridge,
R. Ibrahim, T.A. Smith, D. Cox, L. Welch, T. Foulds, S. Comber,
F. Kelly, C. Morris, C. Bowden, M. Noss.

Scorer: R. Hughes

SUMMARY

The 1st XI had a disappointing season in which no batsmen were able
to consistently score enough runs for the bowlers to have something to
bowl at. The team's solitary win came against the Old Ratcliffians,
when the batting finally fired. 154 was chased successfully for the loss
of just four wickets.

There are some grounds for hope in the future as the XI featured
three 15-year-olds, including leading run-scorer and wicket-keeper,
Freddie Bainbridge. The leading wicket-taker was leg-spinner Richard
Cox, followed by three players including 15-year-old off-spinner
David Cox.

The season's highest score was 78 made by Sachin Jivanji in the
victory over the Old Ratcliffians.

AVERAGES

BATSMAN	INNINGS	NOT OUT	RUNS	H. SCORE	AVERAGE
F. Bainbridge	10	0	221	55	22.1
S. Jivanji	10	0	216	78	21.6
T. Smith	6	1	90	44	18.0
R. Ibrahim	8	1	102	28	14.6
P. Irvine	4	0	54	22	13.5
J. Grant	5	1	47	23	11.8

BOWLER	OVERS	MAIDENS	RUNS	WICKETS	AVERAGE
J. Simpson	6	0	29	2	14.5
T. Smith	25	3	82	5	16.4
D. Cox	38	2	226	9	25.1
S. Smith	54.2	2	248	9	27.6
R. Cox	67	9	341	11	31.0
J. Northover	74	7	320	9	35.6

WICKET-KEEPER	PLAYED	CAUGHT	STUMPED
F. Bainbridge	10	7	2
P. Irvine	4	0	2

NOTABLE BATTING PERFORMANCES

PLAYER	OPPOSITION	SCORE
S. Jivanji	Old Ratcliffians	78
F. Bainbridge	XL Club	55

NOTABLE BOWLING PERFORMANCES

PLAYER	OPPOSITION	FIGURES
D. Cox	Emeriti CC	4-18
R. Cox	Nottingham CC	4-69

READING SCHOOL

Erleigh Road, Reading RG1 5LW

Tel: 0118 901 5600 Fax: 0118 935 2755
Email: alan.walder@readingschool.reading.sch.uk

Master i/c Cricket: A.D. Walder

2005 SEASON

Played: 11   Won: 4   Lost: 5   Drawn: 2

Captain: T. Vaal   Vice-captain: M. Jubb

Team selected from: T. Vaal*, M. Jubb, A. Davidson*, D. Bettes, M. Carson, S. Conroy, A. Farooq, R. Kapoor, A. Lloyd, M. Lloyd, J. Lattimore, V. Kumar, P. Mattingley, R. Mendhir, T. Walder, J. Williams.

SUMMARY

An early season disrupted by bad weather was followed by disappointing performances with the bat. Adam Davidson eventually found some consistency, scoring two centuries. However, batting as a side we never matched a competent bowling attack, and thus the team found games difficult to win.

Despite this, the boys created a good competitive spirit and always gave their all, led by Tom Vaal whose bowling remained consistent throughout.

A number of younger boys were given opportunities in the 1st XI, and this should set us up well for future years.

AVERAGES

BATSMAN	INNINGS	NOT OUT	RUNS	H. SCORE	AVERAGE
A. Davidson	11	0	345	107	31.4
A. Lloyd	7	1	160	57	26.7
J. Williams	6	1	110	55*	22.0
M. Carson	5	0	103	79	20.6

BOWLER	OVERS	MAIDENS	RUNS	WICKETS	AVERAGE
T. Vaal	137.1	36	356	27	13.2
A. Davidson	67.1	18	213	15	14.2
R. Kapoor	41	7	183	10	18.3

WICKET-KEEPER	PLAYED	CAUGHT	STUMPED
T. Walder	7	2	3
A. Lloyd	4	3	2

NOTABLE BATTING PERFORMANCES

PLAYER	OPPOSITION	SCORE
A. Davidson	Aylesbury	106
A. Davidson	Old Redingensians	107
M. Carson	Old Redingensians	79

NOTABLE BOWLING PERFORMANCES

PLAYER	OPPOSITION	FIGURES
T. Vaal	Old Redingensians	5-36
A. Davidson	J.W. Haines' XI	5-41
T. Vaal	Lord Williams's	6-43
A. Davidson	Windsor	4-7

REED'S SCHOOL

Sandy Lane, Cobham, Surrey KT11 2ES

Tel: 01932 869072 Fax: 01932 869072

Email: mrdunn@reeds.surrey.sch.uk

Master i/c Cricket: M.R. Dunn

2005 SEASON

Played: 14 Won: 6 Lost: 4 Drawn: 4

Captain: M. Wakefield

Team selected from: M. Beretta, B. Bullock, S. Cole, T. Coventry,
S. Hussain, J. Langham, L. Macdonald, C. Magoye*,
D. Middleton, J. Raimondo, R. Sachdev, C. Stafford,
T. Streatfeild-Moore, M. Wakefield*.

Scorer: S. Allcock

SUMMARY

With a team that was largely unchanged from the last campaign, it was hoped the promise and success shown last year would continue to develop. Four players fulfilled the expectations quite handsomely - Michael Wakefield with bat and ball, Charlie Magoye with the bat, and James Langham and Sharaz Hussain both with the ball.

The curtain-raiser saw us get the better of a draw against City of London Freemen's School, as Michael Wakefield scored an unbeaten 110 and Ben Bullock took 6-39 with his flighted off-spin. Other draws were aginst Sutton Valence, John Fisher and King's Parramatta. Sutton Valence set a very stiff target with some explosive batting, whilst we did the same to John Fisher, swiftly compiling a big score built around a season's best of 162* from Michael Wakefield. The King's Parramatta game featured a last wicket stand between Ben Bullock and James Langham, over 12 overs, to rescue a result.

Games were lost against King's College Wimbledon, a 40 over match with a tight finish, and Lord Wandsworth College, where our haste to score runs on a tricky pitch against an adequate bowling attack played into the hands of our hosts. Against Old Reedonians and MCC, our approach to the run chases did not seem wholly convincing.

Of the games that were won, the most enthralling was against St. George's. Having dismissed them for 147 on a flat track (Michael Wakefield 7-28), we dominated until a middle-order collapse. With two runs needed and the last pair at the crease, a catch went down. The next ball was a wide, promptly followed by a bye to win the game! Many victories were run chases, and more often than not they were cleverly masterminded by Charlie Magoye. An exception was against Reading Blue Coat School when Sharaz Hussain took 5-24 with his accurate pace bowling.

The season ended on a very sad note with the cancellation of our annual fixture against the Stock Exchange due to the bomb attacks in London. In the history of cricket at Reed's, there cannot have been a more poignant reason for a game not to take place.

AVERAGES

BATSMAN	INNINGS	NOT OUT	RUNS	H. SCORE	AVERAGE
M. Wakefield	14	3	630	162*	57.3
C. Magoye	13	2	567	113	51.6
L. Macdonald	14	0	264	107	18.9
T. Coventry	13	1	174	45	14.5
R. Sachdev	13	2	158	31	14.4

BOWLER	OVERS	MAIDENS	RUNS	WICKETS	AVERAGE
M. Wakefield	151.5	28	477	29	16.5
S. Hussain	67.3	13	218	13	16.8
J. Langham	139.3	24	525	28	18.7
B. Bullock	69.1	9	312	11	28.4

WICKET-KEEPER	PLAYED	CAUGHT	STUMPED
D. Middleton	8	8	0
C. Stafford	6	4	1

NOTABLE BATTING PERFORMANCES

PLAYER	OPPOSITION	SCORE
M. Wakefield	City of London Freemen's	110*
M. Wakefield	John Fisher	162*
L. Macdonald	XL Club	107
C. Magoye	Old Reedonians	113

NOTABLE BOWLING PERFORMANCES

PLAYER	OPPOSITION	FIGURES
B. Bullock	City of London Freemen's	6-39
S. Hussain	Reading Blue Coat	5-24
M. Wakefield	St. George's College Weybridge	7-28
J. Langham	King's Parramatta (Australia)	5-45

REPTON SCHOOL

Repton, Derby DE65 6FH

Tel: 01283 559200 Fax: 01283 559210
Email: fpw@repton.org.uk

Master i/c Cricket: Frank Watson   Coach: Mike Kettle

2005 SEASON

Played: 13   Won: 11   Lost: 2

Captain: C. Paget

Team selected from: P. Borrington*, L. Harvey*, J. Lamb*, C. Paget*,
R. Murrall*, J. Blackwell*, R. Kniveton*, W. Bridgeman*, A. Village,
S. Duggan*, C. Carlile*, G. Dancey, J. Walters.
Scorer: R. Macpherson

SUMMARY

Paul Borrington and Luke Harvey formed a superb opening pair and
amongst their many good partnerships was a stand of 231 in the rain-
ruined Shrewsbury match. However, this was then eclipsed by
Borrington and James Blackwell, who broke the Repton record
partnership for any wicket with an unbeaten first-wicket 314 against
Denstone College.

Borrington, who was selected for the ECB U17 side, finished top of
the batting averages with 551 runs at 68.9, followed by Harvey (627 at
62.7), Jack Lamb (418 at 52.3) and Richard Murrall (268 at 44.7).
Borrington (2), Harvey, Lamb and Blackwell all recorded centuries.
Overall the team scored its runs at 4.53 per over - a major factor in
achieving positive results.

Harvey, last season's top all-rounder, again led the bowling. His leg-
spin and googlies brought him 37 wickets at the remarkably low
average of 12.3 and he took 5 wickets or more on four occasions. He
deservedly gained selection for the ECB Schools team in July and
scored 89 against Sri Lanka U19. Paget's off-spin brought him 21
wickets and the opening pair of Blackwell and Simon Duggan took 20
and 19 respectively.

Ricky Kniveton kept wicket tidily and generally the fielding, with
Lamb outstanding, was of a very high standard. However, as in
previous seasons, the slip catching showed room for improvement.

AVERAGES

BATSMAN	INNINGS	NOT OUT	RUNS	H. SCORE	AVERAGE
P. Borrington	10	2	551	172*	68.9
L. Harvey	12	2	627	125	62.7
J. Lamb	12	4	418	120	52.3
R. Murrall	8	2	268	77	44.7
C. Paget	11	2	286	74	31.8
J. Blackwell	10	4	170	120*	28.3

BOWLER	OVERS	MAIDENS	RUNS	WICKETS	AVERAGE
L. Harvey	138.3	27	457	37	12.4
J. Blackwell	148	23	448	20	22.4
C. Paget	164.2	37	516	21	24.6
S. Duggan	132.5	11	503	19	26.5

WICKET-KEEPER	PLAYED	CAUGHT	STUMPED
R. Kniveton	13	14	8

NOTABLE BATTING PERFORMANCES

PLAYER	OPPOSITION	SCORE
P. Borrington	Denstone College	172*
J. Blackwell	Denstone College	120*
P. Borrington	Shrewsbury	105*
L. Harvey	Shrewsbury	125
J. Lamb	Nottingham HS	120

NOTABLE BOWLING PERFORMANCES

PLAYER	OPPOSITION	FIGURES
L. Harvey	Rugby	6-37
S. Duggan	Worksop College	6-57
L. Harvey	Uppingham	5-44
L. Harvey	Denstone College	5-35
L. Harvey	Free Foresters	6-42

ROYAL GRAMMAR SCHOOL GUILDFORD

High Street, Guildford, Surrey GU1 3BB
Tel: 01483 880600 Fax: 01483 880602
Email: pe@rgs-guildford.co.uk

Master i/c Cricket: S.B.R. Shore   Coach: Monte Lynch

2005 SEASON

Played: 18   Won: 13   Lost: 4   Drawn: 1

Captain: P. Drake

Team selected from: P. Drake*, J. Ackroyd, S. Ackroyd*, R. Bowles,
A. Drake, T. Hickey, C. Homewood, D. Jefferies, C. Neal, C. Nelson*,
C. Peploe, N. Symonds-Baig*, J. Thomas, C. Thomson.
Scorer: J. Collins

SUMMARY

This year we have played new fixtures against Whitgift, St Paul's and
Tonbridge, which were greatly enjoyed.

Before the RGS Cricket Festival, our record was excellent, winning
ten of fourteen matches. Our best fixture was the inaugural match
against St. Paul's. A magnificent bowling display from Tom Hickey (7-
58) ensured that we had a good target to aim for. Chris Nelson duly
obliged with 105* off 101 balls to win the match.

After this excellent 'domestic' season, we made the trip to
Colchester for the Festival, where we started against the hosts.
However, after a useful bowling display, we collapsed seven runs
short. The team was extremely disappointed, and spirits were hardly
lifted after a crushing defeat by RGS Worcester. But the incredible
fighting spirit that the team has exhibited throughout the season shone
through against RGS High Wycombe. Batting first, we were finally on
the right side of a cliffhanger, winning by just six runs. This was
greatly helped by Chris Neal's 60 and Anthony Drake's two
consecutive sixes into the top of the trees. The last match, a victory
against RGS Newcastle, was memorable for Chris Nelson's last innings
for the school - a bludgeoning 111, which typefied his wonderful
batting.

Captain Phil Drake has been a tremendous servant to the XI, with
frequent good batting and mesmerising leg-spin. Naeman Symonds-

Baig's solid opening has often provided a great platform for the middle order. Anthony Drake's development as a fine all-rounder has greatly pleased everyone, and it was a key factor in him succeeding his brother as captain. Simon Ackroyd, Charlie Thomson and Joey Thomas have all been fine players for the RGS and Chris Peploe's strike bowling and timely knocks have proved invaluable for us. Thanks to all the players, coaches Steve Shore and Monte Lynch, and our immaculate scorer Josh Collins. Everyone has contributed to a memorable season.

AVERAGES

BATSMAN	INNINGS	NOT OUT	RUNS	H. SCORE	AVERAGE
C. Nelson	14	3	548	111	49.8
C. Neal	9	2	287	103*	41.0
R. Bowles	11	2	246	64*	27.3
N. Symonds-Baig	16	1	382	83	25.5
P. Drake	13	3	238	55	23.8

BOWLER	OVERS	MAIDENS	RUNS	WICKETS	AVERAGE
T. Hickey	97.1	20	328	23	14.3
P. Drake	55.5	9	153	10	15.3
J. Ackroyd	96.1	14	326	19	17.2
C. Peploe	63.4	7	258	11	23.5
S. Ackroyd	136	22	472	19	24.8
A. Drake	101.4	11	394	15	26.3

WICKET-KEEPER	PLAYED	CAUGHT	STUMPED
C. Homewood	17	12	2
C. Nelson	1	3	0

NOTABLE BATTING PERFORMANCES

PLAYER	OPPOSITION	SCORE
C. Nelson	St. Paul's	105*
N. Symonds-Baig	St. George's	83
C. Neal	Ewell Castle	103*
C. Neal	RGS High Wycombe	69
C. Nelson	RGS Newcastle	111

NOTABLE BOWLING PERFORMANCES

PLAYER	OPPOSITION	FIGURES
T. Hickey	St. Paul's	7-58

ROYAL GRAMMAR SCHOOL WORCESTER

Upper Tything, Worcester WR1 1HP

Tel: 01905 613391   Fax: 01905 726892

Email: office@rgsw.org.uk

Master i/c Cricket: M.D. Wilkinson   Coach: P.J. Newport

2005 SEASON

Played: 24   Won: 17   Lost: 3   Drawn: 4

Captain: D. Harris   Vice-captain: M. Illingworth

Team selected from: D. Harris*, M. Illingworth*, L. O'Driscoll*,
S. Howell*, G. Broadfield, F. Khalid, J. Dovey, A. Ford*, T. Poole,
A. Wilkinson, M. Cunneen, T. Evans, N. Newport, T. Brain,
D. Sproul, N. Pinner.

Scorer: O. Coddington

SUMMARY

This was the most successful year in the school's history, beating the previous highest number of wins by two. The batting relied on youngsters Nathan Newport (son of Phil, ex-Worcestershire and England) and 14-year-old Neil Pinner who is the youngest centurion in our history. The spin attack of Miles Illingworth (son of Richard, ex-Worcestershire and England) and Andy Ford was the difference in many of the wins, as was an excellent team spirit and the astute captaincy by Dominic Harris.

The Chesterton Cup was won at New Road against Cheltenham College and the RGS Festival Trophy was retained at RGS Colchester, winning all four games against Colchester, Newcastle, Guildford and High Wycombe. The highlight of the week was the weight of runs scored on the flat Essex pitches; the XI scored 1082 runs in the week, twice topping 300 runs in the 50 over competition.

Losing only four upper sixth players, there is clear optimism for next year as a number of very promising youngsters push for a place.

AVERAGES

BATSMAN	INNINGS	NOT OUT	RUNS	H. SCORE	AVERAGE
N. Pinner	17	6	544	117*	49.5
N. Newport	23	2	906	113	43.1
M. Illingworth	19	7	384	69	32.0
S. Howell	18	2	484	104	30.3
L. O'Driscoll	22	2	588	72	29.4
T. Brain	23	2	512	105	24.4

BOWLER	OVERS	MAIDENS	RUNS	WICKETS	AVERAGE
M. Illingworth	188	31	596	38	15.7
A. Ford	177.5	33	624	36	17.3
J. Dovey	180.3	30	595	34	17.5
T. Poole	153.5	15	517	26	19.9
A. Wilkinson	108	9	436	17	25.6

WICKET-KEEPER	PLAYED	CAUGHT	STUMPED
S. Howell	22	16	4

NOTABLE BATTING PERFORMANCES

PLAYER	OPPOSITION	SCORE
T. Brain	Hereford Cathedral	105
N. Pinner	Hereford Cathedral	117*
N. Newport	RGS Colchester	113
S. Howell	RGS Colchester	104

RUGBY SCHOOL

Rugby, Warwickshire CV22 5EH

Tel: 01788 556216   Fax: 01788 556219
Email: pjr@rugbyschool.net

Master i/c Cricket: P.J. Rosser Coach: N.C.B. Cook

2005 SEASON

Played: 15   Won: 4   Lost: 4   Drawn: 7

Captain: J. Weaving

SUMMARY

The season relied on team performances with six players scoring 200 runs or more and five bowlers sharing the wickets. Leading player was Ralph Hardwick, who compiled the most runs and wickets.

At the two day match against Marlborough we had the upper hand, but rain prevented any chance of a result. We went on to draw all three matches in a highly competitive festival with Charterhouse, Malvern and Leinster Under 19.

AVERAGES

BATSMAN	INNINGS	NOT OUT	RUNS	H. SCORE	AVERAGE
R. Hardwick	14	2	334	81	27.8
F. Maclehose	12	3	232	40	25.8
J. White	14	5	229	43	25.4
J. Weaving	11	3	200	54*	25.0
A. Davison	16	1	319	75	21.3
C. Price	16	2	220	65*	15.7

BOWLER	OVERS	MAIDENS	RUNS	WICKETS	AVERAGE
N. Khandwala	70	8	290	16	18.1
R. Hardwick	168.1	28	480	23	20.9
F. Maclehose	124	25	339	13	26.1
J. White	108	9	376	14	26.9
J. Weaving	118.5	14	382	14	27.3

RYDAL PENRHOS

Colwyn Bay, North Wales LL29 7BT

Tel: 01492 530155 Fax: 01492 531872
Email: mtleach@rydal-penrhos.com

Master i/c Cricket and Coach: M.T. Leach

2005 SEASON

Played: 6   Lost: 5   Abandoned: 1

Captain: J. Leach

Team selected from: J. Leach*, M. Barnett, T. Blackwell, C. Booth,
J. Coates, A. Fowler, G. Holgate, S. Hughes, Q. Mohammed,
K. Trehan, A. Ward, T. Moore, B. Evans, M. Sorrentino, K. Lau,
A. Jones, W. Hancock.

SUMMARY

A young and inexperienced squad persevered throughout the season
without winning a game. The emphasis was on enjoying their cricket
and provide the opportunities and experience to take forward into next
season, when it is hoped greater success will be forthcoming.

AVERAGES

BATSMAN	INNINGS	NOT OUT	RUNS	H. SCORE	AVERAGE
J. Leach	5	1	204	75*	51.0

NOTABLE BATTING PERFORMANCES

PLAYER	OPPOSITION	SCORE
J. Leach	Ellesmere College	75*
J. Leach	King's Chester	72

NOTABLE BOWLING PERFORMANCES

PLAYER	OPPOSITION	FIGURES
Q. Mohammed	Ellesmere College	13-1-50-3
J. Coates	Oswestry	6-0-38-3

St. ALBANS SCHOOL

Abbey Gateway, St. Albans AL3 2HB

Tel: 01727 855521 Fax: 01727 843447
Email: hm@st-albans-school.org.uk

Master i/c Cricket: C.C. Hudson   Coach: A. McLean

2005 SEASON

Played: 13 Won: 6 Lost: 4 Drawn: 3

Captain: T. Barnard

Team selected from: T. Barnard, J. Mitchell, M. Grimditch,
A. Addison, S. Gregory*, D. Cole, R. Vijh, M. Dobson, T. Cuppello,
M. Burgess, J. Reynolds, A. Jayawardena, M. Alford, M. Rafiee.

Scorer: R. Waller

SUMMARY

Is there life after Lamb? School 1st XIs are essentially transient but the
three year captaincy of Nick Lamb, son of the former ECB Chief
Executive, created an unnatural feeling of permanence. Tom Barnard,
Lamb's successor as captain, was always going to have a difficult time.
Replacing one of the best all-rounders in the country inevitably leads
to negative comparisons.

Simon Gregory, left-hand bat and slow bowler, and Alex Addison,
right-arm fast bowler, were expected to be the stars of the team. It was
felt that if Gregory scored a fifty or Addison took five wickets,
matches would be won. The best laid plans however... Gregory broke
his hand after the second match and was out for six weeks. Current
bowling regulations mean you can afford to play out fast bowlers and
score against change bowlers.

June saw the return of Gregory, who averaged exactly 100 in the
remaining seven matches of the season, with the XI recording six wins.
St. Albans only batted first once in thirteen matches. Gregory's
accident gave an opportunity to 14-year-old Jack Reynolds, who
became the youngest player since Graham Dill (golf and cricket blues)
to play for the 1st XI.

The highlights of the season were the wins over Berkhamsted,
Gordonstoun and an Australian touring side.

AVERAGES

BATSMAN	INNINGS	NOT OUT	RUNS	H. SCORE	AVERAGE
S. Gregory	9	3	359	115*	59.8
D. Cole	10	1	308	57*	34.2
M. Grimditch	6	1	142	47	28.4
J. Reynolds	9	3	131	49	21.8
R. Vijh	11	1	191	50	19.1
J. Mitchell	10	0	160	50	16.0

BOWLER	OVERS	MAIDENS	RUNS	WICKETS	AVERAGE
A. Addison	104	17	272	18	15.1
S. Gregory	68	10	281	15	18.7
M. Dobson	75	9	346	14	24.7
J. Reynolds	50	9	200	8	25.0
T. Cuppello	85	11	302	11	27.5
M. Burgess	58	8	248	9	27.6

WICKET-KEEPER	PLAYED	CAUGHT	STUMPED
R. Vijh	12	11	3

NOTABLE BATTING PERFORMANCES

PLAYER	OPPOSITION	SCORE
S. Gregory	Gordonstoun	115*
S. Gregory	Berkhamsted	70*
D. Cole	Haileybury	57*
D. Cole	Gordonstoun	56

St. GEORGE'S COLLEGE WEYBRIDGE

Weybridge Road, Addlestone, Surrey KT15 2QS

Tel: 01932 839300 Fax: 01932 839301
Email: rambrose@st-georges-college.co.uk

Master i/c Cricket: Richard Ambrose

2005 SEASON

Played: 18 Won: 7 Lost: 7 Drawn: 4

Captain: H. Grant Vice-captain: M. Ford

Team selected from: H. Grant*, M. Ford*, D. McGahon*, A. Willis*,
A. Reynolds, T. Reynolds, W. Bottomley, T. Simonis, J. Hardman,
D. Pope, B. Kenney, D. Rowland, J. Dowell, N. Cole, M. Hawkins.

SUMMARY

This has been a successful season for the 1st XI. The team has played
superbly and there have been many outstanding individual performances.

The XI have been thankful for the all-round talent of captain Henry
Grant. His haul of 44 wickets is a formidable achievement which he
fully deserves, thanks to his fast and penetrative bowling.

The boys have batted far better than last season and opening
batsman Michael Ford has comfortably been the highest run-scorer.

The side achieved seven victories during the season which beats the
number in recent years. With many of the team still at the College next
year, the boys can look forward to another promising season.

AVERAGES

BATSMAN	INNINGS	NOT OUT	RUNS	H. SCORE	AVERAGE
M. Ford	16	1	631	112	42.1
H. Grant	16	2	408	84*	29.1
A. Willis	17	1	409	87*	25.6
A. Reynolds	13	1	282	85	23.5
T. Reynolds	17	0	300	70	17.6
D. McGahon	12	5	97	21*	13.9

BOWLER	OVERS	MAIDENS	RUNS	WICKETS	AVERAGE
H. Grant	172.2	35	582	44	13.2
D. Pope	95.5	15	389	18	21.6
D. McGahon	173.3	29	640	26	24.6
J. Hardman	79	18	304	12	25.3
T. Reynolds	121.1	24	494	19	26.0

WICKET-KEEPER	PLAYED	CAUGHT	STUMPED
A. Willis	17	12	2

NOTABLE BATTING PERFORMANCES

PLAYER	OPPOSITION	SCORE
M. Ford	Hampton	112
A. Willis	Headmaster's XI	87*
A. Reynolds	Old Georgians	85
H. Grant	St. Benedict's	84*
M. Ford	King's College Wimbledon	84
M. Ford	St. Benedict's	75*
T. Reynolds	Grasshoppers CC	70

NOTABLE BOWLING PERFORMANCES

PLAYER	OPPOSITION	FIGURES
H. Grant	Trinity	6-32
T. Reynolds	Frogs CC	6-42
H. Grant	Caterham	5-14
H. Grant	MCC	5-34
H. Grant	Old Georgians	6-61
H. Grant	Christ's Hospital	4-28
D. McGahon	MCC	4-57

St. LAWRENCE COLLEGE

College Road, Ramsgate, Kent CT11 7AE

Tel: 01843 572909 Fax: 01843 572918
Email: nosj@slcuk.com

Master i/c Cricket: N.O.S. Jones

2005 SEASON

Played: 9   Won: 4   Lost: 4   Drawn: 1

Captain: A. Hammond   Vice-captain: A. Gayton

Team selected from: C. Burgess, J. Foot, A. Gayton*, A. Hammond,
J. Lillicrap, A. McConnell, A. Mahmud, Mur. Mahmud*, M. Shahid,
Mus. Mahmud, N. Muncey, G. O'Connell, E. O'Grady, M. Scannell.

Scorer: Miss E. Riley

SUMMARY

The 1st XI comprised experienced players from the previous season
supported by some talented fifth formers. There were good wins
against The British School of Paris, Duke of York's RMS, Dover
College and the MCC. Overall, batting was stronger than the bowling.
Highlights were the 109 by Murtaza Mahmud to set up a great win
over the MCC and Adam Gayton's 100* against the The British School
of Paris.

Batting looked strong but the greatest fault was that batsmen did not
go on to build a big score. The bowling had variation, from genuine
pace to leg-spin, but lacked consistency of line and length.

A large number of the side will return next year, so the prospects
look encouraging.

AVERAGES

BATSMAN	INNINGS	NOT OUT	RUNS	H. SCORE	AVERAGE
Mur. Mahmud	8	2	346	109	57.7
A. Gayton	8	2	301	100*	50.2
G. O'Connell	9	0	206	55	22.9
N. Muncey	8	0	153	28	19.1
Mus. Mahmud	8	0	146	46	18.3
A. Mahmud	5	0	75	32	15.0

BOWLER	OVERS	MAIDENS	RUNS	WICKETS	AVERAGE
A. Gayton	21	2	109	5	21.8
J. Foot	50.5	8	225	10	22.5
A. Mahmud	42	5	206	8	25.7
Mur. Mahmud	63	4	289	11	26.3
N. Muncey	49	1	288	9	32.0

WICKET-KEEPER	PLAYED	CAUGHT	STUMPED
A. Hammond	9	4	0

NOTABLE BATTING PERFORMANCES

PLAYER	OPPOSITION	SCORE
Mur. Mahmud	MCC	109
A. Gayton	British School of Paris	100*

NOTABLE BOWLING PERFORMANCES

PLAYER	OPPOSITION	FIGURES
J. Foot	British School of Paris	5-13
A. Gayton	Duke of York's RMS	5-26
J. Foot	Dover College	4-13
N. Muncey	British School of Paris	4-14
Mur. Mahmud	Dover College	4-14
A. Mahmud	King's Rochester	4-40

St. PETER'S SCHOOL

Clifton, York YO30 6AB

Tel: 01904 527407 Fax: 01904 527302
Email: enquiries@st-peters.york.sch.uk

Master i/c Cricket and Coach: D. Kirby

2005 SEASON

Played: 15   Won: 5   Lost: 4   Drawn: 6

Captain: B. Hough

Team selected from: B. Hough*, J. Bairstow*, E. Hilling*, D. Heaton*,
I. Jarvis*, J. Marsden*, J. Mills*, C. Parry*, J. Scattergood*,
P. Wackett*, W. Butler, M. Down, T. Heaps, S. Macbeth, T. Peet,
P. Steadman, P. Denison, J. Nàdian.

Scorer: A. Lindley and S. Maekawa

SUMMARY

An inexperienced St. Peter's York team made encouraging progress
during the season and played some good positive cricket. The team was
ably captained by all-rounder Ben Hough. He, Jonathan Bairstow and
David Heaton all played some big innings, but the highlight of the
season was Bairstow's 167* against Ampleforth. For a 15-year-old it
was a remarkable innings.

As a whole, the batting was strong with the late batsmen often
playing a valuable part. All five wins came when the team batted
second. When they batted first, they usually built a challenging total,
but the bowling lacked penetration and they struggled to bowl teams
out on good pitches. The leading wicket-takers were two U15 spinners,
Jonathan Bairstow and Jamie Scattergood.

The team fielded well with James Marsden and Peter Wackett
particularly quick and athletic. Edward Hilling was an excellent
wicket-keeper.

AVERAGES

BATSMAN	INNINGS	NOT OUT	RUNS	H. SCORE	AVERAGE
J. Bairstow	12	1	478	167*	43.5
B. Hough	15	2	541	96	41.6
D. Heaton	13	2	429	80	39.0
J. Marsden	11	6	152	28	30.4
E. Hilling	11	2	224	46*	24.9
P. Wackett	9	0	215	78	23.9

BOWLER	OVERS	MAIDENS	RUNS	WICKETS	AVERAGE
J. Bairstow	156.1	40	470	21	22.4
J. Scattergood	93.2	11	432	19	22.7
B. Hough	92.2	13	366	15	24.4
C. Parry	110	27	359	14	25.6
J. Mills	75	15	255	7	36.4
I. Jarvis	53.4	5	197	5	39.4

WICKET-KEEPER	PLAYED	CAUGHT	STUMPED
E. Hilling	13	9	9
T. Peet	2	2	2

NOTABLE BATTING PERFORMANCES

PLAYER	OPPOSITION	SCORE
J. Bairstow	Ampleforth College	167*
J. Bairstow	Leeds GS	117
B. Hough	Cranleigh	96
B. Hough	Scarborough College	86*
B. Hough	Leeds GS	85
I. Jarvis	Old Peterites	81
D. Heaton	Ampleforth College	80

NOTABLE BOWLING PERFORMANCES

PLAYER	OPPOSITION	FIGURES
J. Scattergood	Barnard Castle	5-40
J. Bairstow	Bradford GS	4-24

SEDBERGH SCHOOL

Sedbergh, Cumbria LA10 5HG

Tel: 015396 22271 Fax: 015396 22271
Email: cpm@sedbergh.sch.uk

Master i/c Cricket: C.P. Mahon   Coach: D.J. Fallows

2005 SEASON

Played: 15   Won: 5   Lost: 2   Drawn: 8

Captain: D. Ford   Vice-captain: M. Raikes

Team selected from: D. Ford*, M. Raikes*, O. Pimlott*, B. Graham*,
H. Clerey*, R. Barnby*, T. Harmer, D. Blackburn, J. O'Brien,
C. Drake, P. Raikes, J. Blair, O. Brown.

SUMMARY

Sedbergh started the season in fine form, recording comfortable victories against St. Peter's York, KEQMS Lytham and Giggleswick. All three of these wins were based around the elegant stroke-play of vice-captain Michael Raikes and the powerful hitting of captain Guy Ford.

Unfortunately, the side struggled for fluency during the middle of the season, the weather affecting four games and two others resulting in tame draws. However, some excellent cricket was played in the post exam period.

Kirkham and Birkenhead were bowled out cheaply, with opening bowler Olly Pimlott shining on both occasions. An excellent century by Michael Raikes against King's Macclesfield set up an exciting game which saw King's successfully chase 256 in 49 overs for a deserved victory.

At the end of the day, the side should have won more games, however with all but three of the XI returning and some exciting talent lower down the school, the prospects for the future seem bright.

AVERAGES

BATSMAN	INNINGS	NOT OUT	RUNS	H. SCORE	AVERAGE
H. Clerey	9	5	173	41*	43.3
M. Raikes	14	0	593	115	42.4
D. Ford	12	2	329	67*	32.9
D. Blackburn	13	1	233	50	19.4
O. Pimlott	13	4	166	27	18.4

BOWLER	OVERS	MAIDENS	RUNS	WICKETS	AVERAGE
M. Raikes	179.5	46	461	37	12.5
O. Pimlott	163.2	34	481	29	16.6
J. Blair	69.1	9	285	14	20.4
D. Ford	148.5	41	430	17	25.3
R. Barnby	103	23	377	13	29.0

NOTABLE BATTING PERFORMANCES

PLAYER	OPPOSITION	SCORE
M. Raikes	St. Peter's York	89
D. Ford	St. Peter's York	67*
M. Raikes	KEQMS Lytham	78
M. Raikes	Manchester GS	77
M. Raikes	King's Macclesfield	115

NOTABLE BOWLING PERFORMANCES

PLAYER	OPPOSITION	FIGURES
M. Raikes	XL Club	17-7-28-8

SEVENOAKS SCHOOL

Sevenoaks, Kent TN13 1HU

Tel: 01732 455133 Fax: 01732 456143
Email: cjt@sevenoaksschool.org

Master i/c Cricket and Coach: C.J. Tavaré

2005 SEASON

Played: 15   Won: 9   Lost: 4   Drawn: 2

Captain: N. Tunnell

Team selected from: N. Tunnell*, D. Burden, S. Cox, A. Douglas*,
N. Crombie, J. Dunnett, D. Franklin, D. Haley, J. Parker, A. Quinn,
A. Weston*, P. Sutton-Mattocks, D. Walker*, W. Wilkin.
Scorer: S. Carr

SUMMARY

The 1st XI finished the season with nine wins - one behind the record of 1970. It was very much a group effort, with Nick Tunnell captaining the side superbly, engendering a strong spirit in a team including up to five U15 players. We also had two spinners, Andy Douglas and Will Wilkin, who took 41 wickets between them.

The highlights were victories against King's Canterbury and Sutton Valence, followed by four close wins on the trot, chasing targets between 121 and 174. Sevenoaks were put in by King's Canterbury. The 1st XI slumped to 129 for 7, before a last wicket stand of 49 between Douglas (19) and U15 Wilkin (23) raised the target to 178. King's were in control at 152 for 6, but captain Nick Tunnell returned to the attack to remove Bruce (103) and the final three wickets, producing a nail-biting win by 6 runs.

Against Sutton Valence, only the aggressive David Franklin (37) came to terms with a damp, seaming wicket. 107 was a small target, but outstanding bowling from Andy Douglas (4-11), Dean Walker (2-13) and Jamie Dunnett (2-20), supported by athletic fielding, reduced the opposition to 72 all out and gave the school a remarkable 35 run win.

In the first of the four run chases, Eltham played some excellent shots to reach 187-7 from their 35 overs. Sevenoaks got off to a good start with David Franklin and Dan Haley putting on 66 for the first wicket. The school needed 38 off 5 overs with 2 wickets left. Will Wilkin joined Nick Tunnell in a super stand, making the winning hit with four balls of the final over remaining.

AVERAGES

BATSMAN	INNINGS	NOT OUT	RUNS	H. SCORE	AVERAGE
D. Haley	7	1	205	51*	34.2
D. Franklin	14	1	289	90	22.2
D. Walker	9	1	154	52	19.2
J. Parker	12	3	163	30	18.1
S. Cox	12	1	168	47	15.3
P. Sutton-Mattocks	11	1	109	51*	10.9

BOWLER	OVERS	MAIDENS	RUNS	WICKETS	AVERAGE
D. Walker	78	19	272	20	13.6
A. Douglas	85	11	368	25	14.7
W. Wilkin	85	12	277	16	17.3
N. Tunnell	93	11	394	17	23.2
J. Dunnett	112	14	452	12	37.7

WICKET-KEEPER	PLAYED	CAUGHT	STUMPED
A. Weston	6	7	3
A. Quinn	9	4	3

NOTABLE BATTING PERFORMANCES

PLAYER	OPPOSITION	SCORE
D. Franklin	Melbourne HS (Australia)	90

NOTABLE BOWLING PERFORMANCES

PLAYER	OPPOSITION	FIGURES
D. Walker	Sevenoaks Vine U18	7-3-11-6
A. Douglas	Sutton Valence	6-3-11-4
N. Tunnell	King's Canterbury	13-2-38-5
W. Wilkin	King's Rochester	6-1-15-5

SHERBORNE SCHOOL

Abbey Road, Sherborne, Dorset DT9 3AP

Tel: 01935 810560 Fax: 01935 810426
Email: rwh@sherborne.org

Master i/c Cricket: Rob Hill   Coaches: Alan Willows

2005 SEASON

Played: 18   Won: 13   Lost: 4   Drawn: 1

Captain: S. Crawford   Vice-captain: A. Mackay-James

Team selected from: S. Crawford*, A. Mackay-James*, C. Clifton*,
E. Kelly*, M. Saunders, C. Esson, J. Jenkins, S. Lamb, B. Lyons,
B. Trepess, H. Gibbs, A. Isles, J. Davis.

Scorer: R. Sworder

SUMMARY

The 1st XI have had a very good season. Excellent last over wins against Millfield and Marlborough showed that the team could play for 100 overs in a day. Chasing 267, we lost off the last ball against Taunton, and Canford successfully chased 231 from 35 overs with the help of an outstanding individual performance. There were also losses against a very talented South African touring team and a well organised Winchester College.

The team was led from the front by the captain, Seamus Crawford, who scored 658 runs including two hundreds. He was very well backed up by Ed Kelly, who scored five fifties in his fifteen innings. Ed, batting at number five, finished games off for us by either accelerating the pace when we batted first, or by dominating the bowling in a run-chase. Archie Mackay-James, who kept wicket and batted at four, was another vital member of this successful team. He delivered solid batting performances at crucial times, and put pressure on opposition batsmen when keeping wicket standing up. Charlie Clifton led the bowling with his useful medium-pace, possessing the ability to move the ball both ways and bowl a good yorker at the end of the innings.

The young members, Charlie Esson, Ben Lyons and Jack Jenkins, all showed they can play at this level. With two more years for them, I am hopeful of continued success for the future of cricket at Sherborne.

AVERAGES

BATSMAN	INNINGS	NOT OUT	RUNS	H. SCORE	AVERAGE
E. Kelly	15	4	467	70	42.5
S. Crawford	18	0	658	111	36.6
B. Lyons	9	5	121	28*	30.3
A. Mackay-James	18	1	481	96	28.3
C. Esson	18	1	459	89	27.0
J. Jenkins	18	3	398	106*	26.5

BOWLER	OVERS	MAIDENS	RUNS	WICKETS	AVERAGE
A. Isles	51	7	177	9	19.7
S. Clifton	146	15	515	26	19.8
S. Crawford	127	26	446	18	24.8
E. Kelly	72	11	301	12	25.1
S. Lamb	105.3	12	453	16	28.3
B. Lyons	109.5	14	454	16	28.4

WICKET-KEEPER	PLAYED	CAUGHT	STUMPED
A. Mackay-James	18	13	5

NOTABLE BATTING PERFORMANCES

PLAYER	OPPOSITION	SCORE
S. Crawford	Sherborne CC	111
S. Crawford	Sherborne Old Boys	103
J. Jenkins	Sherborne CC	106*
A. Mackay-James	Cheltenham College	96
C. Esson	MCC	89
E. Kelly	Blundell's	70

NOTABLE BOWLING PERFORMANCES

PLAYER	OPPOSITION	FIGURES
B. Lyons	King's Taunton	10-2-32-5
C. Clifton	Haileybury	10-1-31-5

SHIPLAKE COLLEGE

Henley-on-Thames, Oxon RG9 4BW

Tel: 0118 940 2455 Fax: 0118 940 5204
Email: adix@shiplake.org.uk

Master i/c Cricket and Coach: Andrew Dix

2005 SEASON

Played: 16   Won: 12   Lost: 4

Captain: E. Blanchard   Vice-captain: W. Downing

Team selected from: E. Blanchard, W. Downing, C. Stormont,
G. Moseby, L. Robarts, J. Talbot, G. Braithwaite, R. Lloyd,
R. Donovan, J. Ridgway, S. Pershall, B. Farmar, J. Smith-Jones,
D. Cullen, J. Rankin.

Scorer: C. Gardner

SUMMARY

Although the statistics above reflect a successful season, the feeling is
that this team could have done even better. St. Martin's from South
Africa provided quality opposition and we were not in a position to
match them so early in the season.

We lost a memorable 'time' game to Reed's. After a fine start
between James Talbot and William Downing (47), Shiplake declared on
161 for 7. Downing then bowled two fine spells, probably his quickest
all season, and was ably supported by Grant Moseby.

Despite losing 5 early wickets, the 1st XI beat The OVS. Captain
Edward Blanchard scored 62 and James Smith-Jones 56, to rescue the
situation. OVS were bowled out for 117 with Downing taking 5-11.

The Twenty20 competition added a spark to the season. Victories
against Abingdon and Dauntsey's left us relying on St. Benedict's and
Dauntsey's overall run-rate being lower than ours. The display in the
field at St. Benedict's came back to haunt us!

Special mention must go to captain Edward Blanchard who has
displayed the best cricketing brain during my time at Shiplake. William
Downing has also played superbly in the 1st XI for four years and
scored back-to-back centuries against Bearwood and The Oratory.

The future is bright, especially as Moseby (64*) and Braithwaite
(76) ensured victory in the Shiplake Shield. I would like to thank all the
players for their commitment during an enjoyable season, their parents
for support and Christopher Gardner for scoring. Also thanks to all the
coaches, groundsmen and staff who have helped during the year.

AVERAGES

BATSMAN	INNINGS	NOT OUT	RUNS	H. SCORE	AVERAGE
W. Downing	16	2	656	134	46.9
G. Moseby	14	5	381	84*	42.3
G. Braithwaite	13	3	275	76	27.5
J. Smith-Jones	11	3	187	56	23.4

BOWLER	OVERS	MAIDENS	RUNS	WICKETS	AVERAGE
W. Downing	94.1	9	281	34	8.3
G. Braithwaite	61.2	9	220	18	12.2
B. Farmar	-	-	25	2	12.5
J. Talbot	-	-	268	18	14.9
G. Moseby	-	-	291	16	18.2

WICKET-KEEPER	PLAYED	CAUGHT	STUMPED
E. Blanchard	-	-	-

NOTABLE BATTING PERFORMANCES

PLAYER	OPPOSITION	SCORE
W. Downing	Bearwood College	134
W. Downing	The Oratory	106
G. Moseby	Claire's Court	84*
G. Braithwaite	Reading Blue Coat	76
W. Downing	St. Benedict's	64
G. Moseby	Reading Blue Coat	64*
E. Blanchard	Old Vikings	62

NOTABLE BOWLING PERFORMANCES

PLAYER	OPPOSITION	FIGURES
W. Downing	Old Vikings	5-11
W. Downing	Pangbourne College	4-15
G. Braithwaite	Reading Blue Coat	4-16
J. Talbot	Abingdon	4-12

SHREWSBURY SCHOOL

The School, Shrewsbury SY3 7BA

Tel: 01743 280500 Fax: 01743 340048
Email: asb@shrewsbury.org.uk

Master i/c Cricket: A. Barnard   Coach: P. Pridgeon

2005 SEASON

Played: 17   Won: 11   Lost: 4   Drawn: 2

Captain: T. Cox   Vice-captain: J. Gale

Team selected from: T. Cox*, J. Gale*, P. Duncan*,
T. Corbelt-Winder*, B. Alderson, R. Hawkin, J. Travers,
P. Hutchinson, P. Bailey, E. Jenkins, O. Wood, L. Portsmouth,
A. Parker, E. Taylor, A. Garth, J. Taylor, M. McKeever.
Scorer: Trevor Lloyd

SUMMARY

The 1st XI had a fine season and made progress throughout. The winter tour to South Africa was excellent preparation. A few weeks in the sun during a cold and long winter can do much for the building of team spirit and confidence. Touring is never without merit for schools and schoolboys. They learn so much about themselves and others whilst we learn so much about them. It is pleasing to report that notable contributions to the summer of 2005 were made by players of all ages, but many of the tourists prospered to a greater extent.

The 1st XI season got off to a slow start with our early fixture against the Free Foresters being abandoned. This was followed by a very ordinary performance against RGS Worcester that saw us crash to an early defeat.

A win against King Edward's Birmingham was followed by another disappointing loss at home to Oundle, but then we hit some form and produced a run of five wins before the draw against Manchester GS in late June. We followed that with three wins, before we encountered our first defeat in two months, being just edged out against Eton on the final day of the Silk Trophy.

We returned to school and were well beaten by the MCC, before finding our best form and beating the Saracens on Speech Day.

Our practice regimes were good but as ever disrupted by exams. I will seek to make further progress in this area next season as we aim to build on last year's fine results. Preparation is key to success. Attention to detail is everything and I hope next year's squad will take this on board and work assiduously at all areas of their game.

AVERAGES

BATSMAN	INNINGS	NOT OUT	RUNS	H. SCORE	AVERAGE
T. Cox	17	4	623	128*	47.9
J. Taylor	10	2	357	73*	44.6
L. Portsmouth	12	4	321	90*	40.1
M. McKeever	9	2	173	35	24.7

BOWLER	OVERS	MAIDENS	RUNS	WICKETS	AVERAGE
O. Wood	125.3	35	340	20	17.0
T. Corbelt-Winder	134.9	30	345	20	17.2
M. McKeever	130.5	26	342	17	20.1
P. Duncan	110.4	25	350	17	20.6
J. Gale	120.2	28	377	18	20.9

WICKET-KEEPER	PLAYED	CAUGHT	STUMPED
R. Hawkin	10	8	7
B. Alderson	6	2	5

NOTABLE BATTING PERFORMANCES

PLAYER	OPPOSITION	SCORE
T. Cox	Saracens	128*
L. Portsmouth	Eton College	90*

NOTABLE BOWLING PERFORMANCES

PLAYER	OPPOSITION	FIGURES
T. Corbelt-Winder	King Edward's Birmingham	4-11
M. McKeever	Melbourne HS (Australia)	5-20

SIR JOSEPH WILLIAMSON'S MATHEMATICAL SCHOOL

Maidstone Road, Rochester, Kent ME1 3EL

Tel: 01634 844008 Fax: 01634 818303
Email: office@sirjosephwilliamson.medway.sch.uk

Master i/c Cricket: D.J. Watson   Coach: S.N. Downes

2005 SEASON

Played: 10 Won: 5 Lost: 3 Drawn: 2

Captain: R. Hartley Vice-captain: J. Child

Team selected from: C. Maguire, R. Hartley*, T. Hanman*,
A. Fletcher, J. Rodgers, H. Bahia, J. Child*, D. Fordham*,
A. De Figueiredo, M. Payne, S. Shamshad, A. Khan, M. Kynaston,
B. Curtis, S. Graley.

SUMMARY

The highlight of the season proved to be a hard fought win against the MCC. Tom Hanman, in his final year at the school, spearheaded the bowling attack and also proved to be our most effective batsman, racking up over 300 runs, including an impressive 80 against the MCC.

Ralph Hartley lead the side with aplomb and was ably supported by Jon Child as vice-captain. Child, a Year 12 student, scored 261 runs and took 20 wickets.

***Did you know?* . . .** Ian Botham has the highest number of Test wickets for England. He has taken a total of 383 in 102 Tests at an average of 28.4.

AVERAGES

BATSMAN	INNINGS	NOT OUT	RUNS	H. SCORE	AVERAGE
T. Hanman	7	2	303	80	60.6
J. Child	9	2	261	60*	37.3
R. Hartley	6	2	89	34	22.3

BOWLER	OVERS	MAIDENS	RUNS	WICKETS	AVERAGE
T. Hanman	66	15	162	21	7.7
J. Child	63	6	274	20	13.7

WICKET-KEEPER	PLAYED	CAUGHT	STUMPED
J. Rogers	10	11	1

NOTABLE BATTING PERFORMANCES

PLAYER	OPPOSITION	SCORE
T. Hanman	Gravesend GS	73*
A. Fletcher	Gravesend GS	52
J. Child	Tunbridge Wells GS	61*
T. Hanman	Langley Park GS	64*
J. Child	Harvey GS	60*
T. Hanman	MCC	80

NOTABLE BOWLING PERFORMANCES

PLAYER	OPPOSITION	FIGURES
T. Hanman	Judd	7-2-21-5
T. Hanman	Chislehurst and Sidcup GS	6-0-18-5
T. Hanman	Langley Park GS	6-4-4-4

SOUTH CRAVEN SCHOOL

Holme Lane, Cross Hills, Nr Keighley BD20 7RL

Tel: 01535 632861 Fax: 01535 632859
Email: admin@south-craven.n-yorks.sch.uk

Master i/c Cricket: D.M. Birks

2005 SEASON

Played: 7   Won: 3   Lost: 2   Drawn: 2

Captain: M. Hebden   Vice-captain: R. Wilkinson

Team selected from: M. Hebden*, R. Wilkinson*, C. Barrett*,
R. Butcher*, S. Claridge*, S. Hanson*, A. Hardwick*, P. Rishton*,
S. Roberts*, C. Spencer, T. Waggett*, M. Wiggan*,
R. Walker*, J. Wilkinson.

SUMMARY

Four matches were abandoned due to the weather. Those played were largely contested on damp pitches and low total scores were common. The MCC game was foreshortened by a thunderstorm.

A new fixture was against an Old Boys XI made up of players since the 1st XI started in 1992 and the result was an honourable draw.

Man of the season was vice-captain Robert Wilkinson who top-scored with 128 runs and took 13 wickets.

AVERAGES

BATSMAN	INNINGS	NOT OUT	RUNS	H. SCORE	AVERAGE
S. Hanson	4	3	55	32*	55.0
R. Wilkinson	6	2	128	35	32.0
M. Wiggan	6	1	92	55*	18.4
M. Hebden	7	1	92	45*	15.3
T. Waggett	7	1	91	35	15.2
C. Barrett	6	0	75	24	12.5

BOWLER	OVERS	MAIDENS	RUNS	WICKETS	AVERAGE
M. Wiggan	18	3	58	6	9.7
R. Walker	33	6	128	8	16.0
R. Wilkinson	58	8	243	13	18.7
T. Waggett	59	13	213	10	21.3

WICKET-KEEPER	PLAYED	CAUGHT	STUMPED
M. Hebden	6	3	0
C. Spencer	1	1	0

NOTABLE BATTING PERFORMANCES

PLAYER	OPPOSITION	SCORE
M. Wiggan	Old Boys XI	55*

NOTABLE BOWLING PERFORMANCES

PLAYER	OPPOSITION	FIGURES
M. Wiggan	Rotherham Sixth Form	4-20
R. Wilkinson	Rotherham Sixth Form	4-27
R. Walker	XL Club	4-30
T. Waggett	XL Club	4-38

STEWART'S MELVILLE COLLEGE

Queensferry Road, Edinburgh EH4 3EZ

Tel: 0131 311 1000 Fax: 0131 311 1099
Email: secretary@esmgc.com

Master i/c Cricket: M.R. Burgess   Coach: B.G. Lockie

2005 SEASON

Played: 10   Won: 4   Lost: 6

Captain: S. Parker   Vice-captain: U. Malik

Team selected from: S. Parker*, D. Aitken, S. Ditchfield, R. Logan*, A. Brock, I. Morrison, S. Ahmed, U. Malik, A. McHoul*, C. Gould, N. Waterman, R. Samson, J. Duguid.

SUMMARY

Although the season record does not reflect it, the team produced many positive performances. Three of the six games lost were by 3 wickets or less, and could have gone either way. Steven Parker, the team captain, had another fine season, averaging over 40 with the bat yet again.

With next season in mind, it was pleasing to see fine performances from both Andrew Brock and Steven Ditchfield, who still have another three years in the 1st XI to go. Only three of the team have left school, so we are looking forward to having a more experienced side next season.

AVERAGES

BATSMAN	INNINGS	NOT OUT	RUNS	H. SCORE	AVERAGE
S. Parker	9	2	290	59*	41.4
A. Brock	6	0	138	51	23.0

BOWLER	OVERS	MAIDENS	RUNS	WICKETS	AVERAGE
S. Ditchfield	33	4	117	9	13.0
A. Brock	34	3	174	11	15.8
A. McHoul	61	9	248	15	16.5

NOTABLE BATTING PERFORMANCES

PLAYER	OPPOSITION	SCORE
S. Parker	Fettes College	56
S. Parker	Merchiston Castle	46
A. Brock	George Watson's College	51
S. Parker	Kelvinside Academy	59*
S. Parker	Loretto	46*

NOTABLE BOWLING PERFORMANCES

PLAYER	OPPOSITION	FIGURES
A. McHoul	George Watson's College	4-31
S. Ditchfield	Glasgow Academy	5-27
A. Brock	Loretto	4-26

Did you know? . . . The youngest player to represent England in a Test match was D.B. Close, who played his first in 1949 aged 18 years 149 days. He was still playing Test cricket in 1976 aged 45.

STOCKPORT GRAMMAR SCHOOL

Buxton Road, Stockport, Cheshire SK2 7AF

Tel: 0161 456 9000 Fax: 0161 483 1797
Email: youngr@stockportgrammar.co.uk

Master i/c Cricket: R. Young   Coach: D. Makinson

2005 SEASON

Played: 11   Won: 3   Lost: 7   Drawn: 1

Captain: J. Rice

Team selected from: J. Rice*, C. Jones*, I. Pennington*, J. Holt,
J. Cowley, C. Ripley, M. Fendall, T. Radford, R. Cahill, J. Hewitt,
A. Hope, N. Pennington, A. Clinch, E. Needham, P. Hollingshead,
B. Garside, R. Wilson, M. Barrow, T. Jenkins, S. Jones.

SUMMARY

Although the results did not go our way, the squad were a pleasure to take. Their attitude remained positive and the number of players in regular training made for a healthy competition for places.

Batting prior to our end of season Malta Tour was vulnerable, but Chris Jones, Richard Wilson and John Cowley played key individual performances at various times. Josh Hewitt and John Cowley were the outstanding bowlers. Youngsters like Alex Hope, Neil Pennington, Tim Radford and Edward Needham developed well and should be more than capable next season.

The tour to Malta earned three out of four wins and was memorable once again. We look forward to the new season with our prospects enhanced.

AVERAGES

BATSMAN	INNINGS	NOT OUT	RUNS	H. SCORE	AVERAGE
C. Jones	11	0	372	110	33.8
A. Hope	5	2	91	52	30.3
E. Needham	5	1	91	31	22.8
R. Wilson	5	0	105	41	21.0
J. Holt	6	0	125	42	20.8
T. Radford	8	1	141	83	20.1

BOWLER	OVERS	MAIDENS	RUNS	WICKETS	AVERAGE
J. Cowley	37.4	4	103	7	14.7
R. Cahill	7	0	30	2	15.0
J. Hewitt	38	5	111	7	15.9
J. Holt	9	0	48	3	16.0
C. Ripley	21	1	83	4	20.7
N. Pennington	33	2	149	7	21.3

WICKET-KEEPER	PLAYED	CAUGHT	STUMPED
R. Cahill	7	3	0
A. Hope	4	4	0

NOTABLE BATTING PERFORMANCES

PLAYER	OPPOSITION	SCORE
C. Jones	Marsa (Malta)	110
C. Jones	Cheadle Hulme	91
T. Radford	Marsa (Malta)	83
R. Cahill	Malta	53
A. Hope	Malta	52
J. Cowley	KEQMS Lytham	52
C. Jones	Malta	50

NOTABLE BOWLING PERFORMANCES

PLAYER	OPPOSITION	FIGURES
A. Clinch	Malta	4-33
N. Pennington	Marsa (Malta)	3-28
J. Hewitt	Cheadle Hulme	3-20
J. Hewitt	Manchester GS	3-42

STONYHURST COLLEGE

Stonyhurst, Clitheroe, Lancashire BB7 9PZ

Tel: 01254 826345 Fax: 01254 826370
Email: admissions@stonyhurst.ac.uk

Master i/c Cricket: Gareth Thomas   Coach: Pierre Joubert

2005 SEASON

Played: 8   Won: 4   Lost: 2   Drawn: 2

Captain: M. Richardson   Vice-captain: L. Langford

Team selected from: M. Richardson*, L. Langford*, J. Ryan*,
T. Wood, M. Wild, D. Kumar, P. Beard*, R. Stokes, R. Munro,
B. Knight, J. Haynes, M. Sharples, N. Crouch, D. Layzell, B. Vines,
J. Garlington, J. Dineen, W. Marsden.

Scorer: D. Kent

SUMMARY

The 1st XI's success was highly dependent on the batting of Michael Richardson and the economic bowling of David Kumar and Luke Langford. They were backed up by Paul Beard, James Ryan and 15-year-old Matthew Wild, who played every game and was second highest wicket-taker and run-scorer.

Unfortunately seven regulars leave this year, including the 'run-machine' Michael Richardson, who for the last three seasons has contributed about half our runs.

We are not a strike bowling team so tight fielding and containment have been crucial to achievable targets batting second. Only two teams were bowled out, however one of those was the MCC. The game against them also featured Michael's maiden century; his chanceless 118* was a joy to behold.

So we beat all the adult teams and had the best of a draw with a strong and unbeaten Sedbergh, but lost to the two weakest teams we played. But isn't that unpredictability what makes cricket the great game it is?

AVERAGES

BATSMAN	INNINGS	NOT OUT	RUNS	H. SCORE	AVERAGE
M. Richardson	8	2	400	152	66.7
M. Wild	8	1	126	39	18.0
J. Ryan	6	2	71	29*	17.8
D. Kumar	6	2	61	23	15.3
T. Wood	8	1	87	43	12.4

BOWLER	OVERS	MAIDENS	RUNS	WICKETS	AVERAGE
D. Kumar	78	-	216	18	12.0
M. Wild	41	-	164	10	16.4
P. Beard	27	-	86	5	17.2
L. Langford	69	-	168	6	28.0
J. Ryan	54	-	170	4	42.5
B. Knight	22	-	86	2	43.0

WICKET-KEEPER	PLAYED	CAUGHT	STUMPED
M. Richardson	8	7	4

NOTABLE BATTING PERFORMANCES

PLAYER	OPPOSITION	SCORE
M. Richardson	MCC	118*
M. Richardson	XL Club	67
M. Richardson	Sedbergh	152

NOTABLE BOWLING PERFORMANCES

PLAYER	OPPOSITION	FIGURES
D. Kumar	MCC	5-57
D. Kumar	Giggleswick	4-26
D. Kumar	Sedbergh	4-22

STOWE SCHOOL

Stowe, Buckingham, Bucks MK18 5EH

Tel: 01280 818000 Fax: 01280 818181
Email: enquiries@stowe.co.uk

Master i/c Cricket: James Knott   Coach: Chris Townsend

2005 SEASON

Played: 22   Won: 16   Lost: 3   Drawn: 3

Captain: G. White

Team selected from: G. White, A. Cossins, B. Howgego, M. Nelson,
A. Leon, H. Taylor, R. Lyon, E. Hoy, R. Rowling, G. Coote,
G. Bateman, J. Hinds, C. Carter, C. Sheldon, H. Banks, J. Hirst,
A. Forsdike, C. Fenton, C. Walker.

SUMMARY

However this season is judged, it must rank as one of the finest in the proud history of cricket at Stowe. The 1st XI won a remarkable sixteen matches which is almost certainly an all-time record. The side reached the semi-final of the National Schools' Twenty20 Cup and there were no defeats to schools in regular fixtures. Furthermore, three members of the side have earned national recognition (Graeme White, Mark Nelson and Ben Howgego), the Stowe Twenty20 quadrangular challenge was retained and the school hosted its first ever county cricket (the Totesport League match between Northamptonshire and Gloucestershire).

There is no doubt that this was a talented side, and they were led by one of the outstanding schoolboy cricketers in the country, Graeme White. To score over 700 runs and take 55 wickets in a season is a remarkable effort in itself, but he also led the side with a determination and confidence that gave them a real edge. Graeme was brilliantly supported by Mark Nelson, a wonderfully gifted all-rounder, and Adam Cossins, a most destructive batsman in Twenty20 cricket, and a wicket-keeper with superb hands as his stumping tally shows.

Of those who remain for next year, Ben Howgego stood out, and will captain the side in 2006.

AVERAGES

BATSMAN	INNINGS	NOT OUT	RUNS	H. SCORE	AVERAGE
B. Howgego	18	5	655	110	50.4
G. White	20	3	732	101*	43.1
M. Nelson	19	6	505	102*	38.8
A. Cossins	21	1	529	73	26.5

BOWLER	OVERS	MAIDENS	RUNS	WICKETS	AVERAGE
G. White	217.2	55	659	55	12.0
R. Rowling	121.1	21	439	23	19.1
R. Lyon	144.4	11	570	28	20.4
M. Nelson	132.1	23	489	24	20.4

WICKET-KEEPER	PLAYED	CAUGHT	STUMPED
A. Cossins	22	11	12

NOTABLE BATTING PERFORMANCES

PLAYER	OPPOSITION	SCORE
B. Howgego	Radley	110
M. Nelson	King's College Wimbledon	102*
G. White	Rugby	101*
G. White	Uppingham	97
B. Howgego	St. Edward's Oxford	80

NOTABLE BOWLING PERFORMANCES

PLAYER	OPPOSITION	FIGURES
G. White	St. Edward's Oxford	7-35
G. White	King's College Wimbledon	6-59
G. White	Wycliffe College	6-32
R. Lyon	Westville (South Africa)	5-48
G. White	Westville (South Africa)	5-53

THE TREASURE HOUSE OF LORD'S

by Glenys Williams, MCC Museum archivist and historian

The MCC Museum houses the most comprehensive array of cricketing memorabilia in the world. It was opened in 1953 as a memorial to all cricketers who lost their lives during the two World Wars. Over the past few years it has been extensively redeveloped and in 1993 was reopened by the Rt Hon Sir John Major, who was prime minister at the time. More recent developments include a new exhibition gallery, opened in 1997, and the Brian Johnston Film Theatre, named after the much-loved cricket commentator who lived near the ground. Here visitors can learn more about the history of Lord's and watch some of the great cricket performances of the past. In 2003 the museum celebrated the anniversary of its foundation with a visit from HRH the Duke of Edinburgh – who had also presided at the opening ceremony 50 years earlier.

Undoubtedly the most famous item housed in the museum is the Ashes urn – the symbol of Anglo/Australian cricket rivalry. The Museum also permanently holds the Wisden Trophy, which is awarded to the winners of the Test series between England and West Indies, and the Prudential Cup, last awarded to India in 1983. The museum houses a fine assembly of paintings from all periods, with many modern MCC commissions. These include three Conversation Pieces by Andrew Festing featuring famous cricketers of the past 50 years, and numerous works by MCC 'young artists' who have been appointed to travel overseas and capture the atmosphere of England playing cricket around the world.

Two more unusual exhibits are the sparrow that was killed by a ball bowled by Jehangir Khan at Lord's in 1936 and the Chinese punchbowl (c.1786) depicting the painting *Cricket in the Marylebone Fields*, which was probably made at the behest of Thomas Lord himself. There are also scorebooks of famous matches, boots worn by Sir Donald Bradman and numerous bats, including the one used by Graham Gooch to score his record innings of 333 against India at Lord's in 1990. More recent acquisitions include donations by numerous contemporary cricketers including

Shane Warne, Makhaya Ntini, Graeme Smith, Shivnarine Chanderpaul, Saurav Ganguly, Robert Key, Ashley Giles, Nasser Hussain and Michael Vaughan.

Above the museum is the MCC Library which contains a fine collection of books and manuscripts dating back to the 17th century. MCC attempts to purchase every cricket publication and is an excellent resource for members and students alike.

This sparrow was killed at Lord's by a ball bowled by Jehangir Khan in 1936
(Reproduced by kind permission of The MCC Museum)

For details regarding guided tours, contact 020 7616 8596

Top Left: James Hayward who was captain of the unbeaten Taunton 1st XI
Top Right: Neil Desai (Tiffin) 757 runs and 32 wickets
Bottom Left: Anthony Shales (Tonbridge) 506 runs and 38 dismissals
Bottom Right: Oliver Howick (Tonbridge) 48 wickets at 13.6

SUTTON VALENCE SCHOOL

North Road, Sutton Valence, Nr Maidstone, Kent ME17 3HL

Tel: 01622 845301 Fax: 01622 845306
Email: igglesdena@svs.org.uk

Masters i/c Cricket: Alan Igglesden and Bill Buck

2005 SEASON

Played: 18 Won: 11 Lost: 1 Drawn: 4 Abandoned: 2

Captain: E. Spencer Vice-captain: A. Jackson

Team selected from: E. Spencer, A. Jackson, B. Spencer, O. Peters,
E. Horne, M. Taplin, T. Roberts, S. Knott, A. Carr, B. Richards,
M. Coles, T. Withers-Green, S. Higgins, W. Jackson,
A. Richardson, M. Dodd.

SUMMARY

Sutton Valence enjoyed another rewarding cricket season in 2005, although they never quite reached the dizzy heights of last season. Eleven wins out of eighteen and losing only once is still a very good return for our efforts.

The PCA Twenty20 Cup Competition was a great success and a chance for us to play in coloured clothing with a white ball. It offers new challenges and a completely diverse format of the game.

We had to play two thirds of the season without Ashley Jackson, who was away training and playing for the England U21 Hockey World Cup Squad. He scored nearly 900 runs for us last year and they were very hard to replace. Orlando Peters and Ed Spencer both had productive seasons, batting with great confidence. Toby Withers-Green scored his maiden century for the school against Hurstpierpoint College and Martin Taplin and Ed Horne both contributed to winning matches throughout the summer.

Our bowling department which was without Sam Knott and Ari Richardson - son of the great Richie Richardson - for most of the season, faired really well. Ben Spencer was as metronomic as ever, making important breakthroughs when the team needed them most. It was the 'spin twins', Michael Coles and Simon Higgins, who really caught the eye with over 30 wickets between them.

Great strides were made by some younger members of the team. They will have to step up to the mark again next year if we are to continue with the progress of the last three seasons.

AVERAGES

BATSMAN	INNINGS	NOT OUT	RUNS	H. SCORE	AVERAGE
A. Jackson	5	1	271	98*	67.8
O. Peters	17	4	657	132*	50.5
E. Spencer	18	5	633	101*	48.7
M. Taplin	13	4	320	81*	35.6
T. Withers-Green	14	0	363	100	25.9
E. Horne	12	3	211	63	23.4

BOWLER	OVERS	MAIDENS	RUNS	WICKETS	AVERAGE
S. Higgins	36.1	2	219	12	18.2
S. Knott	66	10	302	15	20.1
M. Coles	105	13	494	21	23.5
B. Spencer	124	15	577	19	30.4

WICKET-KEEPER	PLAYED	CAUGHT	STUMPED
E. Spencer	18	12	2

NOTABLE BATTING PERFORMANCES

PLAYER	OPPOSITION	SCORE
O. Peters	Old Suttonians	132*
E. Spencer	MCC	101*
T. Withers-Green	Hurstpierpoint College	100
A. Jackson	MCC	98*

NOTABLE BOWLING PERFORMANCES

PLAYER	OPPOSITION	FIGURES
M. Coles	St. Dunstan's	4-30

SOUTH CRAVEN SCHOOL

by David Birks, Deputy Head and i/c 1st XI Cricket

South Craven School is an 11-18 mixed comprehensive of 1750 students, located on the boundary of North Yorkshire and Bradford Metropolitan District. By the 1980s very little cricket was being played at the school. However, in 1987 an artificial wicket was installed and this made possible regular cricket fixtures at U12, U13, U14 and U15 levels. Moreover, there emerged a very strong group of cricketers reaching U15 level by 1990, one representing Yorkshire Schools, being in the same team as Michael Vaughan.

As a result I decided to try and set up a 1st XI in 1992, and five matches were arranged with home matches played on local club grounds. Ten fixtures followed in 1993 and three players were selected for the North Yorkshire Schools team, with one appointed captain. The latter subsequently gained three cricket blues for Cambridge and successfully survived facing Andrew Flintoff and Glenn McGrath amongst others.

The MCC offered us a fixture in 1994 and since then we have managed two victories, with the school benefiting enormously from the valuable experience gained. We have also played the XL Club for the last three years. Such fixtures have helped compensate for some problems with school matches, exacerbated by examination pressures.

1994 also saw our first individual hundred, by Mark Chapman, who later went on to play for Worcestershire 2nd XI and we had our exploits recorded in *Wisden* and *The Cricketer*. In one match the following season, captain Neil Spragg took five wickets for no runs. These figures were beaten in 1996 by what remains a school record, 8-18, by debutant Matthew Lloyd, including a hat trick.

In 1997 came the debut of our first female cricketer, Laura Spragg, an all-rounder, and it was a proud moment in 2002 when I was able to watch Laura play for England Women against New Zealand in Durham. Also in 2002, Laura's sister, Anna, kept wicket for the School. In one match the opposing captain, coming out to bat, attempted to whisper sweet nothings in her ear, so she stumped him and sent him off back to the pavilion! The same season saw a school record score of 306-5 declared, a record individual score of 152 by Andrew Sewell and Chris Meehan's fourth hundred for the School. 2005 saw the first Old Boys match, involving some of the original 1992 side and ending in an honourable draw.

As we look forward to the 2006 season we are as dependent as ever on the goodwill of our local cricket clubs for the use of their facilities and we are also very grateful to MCC, the XL Club and *Wisden* for supporting schools cricket so effectively. We are delighted to be able to contribute to the inaugural edition of *The Schools' Cricket Almanac* and wish it every success.

South Craven School v MCC at Keighley Cricket Club

TAUNTON SCHOOL

Staplegrove Road, Taunton, Somerset TA2 6AD

Tel: 01823 349200 Fax: 01823 349201
Email: simon.hogg@tauntonschool.co.uk

Master i/c Cricket: S.T. Hogg   Coach: D. Baty

2005 SEASON

Played: 13   Won: 12   Drawn: 1

Captain: J. Hayward

Team selected from: J. Hayward*, A. Carroll*, A. Mason*,
S. Robinson, P. Roszkowski, J. Bess*, J. Osmond, J. Raistrick,
M. Sutton, S. Toland, J. Todd*, J. Cooper*, H. Kelly, H. Whittington.
Scorer: R. Moore

SUMMARY

Taunton enjoyed a superb unbeaten season for only the second time in the School's proud cricket history.

Having drawn our first fixture with the XL Club, we recorded twelve consecutive victories. Unfortunately, two regular fixtures were lost to the weather and three games against strong touring sides were reduced to 20 over matches.

After winning our games in convincing fashion before half-term, some disappointing bowling and fielding displays led to four thrilling run-chases in our later matches. Several different boys responded with match-winning contributions whilst under pressure, reflecting the team's great strength: they refused to accept defeat.

Josh Bess and Jack Cooper opened the batting and both enjoyed fine seasons. Jack recorded two unbeaten centuries, including 162 against Clifton College and Josh scored over 600 runs. Josh, in particular, along with Hugh Kelly and captain James Hayward, always looked to dominate the opposition bowling and runs were scored at a healthy rate throughout the season.

James, bowling slow left-arm, was our leading wicket-taker, closely followed by Alex Carroll. They were given excellent support by Sean Toland, Andrew Mason and Harry Whittington. Alex enjoyed a fantastic start to the season. Bowling left-arm medium-fast, he always put the opposition under pressure by taking early wickets and conceding very few runs.

Our fielding let us down at times, but it was a real pleasure to watch the excellence of Jonathan Todd's wicket-keeping and the brilliance of James Hayward's fielding. James, who captained the side for the last few years, has thrilled spectators with his all-round ability and many of us have never seen a better schoolboy fielder.

AVERAGES

BATSMAN	INNINGS	NOT OUT	RUNS	H. SCORE	AVERAGE
J. Cooper	11	3	530	162*	66.3
P. Roszkowski	6	3	174	66*	58.0
J. Bess	13	0	622	101	47.8
H. Kelly	9	1	335	108*	41.9
J. Hayward	13	1	346	59	28.8
J. Todd	9	3	149	54*	24.8

BOWLER	OVERS	MAIDENS	RUNS	WICKETS	AVERAGE
A. Carroll	95.5	29	273	22	12.4
J. Hayward	107	15	337	25	13.5
A. Mason	71	9	234	16	14.6
S. Toland	67.1	10	227	10	22.7

WICKET-KEEPER	PLAYED	CAUGHT	STUMPED
J. Todd	13	18	5

NOTABLE BATTING PERFORMANCES

PLAYER	OPPOSITION	SCORE
J. Cooper	Clifton College	162*
H. Kelly	Wellington	108*
J. Cooper	King's Taunton	102*
J. Bess	XL Club	101
H. Kelly	Sherborne	95
J. Bess	Sherborne	80
J. Bess	Dulwich College	74

NOTABLE BOWLING PERFORMANCES

PLAYER	OPPOSITION	FIGURES
J. Hayward	Millfield	7-12
A. Carroll	Clifton College	4-9
A. Mason	Wellington	4-10
S. Toland	Clifton College	4-15
A. Carroll	Blundell's	4-25
A. Mason	Queen's College	4-34
A. Carroll	Canford	4-38

TIFFIN SCHOOL

Queen Elizabeth Road, Kingston-upon-Thames, Surrey KT2 6RL

Tel: 020 8546 4638 Fax: 020 8546 6365
Email: office@tiffin.kingston.sch.uk

Master i/c Cricket: M.J. Williams

2005 SEASON

Played: 17   Won: 12   Lost: 3   Drawn: 2

SUMMARY

The 1st XI had another excellent season. The boys played positive, attacking cricket from the outset and the team was fortunate to have a number of very good all-rounders.

Our leading player was the vice-captain, Neil Desai, who batted and bowled exceptionally, scoring 757 runs and taking 32 wickets with his medium-pace swingers. Arun Harinath, who has completed six seasons in the 1st XI, having played his first as an U13, had another fine year with 598 runs and 22 wickets. Opening bowler Harry Weale claimed 22 wickets and hit 379 runs. Four old colours return next season.

AVERAGES

BATSMAN	INNINGS	NOT OUT	RUNS	H. SCORE	AVERAGE
N. Desai	17	3	757	84*	54.1
A. Harinath	14	0	598	108	42.7
H. Weale	14	3	379	68*	34.5
J. Secker	14	5	256	42	28.4
D. Patel	17	3	346	73	24.7

BOWLER	OVERS	MAIDENS	RUNS	WICKETS	AVERAGE
N. Desai	128	22	474	32	14.8
A. Harinath	99	18	339	22	15.4
H. Weale	132.2	23	511	24	21.3
Z. Tughral	106.5	14	447	20	22.3
J. Mellett	65	6	292	11	26.6

CRICKET AT MALVERN

by George Chesterton

Introduction by Andy Murtagh, Master i/c Cricket

Modesty precludes the author of the following article from paying due heed to his own contributions to the success story of cricket at Malvern. George Chesterton is known quite simply as 'Mr Malvern' to generations of cricketers from the school. He was a colour in the XI in 1939, 1940 and 1941, captaining the side in his final year.

On leaving school, he served in the RAF during the war, flying Stirling bombers and seeing action most notably in the airborn operation known as 'Market Garden' at Arnhem. He then took up his place at Oxford gaining a blue.

Whilst he was a schoolmaster at Malvern, he opened the bowling for Worcestershire for a number of years, during which time he was selected for the Gentlemen against the Players. He became Master i/c Cricket at Malvern in 1951 and remained in that post until 1965, overseeing some of the most talented XIs the school has had. At Malvern, he went on to become housemaster, Second Master and Acting Head before his retirement. He was later elected as President of Worcestershire CCC.

There can be few more spectacular settings for a cricket ground than the Senior Turf at Malvern. Looking to the east is Bredon Hill, the Severn Valley and the Cotswolds and to the west is the backdrop of the Malvern Hills. Within fifteen months of the school's foundation the first matches were played, but with a distinct advantage to the home side, when local knowledge of the one-in-sixteen slope paid dividends. 'Like playing on the side of a house,' as one opponent said. So it was not many years before the first terracing took place in 1872. What a labour this must have been, with pick and shovel, and horse and cart. Rather different from the final widening in 1985, when the work was completed with modern machinery in under a week. With the pitch still slightly on the narrow side, the tradition of no sixes has been maintained.

The quality of Malvern cricket languished until the arrival of Charles Toppin in 1885. For thirty-seven years he was master in charge of cricket, providing inspirational leadership. Through his hands passed a procession of fine players starting with P.H. Latham, the first Malvern blue, who was in the Cambridge side from 1892-4. H.K. Foster was the eldest of seven brothers who dominated Malvern cricket from 1889. Indeed, except for one year, there was a Foster in the XI for fifteen seasons and they all went on to play for Worcestershire. R.E. was the most outstanding and is still remembered for his innings of 287 for England at Sydney on the 1903-4 tour to Australia.

Amongst others who came under Toppin's influence, and who made an impression in the first-class game, were the three Day brothers, S.H., S.E. and A.P., who all played for Kent. G.H. Simpson-Hayward, the last of the great 'lob' bowlers - although he bowled overarm at school - joined Worcestershire. He also nurtured W.S. Bird, who kept wicket for Oxford and the Gentlemen, and the Naumann brothers, who played on opposite sides in the Varsity match. W.H.B. Evans, sadly killed flying with Colonel Cody when only in his twenties, was said to be Malvern's finest all-rounder. All these and many more passed through Toppin's hands. Towards the end of his time, D.J. Knight was selected for the XI as a new boy and then years later played against the great Australian side of 1921. Norman Partridge, another fine all-rounder, was invited to play for the Gentlemen while still at school, an invitation which had to be declined.

Between the wars many fine players emerged from Malvern. Charles Fiddian-Green had taken over from Toppin, and under his guidance there was a string of blues, amongst whom were E.R.T. Holmes who captained Oxford and Surrey, and another county captain, G.B. Legge of Kent. Both went on to play for England. R.G. Stainton and R.H. Maudsley were two highly regarded county players.

In the period following the Second World War, batsmen predominated, including R.K. Whiley, who was five years in the school eleven, J.W.T. Wilcox and B.A. Richardson. The latter represented the Old Malvernians ninety times in the Cricketer Cup - a competition in which Malvern stands only below Tonbridge in its record of success. The Tolchard brothers, J.G., R.C. and R.W., were all outstanding players in the sixties, the last named going on to play four times for England in India. First-class players of more recent times who came under the guidance of A.R. Duff and A.J. Murtagh include H.T. Tunnicliffe and R.M. Ellcock. Ellcock, a Barbadian by birth, suffered a serious back injury which brought his cricket career to an abrupt end while he was a member of the English touring party to the West Indies. David Nash and Mark Hardinges are Malvern's latest contributions to the first-class arena, David with Middlesex and Mark with Gloucestershire.

Malvern has been fortunate over nearly a hundred and fifty years in the loyalty and expertise of a handful of professional coaches. George Arber in the early days, and 'Father' Tate, who bowled endlessly and patiently in the nets for thirty-two years, serving up half volleys to order and Bob Beveridge, late of Middlesex, who succeeded him, wheeled away with almost monotonous accuracy. Then Geoff Morton came to instil generations of Malvernians with skills and impeccable standards of sportsmanship, coupled with his own endearing breed of malapropisms; he in turn passed the mantle on to Roger Tolchard, a Malvernian and outstanding sportsman.

Malvern's main rivals remain, as they have for scores of years, Repton, Shrewsbury, Cheltenham, Clifton and Harrow. The last named maintain Malvern's war time association with that school. In common with so many other schools an annual festival winds up the season. Currently the festival quartet is made up with Malvern, Rugby, Charterhouse and a combined Irish team. Overseas tours from time to time have given an exciting addition to the programme, including visits to the West Indies and South Africa.

It is remarkable that so unpromising a location on the side of a hill has been transformed into a beautiful cricket ground, where such a fine tradition for the best of cricket has been able to develop.

Cricket on The Senior at Malvern College

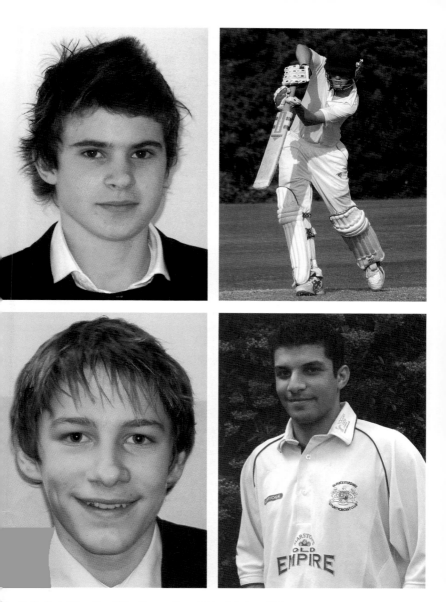

Top Left: Josh Wheatley (Woodhouse Grove) 44 wickets at 15.1
Top Right: Luc Durandt (Wellington College) 912 runs at 57.0, including five centuries
Bottom Left: Tom Ullyott (Worksop College) 41 wickets at 13.0
Bottom Right: Asif Sultan (Wrekin College) 473 runs and 47 wickets

TONBRIDGE SCHOOL

Tonbridge, Kent TN9 1JP

Tel: 01732 365555 Fax: 01732 304277
Email: arw@tonbridge-school.org

Master i/c Cricket: James Hodgson   Coach: Derek Chadwick

2005 SEASON

Played: 18   Won: 4   Lost: 9   Drawn: 5

Captain: O. Howick   Vice-captain: A. Shales

Team selected from: O. Howick*, A. Shales*, C. Hammond*,
A. Howeson*, C. Makepeace*, E. Hill*, O. Durell*, J. Middleton*,
A. Botting*, R. McDonald*, S. Kapila*, H. Hill, E. Bugge,
C. Pierce, A. Trigg.

Scorer: N. Wakeling

SUMMARY

Tonbridge played some excellent cricket this season. Unfortunately the results do not do justice to the talent in this side, which included five returning players from the successful 2004 1st XI.

There were several very close matches which could have gone either way, however all went against Tonbridge this year. Too often the side did not score enough runs, which left challenging goals for the team in the field. In this department, the XI were outstanding and they were well led by the captain, Howick. His bowling performances throughout the season deserve a special mention. He consistently led the attack and his tally of 48 wickets is the most recorded for some time at Tonbridge.

Tonbridge's Cowdrey Cup campaign got off to a poor start by losing to Charterhouse at home. This was followed by an abandoned match at Eton due to the rain and then a convincing win at home against Wellington. The final match against Harrow was an excellent one. Tonbridge made a great effort to defend their modest total of 158 but sadly did not quite manage to remove Harrow's second last pair, who overcame the target with two overs to spare.

The school would like to thank Derek Chadwick for all he has done as coach over the last seven years for Tonbridge, and wish him all the best in his retirement.

AVERAGES

BATSMAN	INNINGS	NOT OUT	RUNS	H. SCORE	AVERAGE
A. Shales	17	2	506	129*	33.7
C. Hammond	16	2	457	78*	32.6
A. Howeson	17	2	442	110	29.5
O. Howick	16	1	398	78	26.5
E. Hill	12	2	228	58	22.8
C. Makepeace	17	3	279	52	19.9

BOWLER	OVERS	MAIDENS	RUNS	WICKETS	AVERAGE
O. Howick	209.3	39	652	48	13.6
A. Botting	111	13	407	16	25.4
S. Kapila	60.3	2	331	12	27.6
A. Howeson	116	17	505	18	28.1
C. Hammond	155	21	572	20	28.6
O. Durell	139	20	520	18	28.9

WICKET-KEEPER	PLAYED	CAUGHT	STUMPED
A. Shales	18	33	5

NOTABLE BATTING PERFORMANCES

PLAYER	OPPOSITION	SCORE
A. Shales	Sevenoaks	129*
A. Howeson	SERC	110
A. Shales	Millfield	104
C. Hammond	Cranleigh	78*
O. Howick	Band of Brothers	78

NOTABLE BOWLING PERFORMANCES

PLAYER	OPPOSITION	FIGURES
O. Howick	Dulwich College	6-47
O. Howick	Tonbridge CC	5-13
O. Howick	Bedford	5-34
O. Howick	Haileybury	4-10
O. Howick	Millfield	4-56
A. Howeson	Bedford	4-22

TRENT COLLEGE

Derby Road, Long Eaton, Nottingham NG10 4AD

Tel: 0115 849 4949 Fax: 0115 849 4997
Email: enquiries@trentcollege.net

Master i/c Cricket: C.P. Seal   Coach: J.A. Afford

2005 SEASON

SUMMARY

We reached the semi-final of the National Schools Twenty20 Cup where we lost to Felsted. This young side made good progress and will be touring Australia at Christmas 2005-6.

AVERAGES

BATSMAN	INNINGS	NOT OUT	RUNS	H. SCORE	AVERAGE
M. Swann	19	2	447	96*	26.3
T. Good	18	1	364	51	21.4
J. Hemstock	11	2	190	80*	21.1
M. Pavis	20	4	269	34	16.8
T. Crosse	16	5	166	52	15.1
M. Spurr	13	0	182	37	14.0

BOWLER	OVERS	MAIDENS	RUNS	WICKETS	AVERAGE
G. Roberts	112.1	18	477	29	16.4
P. Robinson	78	7	336	18	18.7
N. McKeown	113.1	15	433	20	21.6
M. Pavis	109.3	8	460	20	23.0
T. Crosse	142.2	15	554	23	24.1

NOTABLE BATTING PERFORMANCES

PLAYER	OPPOSITION	SCORE
M. Swann	Headmaster's XI	96*
J. Hemstock	Mornington (Australia)	80*

NOTABLE BOWLING PERFORMANCES

PLAYER	OPPOSITION	FIGURES
T. Crosse	Silcoates	5-14
P. Robinson	Solihull	5-26
N. McKeown	Repton	5-27

TRINITY SCHOOL

Shirley Park, Croydon CR9 7AT

Tel: 020 8662 5197 Fax: 020 8656 8229
Email: mdf@trinity.croydon.sch.uk

Master i/c Cricket and Coach: M.D. Ferran

2005 SEASON

Played: 14   Won: 3   Lost: 11

Captain: P. Dolby   Vice-captain: T. Carter

Team selected from: J. Mugridge, C. Bond, P. Dolby, A. De Warrenne,
K. Ganatra, T. Carter*, D. Stoneman, C. Hall, S. O'Connell,
S. Glassington, R. Jones, D. Amin, C. Turner, M. Winter, K. Patel.
Scorer: J. Piggot

SUMMARY

A very young and inexperienced side let themselves down at crucial
points during the early part of the season. The highlight was T. Carter's
century (106) during the celebrations of a centenary of cricket being
played between Colfe's and Trinity - we won by 6 wickets.

The prospects for next year are good as we will retain the majority
of the 1st XI.

AVERAGES

BATSMAN	INNINGS	NOT OUT	RUNS	H. SCORE	AVERAGE
C. Turner	11	1	366	86	36.6
A. De Warrenne	13	1	228	49	19.0
T. Carter	10	0	182	106	18.2
K. Patel	11	0	161	38	14.6
P. Dolby	13	0	166	39	12.8

BOWLER	OVERS	MAIDENS	RUNS	WICKETS	AVERAGE
D. Amin	90.3	15	295	15	19.7
A. De Warrenne	86	8	439	22	20.0
R. Jones	101.4	15	382	15	25.5
M. Winter	79.5	9	342	10	34.2

WICKET-KEEPER	PLAYED	CAUGHT	STUMPED
T. Carter	13	15	3

NOTABLE BATTING PERFORMANCES

PLAYER	OPPOSITION	SCORE
T. Carter	Colfe's	106

UNIVERSITY COLLEGE SCHOOL

Frognal, Hampstead, London NW3 6XH

Tel: 020 7435 2215   Fax: 020 7433 2111
Email: office@ucs.org.uk

Master i/c Cricket: S.M. Bloomfield   Coach: J.P. Cooke

2005 SEASON

Played: 13   Won: 6   Lost: 6   Drawn: 1

Captain: B. Bloom

Team selected from: B. Bloom, D. Goodstone, D. Goldsmith,
G. Gedroyc, V. Nair, T. Ricketts, A. Alibhai, R. McKay, B. Kirmani,
D. Sanford, B. Dymant, A. Connick, A. Choraria, M. Rodger,
H. Armberg-Jennings, E. Barnard, M. Jesnick, J. Lawrence.

SUMMARY

The 1st XI had a moderately good season with victories over Enfield GS, Latymer, Mill Hill, Highgate, St. Benedict's and KEQMS Lytham. There was, however, a sense of underachievement as a few winning positions were not converted.

A mature side with plenty of experience was led enthusiastically by Ben Bloom. The batting let us down a bit with too many batsmen unable to turn starts into substantial scores; the exception was Vishal Nair, but even he failed to score the century his talent deserved.

The strength of the side lay in its bowling with a varied attack which could adapt to all conditions. In particular it was accurate, but the fielding and catching did not lend enough support.

AVERAGES

BATSMAN	INNINGS	NOT OUT	RUNS	H. SCORE	AVERAGE
V. Nair	11	1	343	70*	34.3
G. Gedroyc	11	2	234	49	26.0
D. Goldsmith	13	1	282	45	23.5
T. Ricketts	10	1	181	37	20.1
A. Alibhai	7	1	108	44	18.0
R. McKay	11	5	80	30*	13.3

BOWLER	OVERS	MAIDENS	RUNS	WICKETS	AVERAGE
V. Nair	129.2	14	343	29	11.8
D. Goldsmith	58	3	216	13	16.6
D. Sanford	50	5	174	10	17.4
B. Bloom	128.2	14	388	21	18.5
R. McKay	122.1	22	303	11	27.6
B. Kirmani	59.2	8	180	6	30.0

WICKET-KEEPER	PLAYED	CAUGHT	STUMPED
B. Dymant	8	9	3
J. Lawrence	5	4	0

NOTABLE BATTING PERFORMANCES

PLAYER	OPPOSITION	SCORE
V. Nair	KEQMS Lytham	70*
V. Nair	Merchant Taylors'	61
V. Nair	Haberdashers' Aske's	59

NOTABLE BOWLING PERFORMANCES

PLAYER	OPPOSITION	FIGURES
V. Nair	Merchant Taylors'	5-39
V. Nair	Enfield GS	4-26
B. Bloom	St. Benedict's	4-36

UPPINGHAM SCHOOL

Uppingham, Rutland LE15 9QE

Tel: 01572 822216 Fax: 01572 822332
Email: ccs@uppingham.co.uk

Master i/c Cricket: C.C. Stevens Coach: T.R. Ward

2005 SEASON

Played: 18 Won: 5 Lost: 7 Drawn: 6

Captain: H. Barton Vice-captain: T. Higgs

Team selected from: H. Barton*, T. Higgs*, S. Peters*, A. Collins*,
B. Barnett*, T. Stevens, A. Barton, C. Bennett Baggs, C. Paxton,
D. Astle, A. Taylor, F. Barnson, J. Barnett, D. Dean, M. Heslop,
J. Gorman, H. Morrissey, E. Morrison, W. Wallace.

Scorer: D. Darroch-Thompson

SUMMARY

It proved to be a very busy season with twelve day games, six afternoon games and four Twenty20 matches. Fewer days than usual were affected by the weather and batsmen generally flourished on the excellent surfaces of the 'Upper' at Uppingham, where thirteen of our games were played.

The two centuries scored by Ben Barnett and Alex Collins were the highlights of the season - the latter sealing a narrow victory in thrilling circumstances over Oundle. Both boys scored runs throughout the term and topped the averages, although it was good to see six different players scoring fifties. Third in the averages was Tom Stevens, whose superb innings against Haileybury nearly turned a match in which Uppingham were 69-6 chasing 271. Sadly the run chase ended on 258 with Tom stranded on 78*.

Bowling on such good tracks required real discipline, with almost every bowler going for four runs an over or more. As such, the efforts of Tom Higgs with 30 wickets in his fourth season in the XI were especially noteworthy. Leading the bowling averages, however, was captain (and primarily batsman!) Hamish Barton, who snared 22 wickets - often at the 'death' - with his nagging line and length. Along with 358 runs, this made him the leading all-rounder of the term.

Nonetheless, Duncan Darroch-Thompson was probably the busiest team member, producing wagon-wheels, immaculate scoresheets and updated averages on the evening of each match.

Against other schools, the team ended level on wins, draws and losses. This is probably a fair reflection of a good XI, perhaps lacking the one star player needed to force more victories.

AVERAGES

BATSMAN	INNINGS	NOT OUT	RUNS	H. SCORE	AVERAGE
B. Barnett	14	3	469	104*	42.6
A. Collins	13	2	426	133*	38.7
T. Stevens	10	4	194	78*	32.3
H. Barton	15	0	358	62	23.9
A. Barton	12	3	201	51	22.3
C. Bennett Baggs	14	3	204	30	18.6

BOWLER	OVERS	MAIDENS	RUNS	WICKETS	AVERAGE
H. Barton	99	8	423	22	19.2
T. Higgs	165	16	659	30	22.0
D. Astle	106	13	425	13	32.7
C. Paxton	116	5	440	13	33.8
A. Taylor	92	7	464	11	42.2

WICKET-KEEPER	PLAYED	CAUGHT	STUMPED
C. Bennett Baggs	17	16	4

NOTABLE BATTING PERFORMANCES

PLAYER	OPPOSITION	SCORE
A. Collins	Oundle	133*
B. Barnett	Old Uppinghamians	104*
B. Barnett	Bedford	81
T. Stevens	Haileybury	78*
J. Barnett	Bishop's (South Africa)	67
B. Barnett	Paarl Boys' (South Africa)	66
H. Barton	Bedford	62

NOTABLE BOWLING PERFORMANCES

PLAYER	OPPOSITION	FIGURES
H. Barton	Bishop's Stortford HS	5-15
J. Higgs	Shrewsbury	5-30
H. Barton	Loughborough	4-18
C. Paxton	Paarl Boys' (South Africa)	4-36
T. Higgs	Gentlemen of Leicestershire	4-64

WARWICK SCHOOL

Myton Road, Warwick CV34 6PP

Tel: 01926 776400 Fax: 01926 401259
Email: gat@warwickschool.org

Master i/c Cricket: Geoff Tedstone
Coaches: Neil Smith and Francois Klopper

2005 SEASON

Played: 16   Won: 9   Lost: 5   Drawn: 2

Captain: K. Chhibber   Vice-captain: A. Harris

Team selected from: C. Carr*, K. Chhibber*, J. Collins*,
C. Deverell-Smith, D. Dhillon, T. Grimes, A. Harris*, C. Hayter,
C. Hazell, A. Higgens, C. Kroeger, R. Rigby, D. Russell, T. Whiteside,
A. Wilkinson, D. Wood*, S. Wood.

Scorer: Mr Harris

SUMMARY

A good many cold, grey match days did not prevent this talented squad producing performances that were always either black or white - abysmal one day and outstanding the next. Inconsistent and, at times, infuriating, they were outplayed by Loughborough GS and RGS Worcester, but overcame both the MCC and the Old Warwickians.

A fragile top order led to several batting collapses. The captain, Kamal Chhibber, was the exception. His excellent season total of 650 runs was due to a combination of grit, focus and ability. He scored two centuries, against Trent College and the Old Warwickians. Sam Wood made some useful contributions and Dan Wood and Jamie Collins both had days when they destroyed the opposition bowlers with their flamboyant stroke-play.

Andy Harris took 27 wickets this year. He is a talented and genuinely enthusiastic all-rounder who will surely have many more successful seasons. Of the other front line bowlers, Chris Carr was the most impressive in his control and deserved to take more wickets. The spinners, Dilip Dhillon and Chris Kroeger, also had good days. Both show considerable promise, but still lack the control to bowl regular long spells economically.

The fielding was as inconsistent as the other disciplines. Several individuals took brilliant catches but there were too many elementary errors. Wicket-keeper Charlie Hayter similarly had sessions when he really looked like a Warwickshire player, but he also had periods when, had it been available, we may have implemented the new substitute rule!

Looking optimistically ahead to next season, eleven boys are still at school who have 1st XI experience. With the prospect of a warmer summer term, roll on April!

AVERAGES

BATSMAN	INNINGS	NOT OUT	RUNS	H. SCORE	AVERAGE
K. Chhibber	16	3	650	128*	50.0
D. Wood	11	2	332	88	36.9
J. Collins	15	1	488	68	34.9
S. Wood	14	2	275	57	22.9
C. Carr	13	1	150	38	12.5

BOWLER	OVERS	MAIDENS	RUNS	WICKETS	AVERAGE
A. Harris	106.3	22	417	27	15.4
D. Wood	92.5	20	332	18	18.4
D. Dhillon	74.5	2	343	18	19.1
C. Carr	93.3	9	363	18	20.2
C. Kroeger	104.5	15	386	18	21.4
A. Wilkinson	69	12	312	12	26.0

WICKET-KEEPER	PLAYED	CAUGHT	STUMPED
C. Hayter	16	19	6

NOTABLE BATTING PERFORMANCES

PLAYER	OPPOSITION	SCORE
K. Chhibber	Trent College	100*
K. Chhibber	Old Warwickians	128*
K. Chhibber	Bloxham	70
D. Wood	Bishop Vesey's	88
J. Collins	Bablake	68
A. Harris	Loughborough GS	66*

NOTABLE BOWLING PERFORMANCES

PLAYER	OPPOSITION	FIGURES
A. Harris	Bloxham	4-2
D. Wood	Bloxham	3-13
C. Kroeger	MCC	3-15
A. Wilkinson	Bablake	3-21
C. Carr	Trent College	3-22
D. Dhillon	Old Swinford Hospital	3-30

WATFORD GRAMMAR SCHOOL

Rickmansworth Road, Watford WD18 7JF

Tel: 01923 208900 Fax: 01923 208901
Email: admin@watfordboys.herts.sch.uk

Master i/c Cricket and Coach: Paul Smith

2005 SEASON

Played: 12   Won: 6   Lost: 4   Drawn: 2

Captain: Z. Hussain   Vice-captain: D. Grahame

Team selected from: Z. Hussain, D. Grahame, D. Hawes, J. Rose,
M. Needham, C. Nicol, J. Blackwell, P. Clay. B. van Ryneveld,
D. Harrison, K. Hussain, U. Nawaz, T. Aziz, M. Jackson, R. Williams,
R. Desai, W. Jones, A. Lewis.

SUMMARY

There have been some outstanding team and individual performances this year. The quality of our opposition has been consistently excellent and has provided much exciting cricket. Notable matches were against a strong Gentlemen of Hertfordshire team, MCC and Geelong College from Melbourne.

Against the XL Club, the undefeated opening partnership of Z. Hussain and D. Hawes (255) broke a school record. Both went on to score centuries. Hussain hit another hundred and ended the season as the school's premier batsman. He was selected for Middlesex 2nd XI versus Nottinghamshire.

In the bowling department, the combination of Hussain's pace and the guile of J. Rose and M. Needham caused lots of problems. They accounted for 53 of the wickets taken, with Rose claiming 7-34 against Geelong College - his all-time best figures.

Eighteen players have represented the 1st XI, including W. Jones from the U13 XI. We look forward to next year as we begin the development of a talented young side.

AVERAGES

BATSMAN	INNINGS	NOT OUT	RUNS	H. SCORE	AVERAGE
Z. Hussain	11	3	525	129*	65.6
D. Hawes	11	3	458	103*	57.3
J. Blackwell	5	2	63	31*	21.0
K. Hussain	4	1	50	22*	16.7
D. Grahame	8	1	111	45	15.9
C. Nicol	8	0	114	39	14.3

BOWLER	OVERS	MAIDENS	RUNS	WICKETS	AVERAGE
Z. Hussain	87.3	19	184	25	7.4
D. Harrison	26	1	86	8	10.7
J. Rose	79.2	13	278	20	13.9
M. Needham	83.1	11	296	13	22.8
C. Nicol	68	11	196	7	28.0
K. Hussain	34	7	91	3	30.3

WICKET-KEEPER	PLAYED	CAUGHT	STUMPED
D. Grahame	13	9	7

NOTABLE BATTING PERFORMANCES

PLAYER	OPPOSITION	SCORE
Z. Hussain	XL Club	129*
Z. Hussain	Bishop's Stortford HS	122*
D. Hawes	XL Club	103*

NOTABLE BOWLING PERFORMANCES

PLAYER	OPPOSITION	FIGURES
J. Rose	Geelong College (Australia)	7-34
Z. Hussain	Latymer Upper	5-14
Z. Hussain	Dr Challoner's	5-15

WELLINGTON COLLEGE

Crowthorne, Berkshire, RG45 7PU

Tel: 01344 444001 Fax: 01344 444002
Email: tpn@wellington-college.berks.sch.uk

Master i/c Cricket: C.M. Oliphant-Callum   Coach: T.P. Newman

2005 SEASON

Played: 16   Won: 8   Lost: 8

Captain: S. Stitcher   Vice-captain: A. Barker

Team selected from: S. Stitcher*, R. Gotla*, L. Durandt*,
B. Kingsnorth*, J. Fuller*, E. Young*, B. Marchant*, A. Barker*,
M. Nockles*, A. Gray*, R. Shepherd*, S. Skeates*.

Scorer: S. Berkeley

SUMMARY

The 1st XI enjoyed a mixed season. Wins against the Free Foresters, Winchester, Old Wellingtonians, Radley, Brighton College, Melbourne GS, Solihull and Bedford saw four members of the side score centuries, including Luc Durandt, aged 15, who hit five hundreds. He went on to score 912 runs and represent the Surrey Academy and the South of England U15 - certainly a name for the future.

Many limited-overs games saw us play positive and competitive cricket. The record for the season could have been so much better had we won the tight games.

We are looking forward to our tour of South Africa in February.

AVERAGES

BATSMAN	INNINGS	NOT OUT	RUNS	H. SCORE	AVERAGE
L. Durandt	16	0	912	129	57.0
J. Fuller	10	2	329	100*	41.1
S. Stitcher	12	1	357	112	32.5
B. Kingsnorth	14	3	356	105*	32.4
B. Marchant	11	3	257	63*	32.1
R. Gotla	13	1	328	96*	27.3

BOWLER	OVERS	MAIDENS	RUNS	WICKETS	AVERAGE
E. Young	155	33	504	22	22.9
M. Nockles	81	14	347	13	26.7
L. Durandt	103	7	463	16	28.9
A. Barker	110	10	457	12	38.1

NOTABLE BATTING PERFORMANCES

PLAYER	OPPOSITION	SCORE
L. Durandt	Free Foresters	109
L. Durandt	Eton College	129
L. Durandt	Charterhouse	128
L. Durandt	Radley	122
L. Durandt	Caulfield GS	124
S. Stitcher	Old Wellingtonians CC	112
B. Kingsnorth	Free Foresters	105*
J. Fuller	Brighton College	100*

NOTABLE BOWLING PERFORMANCES

PLAYER	OPPOSITION	FIGURES
E. Young	Brighton College	10-2-28-4

WELLINGTON SCHOOL

South Street, Wellington, Somerset TA21 8NT

Tel: 01823 668719 Fax: 01823 668719
Email: admin@wellington-school.org.uk

Master i/c Cricket and Coach: M.H. Richards

2005 SEASON

Played: 13   Won: 5   Lost: 8

Captain: J. Crowther

Team selected from: J. Crowther*, J. Clarkson, H. Yeomans,
P. Hutchinson, N. Smith, A. Vaughan, M. Burton, M. Guest, C. Kitto,
J. Mayes, M. Bramhall, D. Addicott, T. Carson.

Scorer: C. Meredith

SUMMARY

This year's 1st XI was a young development team, lacking depth both
in batting and bowling. The boys were excellently led by the retiring
captain James Crowther in quite trying circumstances. However, the
season finished appropriately on a high note with an excellent and
exciting two run victory over Truro School, skillfully engineered by
the captain.

Did you know? . . . Two players hold records for the
fastest fifty in Tests for England. In terms of time, it is the
twenty-eight minutes it took for J.T. Brown at Melbourne in
1894/5. Ian Botham's 26 ball half-century at Delhi in 1981/2 is
the quickest by the measure of deliveries faced.

The fastest century is the 75 minutes (76 balls) it took for
Gilbert Jessop against the Australians at the Oval in 1902.

AVERAGES

BATSMAN	INNINGS	NOT OUT	RUNS	H. SCORE	AVERAGE
J. Crowther	12	2	351	112*	35.1
A. Vaughan	8	3	138	64*	27.6
H. Yeomans	9	1	160	47	20.0
M. Guest	10	0	163	32	16.3
J. Clarkson	10	1	137	61	15.2

BOWLER	OVERS	MAIDENS	RUNS	WICKETS	AVERAGE
H. Yeomans	81	13	407	17	23.9
P. Hutchinson	29.5	3	267	14	19.1
J. Crowther	70	7	318	13	24.5
N. Smith	65	9	313	11	28.5

WICKET-KEEPER	PLAYED	CAUGHT	STUMPED
M. Bramhall	8	6	0
D. Addicott	2	1	0

NOTABLE BATTING PERFORMANCES

PLAYER	OPPOSITION	SCORE
J. Crowther	West Buckland	112*

WEST BUCKLAND SCHOOL

Barnstaple, Devon EX32 0SX

Tel: 01598 760130 Fax: 01598 760546
Email: lww@westbuckland.devon.sch.uk

Master i/c Cricket: Lawrence Whittal-Williams   Coach: M.T. Brimsom

2005 SEASON

Played: 11   Won: 5   Lost: 6

Captain: A. Whiteley   Vice-captain: T. Wallace

Team selected from: J. Bouquet, A. Whiteley, J. Singh, H. Haydon,
I. Crombie, S. Cassidy-Seed, C. Kingdon, W. Moor, T. Wallace,
B. Palin, H. Chapman-Walker, G. Hursey, B. Newell, S. Lebarth.

Scorer: K. Li

SUMMARY

This was a slightly disappointing season in which the batting matched the weather - both were poor! Our opening pair, captain Aaron Whiteley and Jack Bouquet, often took the shine off the ball, but our middle-order, which has great potential, proved to be rather brittle.

Throughout the season, opening bowler Chris Kingdon bowled with pace and swing. He was joined later in the season by Branton Palin, from our U15 XI, who shows great promise. They should form a very good bowling attack next season. Another success was Harry Chapman-Walker, who was also promoted from the U15 XI and averaged 30.7 from four innnings.

AVERAGES

BATSMAN	INNINGS	NOT OUT	RUNS	H. SCORE	AVERAGE
H. Chapman-Walker	4	1	92	77*	30.7
A. Whiteley	12	1	242	67	22.0
I. Crombie	10	0	174	39	17.4

BOWLER	OVERS	MAIDENS	RUNS	WICKETS	AVERAGE
T. Wallace	71	12	318	16	19.9
C. Kingdon	74.2	10	314	15	20.9
I. Crombie	62	2	280	11	25.5

WICKET-KEEPER	PLAYED	CAUGHT	STUMPED
S. Cassidy-Seed	7	6	2
S. Lebarth	5	5	0

NOTABLE BATTING PERFORMANCES

PLAYER	OPPOSITION	SCORE
H. Chapman-Walker	Devon Dumplings	77*
A. Whiteley	Devon Dumplings	67

NOTABLE BOWLING PERFORMANCES

PLAYER	OPPOSITION	FIGURES
C. Kingdon	North Devon CC	5-1-6-0
I. Crombie	Filleigh CC	6-0-27-3
C. Kingdon	Plymouth College	7.2-1-24-3
T. Wallace	Plymouth College	7-4-4-2

THE WINDSOR BOYS' SCHOOL

1 Maidenhead Road, Windsor, Berkshire SL4 5EH

Tel: 01753 716060 Fax: 01753 833186
Email: admin@twbs.co.uk

Master i/c Cricket and Coach: R.J. Endacott

2005 SEASON

Played: 10   Won: 8   Lost: 2

Captain: K. Sheikh   Vice-captain: N. Cornish

Team selected from: M. Gould*, T. Jones*, R. Woodward*, R. Doye,
F. Raja, O. Smith*, N. Cornish, S. Ahmed, D. Riches, H. McCreanor*,
S. Ali, K. Sheikh*.

Scorer: Mr C.H. Smith

SUMMARY

The performances of Sussex Academy player Michael Gould helped
the Windsor Boys' School to their most successful season to date.
Some very impressive wins were recorded over RGS High Wycombe,
St. Benedict's and Langley GS.

For a state school such as ours, we take pleasure in hosting the
MCC in an annual 'blue riband' fixture. Unfortunately, despite a tense
encounter, the Windsor Boys' narrowly lost by 15 runs - their first taste
of defeat since May 2003.

As we lose a number of our players this year, we will be rebuilding,
hoping to regain strength for a 2006 tour to Australia. Players such as
Kashif Sheikh, Nick Cornish and Saud Ahmed will be keen to carry the
success of the team into 2006 and beyond.

AVERAGES

BATSMAN	INNINGS	NOT OUT	RUNS	H. SCORE	AVERAGE
D. Riches	6	3	193	52	64.3
M. Gould	10	2	427	65	53.4
R. Woodward	7	2	230	108	46.0
T. Jones	10	3	316	52	45.1
F. Raja	10	1	375	48	41.7
R. Doye	5	2	108	32	36.0

BOWLER	OVERS	MAIDENS	RUNS	WICKETS	AVERAGE
M. Gould	33	17	89	14	6.4
K. Sheikh	129.2	31	451	22	20.5
N. Cornish	112	24	448	19	23.6
S. Ahmed	93	14	338	12	28.2
S. Ali	87	9	461	9	51.2

WICKET-KEEPER	PLAYED	CAUGHT	STUMPED
O. Smith	10	14	2

NOTABLE BATTING PERFORMANCES

PLAYER	OPPOSITION	SCORE
R. Woodward	St. Benedict's	108
M. Gould	MCC	65
M. Gould	RGS High Wycombe	63
K. Sheikh	RGS High Wycombe	56
D. Riches	Langley GS	52
T. Jones	St. Benedict's	52

NOTABLE BOWLING PERFORMANCES

PLAYER	OPPOSITION	FIGURES
N. Cornish	MCC	4-62
S. Ahmed	MCC	4-71
K. Sheikh	Eton College	5-34
M. Gould	Langley GS	5-8

WOODBRIDGE SCHOOL

Burkitt Road, Woodbridge, Suffolk IP12 4JH

Tel: 01394 615000 Fax: 01394 380944
Email: admissions@woodbridge.suffolk.sch.uk

Master i/c Cricket and Coach: D.A. Brous

2005 SEASON

Played: 12   Won: 2   Lost: 7   Drawn: 3

Captain: J. Bloomfield   Vice-captain: D. Walsh

Team selected from: J. Bloomfield, G. Slade, D. Walsh, O. Shekhar,
J. Reiss, M. Cade, G. Warden, J. Pugh, E. Cartwright, S. Watson,
R. Edwards, R. Nicholls, O. Randall, B. Grave, O. Smith,
O. Jones, R. Crowther.

SUMMARY

This season has been a big learning curve for a young side. Only three players will be leaving at the end of the season and to begin with, this showed. Inexperience let us down in taking vital catches and placing pressure on the opposition at right times. Our batting showed lack of concentration for periods of time. Most of our batsmen managed to get themselves in, and there were a lot of thirties and forties scored, but few went on to get their fifties.

Ned Cartwright could always be relied on to anchor the innings and scored three fifties. The top score of the season came from Greg Slade with an excellent 86.

Our bowlers performed well at times, with exceptional displays from Sam Watson. Joe Bloomfield ably captained the side and also delivered one or two captain's innings.

The team's ground-fielding improved considerably over the season. Unfortunately this was not always matched by our standard of catching. Towards the end of the season, we produced several excellent performances and with the improvement we made, I look forward to the next season.

AVERAGES

BATSMAN	INNINGS	NOT OUT	RUNS	H. SCORE	AVERAGE
E. Cartwright	8	1	202	56*	28.9
G. Slade	10	0	238	86	23.8
J. Bloomfield	11	0	230	62	20.9
D. Shekhar	11	0	186	37	16.9

BOWLER	OVERS	MAIDENS	RUNS	WICKETS	AVERAGE
S. Watson	77	8	307	12	25.6
J. Bloomfield	67	3	273	10	27.3
J. Pugh	67	2	404	13	31.1

WICKET-KEEPER	PLAYED	CAUGHT	STUMPED
G. Warden	5	4	0
D. Walsh	7	3	0

NOTABLE BATTING PERFORMANCES

PLAYER	OPPOSITION	SCORE
G. Slade	Sunshine Coast GS (Australia)	86
J. Bloomfield	MCC	62
E. Cartwright	Culford	56
E. Cartwright	Royal Hospital	56*
E. Cartwright	XL Club	51

NOTABLE BOWLING PERFORMANCES

PLAYER	OPPOSITION	FIGURES
R. Nicholls	Royal Hospital	3-15
S. Watson	Sunshine Coast GS (Australia)	3-10
J. Bloomfield	Sunshine Coast GS (Australia)	3-31

WOODHOUSE GROVE SCHOOL

Apperley Bridge, West Yorkshire BD10 0NR

Tel: 0113 250 2477 Fax: 0113 250 5290
Email: enquiries@woodhousegrove.co.uk

Master i/c Cricket: R.I. Frost Coach: G.R.J. Roope

2005 SEASON

Played: 17 Won: 9 Lost: 2 Drawn: 6

Captain: U. Mahomed Vice-captain: J. Lindley

Team selected from: U. Mahomed*, J. Lindley*, J. Wheatley*,
N. Davy, T.K. Dalton, T.E. Dalton, L. Brown, D. Henry, N. Lindley,
G. Phillips, W. Hatfield, O. Szymanski, J. Dickinson, P. Genders,
P. Macnamara, A. Milne, A. Griffin, A. Pue, A. Sattar, G. Moore.

SUMMARY

A very young 1st XI enjoyed a lengthy unbeaten run before losing to the MCC. Only one game was lost to schoolboy opposition.

Captain Uzair Mahomed was awarded an academy contract with Durham mid-way through the season and represented ECB Schools West in a trial match at Loughborough University.

Jonathan Lindley, Josh Wheatley, Tom Dalton, Gareth Phillips, Nick Lindley and Will Hatfield all played for Yorkshire schools at different age group levels. 14-year-old Gareth Phillips was also in the North of England squad and became the first player from Woodhouse Grove to score a century against the MCC. 13-year-old Will Hatfield scored 151* on his debut for Yorkshire schools, beating Anthony McGrath's twenty year record.

Off-spinner Josh Wheatley broke the school record for wickets in a season (44) whilst still having two more years at school.

AVERAGES

BATSMAN	INNINGS	NOT OUT	RUNS	H. SCORE	AVERAGE
U. Mahomed	7	1	356	110*	59.3
T.K. Dalton	14	5	389	79*	43.2
G. Phillips	12	1	351	101	31.9
J. Lindley	17	0	465	80	27.4
N. Lindley	11	4	167	41	23.9
N. Davy	15	1	302	56	21.6

BOWLER	OVERS	MAIDENS	RUNS	WICKETS	AVERAGE
J. Wheatley	203.4	44	663	44	15.1
G. Phillips	58.2	6	201	11	18.3
T.K. Dalton	78	9	347	18	19.3
T.E. Dalton	91.4	17	336	16	21.0
N. Lindley	72.2	5	267	12	22.2

WICKET-KEEPER	PLAYED	CAUGHT	STUMPED
J. Lindley	17	19	8

NOTABLE BATTING PERFORMANCES

PLAYER	OPPOSITION	SCORE
U. Mahomed	Ampleforth College	104
U. Mahomed	St. Aidan's Harrogate	110*
G. Phillips	MCC	101
T.K. Dalton	Manchester GS	79*

NOTABLE BOWLING PERFORMANCES

PLAYER	OPPOSITION	FIGURES
J. Wheatley	Arnold	6-27
J. Wheatley	Silcoates	5-68

WORKSOP COLLEGE

Worksop, Nottinghamshire SB0 3AP

Tel: 01909 537100 Fax: 01909 537102
Email: headmaster@worksopcollege.notts.sch.uk

Master i/c Cricket: I. Parkin   Coach: A. Kettleborough

2005 SEASON

Played: 17   Won: 9   Lost: 2   Drawn: 6

Captain: D. Brown   Vice-captain: L. Carlisle

Team selected from: D. Brown*, L. Carlisle*, S. Parkin*, S. Cowles*,
B. Stroud*, C. Mierkalns, M. Dalton, A. Qadoos, I. Qadoos,
W. Ullyott, T. Ullyott, M. Verjee, A. Latham, G. Purshouse.

Scorer: S. McGlen

SUMMARY

A young team with only two upper sixth leavers continues to improve. Nine games were won with the side working on positive intent. The highlights were convincing victories over Denstone, Bishop Vesey's, the Old Boys, Hurstpierpoint College and Wickersley. The major successes came over Repton and King's Grantham - both coming in close run chases. After Repton made 229-7, Worksop reached the target with one ball to spare and nine wickets down. It was a really great game in which Carlisle made a match-winning 97.

Ben Stroud had a particularly good season, ending up winning player of the tournament at the Woodard Cricket Festival and receiving the Player of the Year award. He made two important contributions against King's Grantham (97*) and Bishop Vesey's (122).

Tom Ullyott proved to be the bowler of the season taking 41 wickets with his accurate off-spin. As a 16-year-old, he is clearly one to watch for the future.

The team has worked hard throughout the season and gelled as a unit. We have reaped the benefits of having no superstars but a real team ethic where everyone knows their role.

AVERAGES

BATSMAN	INNINGS	NOT OUT	RUNS	H. SCORE	AVERAGE
B. Stroud	15	3	539	122	44.9
L. Carlisle	11	0	460	97	41.8
D. Brown	12	5	214	54*	30.6
S. Parkin	13	5	213	40*	26.6
C. Mierkalns	14	2	296	46*	24.7
M. Dalton	13	3	244	35*	24.4

BOWLER	OVERS	MAIDENS	RUNS	WICKETS	AVERAGE
T. Ullyott	162	30	531	41	13.0
M. Verjee	36	5	91	7	13.0
W. Ullyott	30	3	89	5	17.8
C. Mierkalns	77.1	12	278	15	18.5
B. Stroud	31.1	3	141	7	20.1
D. Brown	138.5	34	460	22	20.9

WICKET-KEEPER	PLAYED	CAUGHT	STUMPED
S. Cowles	16	16	0
G. Purshouse	1	1	0

NOTABLE BATTING PERFORMANCES

PLAYER	OPPOSITION	SCORE
B. Stroud	Bishop Vesey's	122
B. Stroud	King's Grantham	97*
L. Carlisle	Repton	97
L. Carlisle	Bishop Vesey's	93
L. Carlisle	Wickersley	77
W. Ullyott	Nottinghamshire U16	60
D. Brown	Denstone College	54*

NOTABLE BOWLING PERFORMANCES

PLAYER	OPPOSITION	FIGURES
T. Ullyott	Wickersley	6-19
T. Ullyott	Bishop Vesey's	5-38
B. Stroud	Ellesmere College	4-28
T. Ullyott	Denstone College	4-26
S. Parkin	Old Worksopians	4-20
T. Ullyott	XL Club	4-5
T. Ullyott	Nottingham HS	4-55

WORTH SCHOOL

Paddockhurst Road, Turner's Hill, West Sussex RH10 4SD

Tel: 01342 710200 Fax: 01342 710201
Email: registry@worth.org.uk

Coach: R. Chaudhuri

2005 SEASON

Played: 11   Won: 5   Lost: 5   Drawn: 1

Captain: N. Hopkins   Vice-captain: H. Bashall

Team selected from: N. Hopkins, H. Bashall, B. Stemp*, W. Symcox,
M. Sullivan, J. Triay, E. Armstrong, M. Bilbe, T. Bilbe, T. Woodman,
T. Mitchell, L. Hegarty.

SUMMARY

In my second season at Worth, first and foremost in my mind was to change the mindset of the boys and increase their cricketing awareness on the field. After a lot of talking and convincing, things started to look up as the season progressed. If the game against the Old Boys before half-term was the turning point, the Ardingly match just proved the point that if we kept faith in ourselves, we could achieve what we wanted. After that the spirit in the dressing-room was just fantastic. What a pleasure it was to see the Worth boys turning up for a game to win, rather than just go through the motions. The last fixture of the season against Reigate GS proved what a turn around the season had been for the Worth cricketers. Struggling at 16-4, we fought back hard with an excellent knock from Warwick Symcox, who got his maiden unbeaten hundred and took us to 216-6 from 40 overs. In the face of some very accurate bowling, Reigate only reached 108-9, leaving us victors by 108 runs.

As a coach I was suddenly feeling elated - all of a sudden the penny had started to drop. The boys were sitting together as a team, talking cricket as they were waiting to go in to bat. They discussed targets, the nature of the wicket and field placing. Batsmen were trying to build an innings rather than score boundaries off every ball and bowlers were trying to dry up the supply of runs rather than show a David Blaine bag of tricks! Here we were, a schoolboy side behaving like professionals! What more can a coach ask for?

They say that statistics never lie, but I feel that our record this year does not reflect the quality of our cricket. Two of the games that we lost, against Reed's and Sevenoaks, could have gone our way but we lost both in the last over - one on the penultimate ball. Our bowling was very disciplined, with Javier Triay being the most economical bowler. Warwick was the leading wicket-taker, followed by Bertie. They were well supported by the Bilbe brothers, Ed Armstrong and skipper Hopkins.

On the batting front, Warwick ended up as the leading run-scorer again, and was well supported by Sullivan and Hopkins. A special mention must be made of our wicket-keeper/batsman Tom Mitchell. Tom kept brilliantly and more often than not contributed usefully with the bat.

So where does Worth cricket go from here? Considering that only Nick and Bertie will be leaving, I am delighted that we shall have more or less the same team next year. With some work on the technical side in the off-season, coupled with extra emphasis on our running between the wickets and attacking fielding, I am confident that this side is going to make all the other schools sit up and take notice of our cricket - as well as stop me from wandering around the boundary like a lunatic! Well done boys - there can be no looking back from here.

AVERAGES

BATSMAN	INNINGS	NOT OUT	RUNS	H. SCORE	AVERAGE
W. Symcox	10	3	277	120*	39.6
N. Hopkins	9	0	164	52	18.2
M. Sullivan	10	0	181	43	18.1

BOWLER	OVERS	MAIDENS	RUNS	WICKETS	AVERAGE
J. Triay	62.2	8	147	12	12.2
B. Stemp	62	6	214	14	15.3
E. Armstrong	70	3	278	13	21.4
W. Symcox	91.3	13	322	15	21.5

NOTABLE BATTING PERFORMANCES

PLAYER	OPPOSITION	SCORE
W. Symcox	Reigate GS	120*

NOTABLE BOWLING PERFORMANCES

PLAYER	OPPOSITION	FIGURES
B. Stemp	Seaford College	10-1-31-4
E. Armstrong	Worth Old Boys	7-1-13-4

WREKIN COLLEGE

Sutherland Road, Wellington, Telford, Shropshire TF1 3BH

Tel: 01952 242305 Fax: 01952 240338
Email: mdeweymarn@wrekincollege.ac.uk

Master i/c Cricket: M. de Weymarn   Coach: P. Dawson

2005 SEASON

Played: 16   Won: 11   Lost: 3   Drawn: 2

Captain: A. Sultan   Vice-captain: C. Sheperd

Team selected from: A. Sultan*, C. Sheperd*, R. Eatough*, S. Black,
H. Wilson, T. Baker, A. Smith, C. Mills, G. Scott, N. Fern, S. Harding,
A. Bacon, F. Oakey, C. Howard, D. Whibley-Law.

Scorer: Miss N. Jones

SUMMARY

This was an outstanding summer for the 1st XI. The side played more
limited overs games, thus inflating the 'win' factor, but it was a vintage
side which broke all recent records.

The team was ably led by Asif Sultan, whose figures speak for
themselves. He has now completed four years in the XI and is playing
regularly for Wellington CC (current Birmingham League Champions),
Shropshire and Gloucestershire 2nd XI. He was also awarded an
England U17 cap last year. However, he was well supported by other
very promising players, notably Chris Sheperd, Adam Smith (captain
of Staffordshire U16) and Chad Mills.

The highlights of the season included convincing wins against
King's Worcester, King's Macclesfield and Hereford Cathedral School;
a dramatic win by 26 runs in a low scoring match against
Wolverhampton GS; an exciting loss by 2 wickets, with 2 balls to
spare, against Shrewsbury; a rather disappointing performance against
Denstone and a draw with Ellesmere when we did not know how to
'winkle them out'.

As the figures show, everyone contributed - even those who, like
Henry Wilson, only fielded. They all did great credit to a small school.

AVERAGES

BATSMAN	INNINGS	NOT OUT	RUNS	H. SCORE	AVERAGE
A. Sultan	12	5	473	116*	67.6
C. Sheperd	14	5	514	103*	57.1
A. Smith	8	3	283	71*	56.6
R. Eatough	9	0	293	60	32.6

BOWLER	OVERS	MAIDENS	RUNS	WICKETS	AVERAGE
A. Sultan	193	39	479	47	10.2
C. Mills	73.2	12	199	13	15.3
T. Baker	73	12	211	11	19.2
S. Black	83.3	8	316	16	19.7
G. Scott	78.1	9	213	10	21.3
N. Fern	111.4	12	381	15	25.4

WICKET-KEEPER	PLAYED	CAUGHT	STUMPED
R. Eatough	14	8	2
F. Oakey	2	2	0

NOTABLE BATTING PERFORMANCES

PLAYER	OPPOSITION	SCORE
A. Sultan	Hereford Cathedral	105*
C. Sheperd	Adams' GS	103*
A. Sultan	Ellesmere College	116*

NOTABLE BOWLING PERFORMANCES

PLAYER	OPPOSITION	FIGURES
A. Sultan	King's Macclesfield	4-8
C. Mills	Old Swinford Hospital	3-4
A. Sultan	Wolverhampton GS	5-34
A. Sultan	Glen HS (South Africa)	6-32
A. Smith	Adams' GS	4-8

HAND-CRAFTED CRICKET BATS

*Alastair Watkins writes about A&D Bats, the cricket bat firm that
he and Daffyd Hughes run in Gloucestershire.*

Whilst still at school, Daffyd and I, both keen batsmen, had the opportunity to do work experience at County Bats, where we picked up the basic knowledge of how to make a bat. About five or six years ago we started experimenting with making our own. Gradually, team-mates and opposition players showed more and more interest in our production and the business grew.

When we first started making bats, we agreed that we did not want to make a 'run of the mill' product. The quality of willow used to make a bat is measured between Grades 1-12, with 1 being the best. We opted to purchase only Grade 1 and 2 willow and have continued to offer these two categories of bat ever since.

The process of making a cricket bat begins with a pressed block of willow with a 'V' cut in it where the handle will be inserted. We reduce the size of the willow with a draw-knife and hand plane. This process is repeated until a desired weight and shape are reached according to an individual customer's requirements. As we are both batsmen, we are able to advise when the bat has the right 'pick up' - a term used to explain how a bat feels when lifted to face a ball.

The willow is sanded and then the bat goes on to a machine, which is like a lathe, where the handle is strung by hand. Once dry, the stickers and the grip are added, with a protective face if required. When your bat has been 'knocked in', it is ready for action!

The D'Abitot Conqueror is a Grade 1 bat and retails at £130. The D'Abitot Quest is Grade 2 and retails at £90. Due to the large amount of junior cricket in our area, we have also recently introduced a Harrow bat, retailing at £60. The name D'Abitot comes from the local village team we play for, Redmarley D'Abitot.

For more information contact: 01452 840803

The Schools'
CRICKET
ALMANAC

"WANTS
YOU"

Please spread the word by encouraging other senior schools to contact us for inclusion in next year's edition

The Editors, Wisteria Books, Wisteria Cottage, Birt Street,
Birtsmorton, Malvern, Worcs WR13 6AW. Tel/fax 01684 833578
sca@wisteriabooks.co.uk   www.wisteriabooks.co.uk